THE BORN-EINSTEIN LETTERS

A. Einstein.

W. Born

DRAWING OF ALBERT EINSTEIN BY WOLGANG BORN, 1924

The
BORN-EINSTEIN
Letters

Correspondence between Albert Einstein
and Max and Hedwig Born
from 1916 to 1955
with commentaries by
MAX BORN

Translated by **Irene Born**

WALKER AND COMPANY
New York

First published in the United States of America in 1971 by the
Walker Publishing Company, Inc.

Library of Congress Catalog Card Number: 76-126107

Printed in the United States of America from type set in the United
Kingdom.

ISBN: 0-8027-0326-7

Foreword

by Bertrand Russell

The correspondence of Albert Einstein and Max Born will provoke the greatest interest, both among men of science and a far wider public. Not only are they among the most eminent scientists of our century, but they had wide interests and an uncommon awareness of the social responsibility of the scientist.

These letters, which clearly were not written for publication, record their hopes and anxieties in war and peace, their private thoughts about the progress of their work and that of colleagues, and much that will prove invaluable source material in the history of science.

Something of the nobility of their lives is also revealed. I have deeply valued their friendship over many years. Both men were brilliant, humble and completely without fear in their public utterances. In an age of mediocrity and moral pygmies, their lives shine with an intense beauty. Something of this is reflected in their correspondence, and the world is the richer for its publication.

1 December 1968

Introduction

by Werner Heisenberg

The relativity and quantum theories, the theoretical foundation of modern physics, are generally held to be abstract systems of ideas, inaccessible to the layman, which no longer show much evidence of their human origin. It is, however, the human aspect of the developing science, more than anything else, which this correspondence between Albert Einstein and Max Born renders intelligible. Einstein and Born were both in the front rank of those who contributed towards the formation of modern physics. In the year 1916, at the beginning of the correspondence, Einstein had just completed his papers about the general theory of relativity, and was concentrating his efforts on the then still very puzzling quantum phenomena. During the years which followed Born, together with his pupils in Göttingen, took a number of decisive steps which led to an understanding of these very phenomena. Nothing demonstrates more clearly the exceptional difficulties which stood in the way of a clearer understanding of atomic phenomena – in spite of the considerable amount of experimental data already obtained – than the fact that these two scientists, who on the human level were on such intimate terms, failed to agree about the final interpretation of the quantum theory.

But their correspondence does not merely bear witness to the dramatic argument about the correct interpretation of atomic phenomena. It also shows the way in which human, political and ideological problems are intermingled in this discussion, and for this reason the contemporary history of the years 1916 to 1954 plays an important part in these letters. Einstein and Born, both interested in the social structures around them, actively participated in the history of their time, suffering and hoping, and many people who have suffered in different ways and hoped for other things during this epoch will find it instructive to have a look at the world of those days through the eyes of these two eminent scientists.

In the year 1916 Einstein and Born were both in Berlin. Einstein had a research appointment at the Prussian Academy of Sciences; Born was Professor Extraordinarius for theoretical physics at the University of Berlin, but was then on wartime service as scientific collaborator of the Artillery-Testing Commission in Berlin. Soon after the end of the war Born became Professor Ordinarius for theoretical physics at the University of Berlin; Einstein undertook extended lecture tours to many universities in America, Asia and Europe.

The working methods of these two scientists were rather different. Einstein basically worked alone. However, he liked to talk to other physicists about his problems; now and again he called upon individual young collaborators, predominantly mathematicians, to help with difficult mathematical investigations. But Einstein did not teach according to the usual custom at universities; rather, one gained the impression that, even in most of the papers he published in collaboration with other people, the inspiration and direction were his.

Born, on the other hand, founded a school of theoretical physics in Göttingen. He held the normal courses of lectures, organised seminars, and soon succeeded in collecting a fairly large band of excellent younger physicists about him, with whom he tried to penetrate the unknown territory of the quantum theory. Göttingen was then one of the world's most important centres of modern physics. In the small university town the mathematical tradition had been carried on for more than a century by some of the most illustrious of names: Gauss, Riemann, Felix Klein and Hilbert all taught in Göttingen. Göttingen thus offered most of the prerequisites for the search for the mathematical laws describing the atomic phenomena. James Franck, the experimental physicist, awakened the interest of young physicists in the curious behaviour of atoms exposed to radiation by his experiments there into electronic collisions. Born and his pupils were striving for insight into the fundamental laws of nature underlying these experiments. In this way a lively intellectual atmosphere was generated, where conversation revolved more frequently around the behaviour of electrons within the atom than the events of the day or political questions. Born and his wife Hedwig, whose letters to Einstein constitute a considerable portion of this correspondence, looked after this group of young physicists, in both the scientific and the human sense. Born's house was always open for social gatherings with young people, and anyone who happened to meet this group of youngsters, in the university, or on the ski-slopes of the Harz Mountains, may well have wondered how the academic staff succeeded in focusing interest so exclusively on such a difficult and abstract science. It was part of Germany's great tragedy that the revolution of 1933 put a sudden and violent end to this scientific life. Born and Franck had to leave Germany. Born found a new sphere of activity in England, Franck in America.

In 1923 Einstein returned to Berlin from his great round-the-world trip. He participated regularly in the colloquia where the élite of Berlin physicists, among them Planck, v. Laue and Nernst, gathered to discuss topical research problems. Einstein's contributions to these discussions in the colloquia, and his private conversations with individual scientists which often took place in his private apartment, may well have been the most important part of his educational activity at that time. But what limited effectiveness he was still able to achieve within a small circle was soon curtailed by political developments and their consequences, which were less easily evaded in a large city like Berlin than in the friendly little university town of Göttingen. Einstein predicted the political catastrophe very early on. He therefore assumed new responsibilities in California, and after 1933 found his ultimate sphere of activity in Princeton, which developed into one of the most important American research centres during the following decades.

Relativity theory and quantum theory were the central scientific themes of the time. As there were no differences of opinion between Einstein and Born about the theory of relativity and the corresponding formulation of space and time, the most interesting discussions are concerned with the interpretation of the quantum theory. Einstein agreed with Born that the mathematical formulation of quantum mechanics, developed in Göttingen and consolidated further in Cambridge and Copenhagen, correctly described the phenomena within the atom. He may also have been willing to admit, for the time being at least, that the statistical interpretation of Schroedinger's wave function, as formulated by Born, would have to be accepted as a working hypothesis. But Einstein did not want to acknowledge that quantum mechanics represented a final, and even less a complete, description of these phenomena. The conviction that the world could be completely divided into an objective and a subjective sphere, and the hypothesis that one should be able to make precise statements about the objective side of it, formed a part of his basic philosophical attitude. But quantum mechanics could not satisfy these claims, and it does not seem likely that science will ever find its way back to Einstein's postulates. The whole trickiness of this central problem is shown clearly in Born's commentaries on the individual letters, which also give us much information about the social and political circumstances connected with the development of physics at that time. All scientific work is, of course, based consciously or subconsciously on some philosophical attitude; on a particular thought structure which serves as a solid foundation for further development. Without a definite attitude of this kind, the concepts and associations of ideas produced would be unlikely to attain the degree of clarity and lucidity essential for scientific work. Most scientists are willing to accept new empirical data and to recognise new results, provided they fit into their philosophical framework. But in the course of scientific progress it can happen that a new range of empirical data can be completely understood only when the enormous effort is made to enlarge this framework and to change the very structure of the thought processes. In the case of quantum mechanics, Einstein was apparently no longer willing to take this step, or perhaps no longer able to do so. The letters between Einstein and Born, and Born's subsequently added commentaries, movingly demonstrate the degree to which the work of the scientist, which in its subject matter seems to be so far removed from all things human, is fundamentally determined by philosophical and human attitudes.

But this correspondence should not only be rated an extremely valuable document in relation to the history of modern science; it also bears witness to a human attitude which, in a world full of political disaster, tries with the best of intentions to help wherever possible, and which considers love for one's fellow men to be fundamentally of far greater importance than any political ideology.

W. Heisenberg

Acknowledgments

I am greatly obliged to Einstein's executor Dr Otto Nathan in New York for permission to use Einstein's letters. I also thank Miss Helen Dukas, Einstein's former secretary, for preparing and sending copies of these letters to Europe. Mrs Franca Pauli very kindly allowed me to use letters of her late husband Professor Wolfgang Pauli, for which I am very grateful. I would further like to thank Professor Armin Hermann in Stuttgart for his valuable help in reading the proofs. I am very grateful to Earl Russell for his warm-hearted preface and Professor Werner Heisenberg for his perceptive, sympathetic foreword. I thank my daughter Mrs Irene Newton-John for her excellent translation of the original letters. I would like to thank Mrs Hedwig Geib for her careful typing of this manuscript, which was often illegible. Finally I would like to thank my son Professor Gustav V. R Born in London for the efforts he made in dealing with the problems which arose in the course of publication.

Max Born.

The publishers thank Paul Atkins for his careful work in editing the letters and commentaries.

The Born-Einstein Letters

Einstein's famous paper[1] containing the fundamentals of his theory of relativity appeared in 1905. The same volume of *Annalen der Physik* contained two more epoch-making papers by him on the hypothesis of the light quantum[2] and the statistical theory of Brownian movement.[3] At that time I was a student in Göttingen and attended a seminar conducted by the mathematicians David Hilbert and Hermann Minkowsky. They dealt with the electrodynamics and optics of moving bodies – the subject that was Einstein's point of departure for the theory of relativity. We studied papers by H. A. Lorentz, Henri Poincaré, G. F. Fitzgerald, Larmor and others, but Einstein was not mentioned. I found these problems so fascinating that I decided to concentrate on theoretical physics. However, I had to postpone any deeper investigation into electrodynamics for other reasons.[4,5,6] After graduating in 1906 I took up the threads again and attended lectures by Larmor in Cambridge, England, on more recent developments in the Maxwellian theory of electromagnetism, and by J. J. Thomson on the experimental progress of the theory of electrons. Again Einstein's name was not mentioned.

When I later (1907–1908) tried to develop my experimental skills at the Institute presided over by Lummer and Pringsheim in my home town of Breslau, I joined an active group of young physicists, including Rudolf Ladenburg, Fritz Reiche and Stanislaus Loria. We studied the more recent physics literature and reported on what we had read. When I mentioned Minkowsky's contributions to the seminars in Göttingen, which already contained the germ of his four-dimensional representation of the electromagnetic field, published in 1907–8, Reiche and Loria told me about Einstein's paper and suggested that I should study it. This I did, and was immediately deeply impressed. We were all aware that a genius of the first order had emerged. But nobody knew anything about his personality or his life, except that he was a civil servant at the Swiss Patent Office in Berne. Then Ladenburg decided to look him up during a holiday trip, and his account was the first I heard of Einstein the man. Even then he was as he appeared later: completely unpretentious, simple and modest in his habits, kind and friendly, yet witty and humorous. Ladenburg was enthusiastic and made us curious about the great unknown.

But some time passed before I met him. This was in 1909 at the conference of natural scientists in Salzburg. As I have described this incident and the years following, during which our friendship developed, on various occasions,[6,7,8] I shall not repeat it here. I shall recount only the events which brought us together. In 1913 Einstein was appointed as successor to J. H. van't Hoff in a research post at the Berlin Academy of Sciences, and he was made an ordinary member of the mathematical physics division. One year later, shortly after the outbreak of the first world war, I became Extraordinarius for theoretical physics at the University of Berlin, a position which was created in order to relieve Planck of teaching duties. Nothing much came of this, as I was called up for military service shortly afterwards (summer 1915). After a short training course as an aircraft wireless operator at the Döberitz Camp, I was sent to the artillery inspectorate in Berlin as a scientific assistant. The office building in Spichernstrasse was quite close to Einstein's flat at Haberlandstrasse 5. Thus it happened that I was able to visit him and talk with him frequently.

We understood each other not only scientifically, but also politically and in our attitude towards human relationships. I cannot say with certainty whether any correspondence existed between Einstein and myself during the preceding years, for nothing has been preserved. But I find it hard to believe that, when I was working with Theodor von Karman on the further development of Einstein's theory of specific heat of solid bodies (1912), I did not write to Einstein about it. Presumably I did not keep any letters at that time. The first letter from Einstein to my wife and myself dates from the year 1916, and no letters from us to Einstein exist before 1920. The commentary I wrote in 1965 therefore depends entirely on my memory for this period. The first item which has been preserved is a postcard addressed to me which deals with scientific matters. It was obviously sent from Einstein's flat in Wilmersdorf to mine in Teplitzerstrasse, Grunewald.

I   *Sunday*
                                          27 February, 1916

Dear Born

This morning I received the corrected proofs of your paper for *Physikalische Zeitschrift*, which I read with a certain embarrassment but at the same time with a feeling of happiness at being completely understood and acknowledged by one of the best of my colleagues. But, quite apart from the material contents, it was the spirit of positive benevolence radiating from the paper which delighted me – it is a sentiment which all too rarely flourishes in its pure form under the cold light of the scholar's lamp.

I thank you with all my heart for this happiness which you have allowed me to share.

With kind regards
Yours
A. Einstein

The article which Einstein was so pleased with was on his theory of gravitation and general relativity;[9] I would not write very differently about this subject to-day. Since then it has become fashionable to regard the relativity aspect of Einstein's general theory as of secondary importance and to consider the new law of gravitation as the essential part. I cannot share this point of view, which is represented particularly by my Russian friend and former collaborator, V. Fock. Einstein's starting point was the empirical fact of the equality of inertial and gravitational mass. It follows that an observer enclosed inside a box is unable to distinguish whether the acceleration of a body inside the box is caused by an external gravitational field or by the acceleration of the box itself in the opposite direction. The existence and the size of a gravitational field inside a small space can thus be assumed only in relation to a certain (accelerated) system of reference. This was the historical basis of the theory, and it is still today, in my opinion, the rational approach. I used it in my book *Die Relativitätstheorie Einsteins*,[10] which was first published in 1920, and also retained it in the recently published new edition. I believe that this is justified, both in regard to Einstein's own intention and objectively.

The following letter to my wife can be understood only if the friendly intercourse between Einstein's house and ours is appreciated. My wife described this in an article which appeared in the journal *Weltwoche* a few years ago.[8] It explains the references to the poem and the 'Flemish sow'. The book he mentions is probably one by Max Brod.

2

8 September, 1916

Dear Mrs Born

Your poem gave me much pleasure, mainly because it is an indication of your happy state of mind, but also because it shows that you are on the best of terms with both the Muse of Parnassus and the 'Flemish sow'. The latter, though, is not really needed to make a few cosy evening hours spent in your and Max's den appear to me in the most alluring colours!

I read the book with great interest. It is certainly entertainingly written by a man who knows the depths of the human soul. Incidentally, I believe that I met him in Prague. I think he belongs to a small circle there of philosophical and Zionist enthusiasts, which was loosely grouped around the university philosophers, a medieval-like band of unwordly people whom you got to know by reading the book.

   Best regards to you both
     Yours
       Einstein

The two papers you wanted are enclosed. The book I will return personally.

Einstein's next letter is again addressed to my wife, but its subject matter concerns me just as much. Presumably I was absent on a lengthy official trip.

3

8 February, 1918

Dear Mrs Born

Your detailed letter with its comforting expression of sympathy and confidence gave me much pleasure. My answer will take the form of a monologue, thereby completely eliminating the ugly chasm between 'you' and 'I'.

Laue wants to come here. Some time ago he had the chance of obtaining a sort of research post here, free from teaching duties, through a private award. His effort to get to Berlin then was, according to him, based on his dislike of teaching activities. Now that this plan will apparently not come off, he is thinking of an exchange of posts with your husband. Primary motive, therefore: 'Berlin'. Motivation: ambition (of the wife?). Planck knows about this, the Ministry probably not. I have not yet talked about it with Planck. I suppose his efforts are directed towards becoming Planck's successor. The poor fish. Nervous subtlety. To strive for an aim which is in direct contradiction with his natural desire for a quiet life, free from complicated human relationships. In this connection please read Andersen's pretty little fairytale about the snails. Seen objectively, the chance of Laue's plan being successful depends on two conditions:

1. Sufficient income for Laue from your post,
2. Your husband's inclination to exchange jobs.

Just assuming that 1. is fulfilled, there remains the question of whether you should agree; this is, of course, the question which worries you already. My opinion is:

Accept unconditionally.

I have no need to assure you how fond I am of you both and how glad I am to have you as friends and kindred spirits in this . . . desert. But one should not refuse such an ideal post, where one is completely independent. There is a wider and freer sphere of activity than here, and it gives your husband a better chance to display his powers. And most important of all: to be near to Planck is a joy. But when Planck eventually retires, you cannot be certain, even if you remain there, that your husband will succeed to his position. If, on the other hand, it were to be someone else, it would be rather less pleasant. One has to be prepared for every eventuality. You should not expose yourselves to this unless it is necessary.

Look after yourself, and let my example be a warning to you. For me the 'sudden jerk upwards' is no longer possible.

Sincerest greetings to you, to your children, and to your, I hope, soon-to-return lord and master.

Yours
Einstein

I do not believe that Einstein would later have persisted in attributing the motive of ambition to Laue. He probably did not yet know Laue well at that time. Later, he acknowledged him not only as a physicist but also as an upright and thoroughly honourable human being, as is shown in a later letter (No. 81). To me Laue maintained that his efforts to get to Berlin were due less to his dislike of teaching than to his wish to be near his admired and much loved teacher, Planck.

The next letter is without an address, but was presumably sent between our two flats in Berlin.

4

24 June, 1918

Dear Born

Tomorrow we *must* be off to our summer holiday resort at Ahrenshoop (at a Mrs Nieman's, *née* Ronow). These lines come as a solemn farewell. A Danaean present too. With Haber's help I have managed to obtain a travel permit to Finland for Nordström (from the General Staff). Now he wants to return to Holland, but unfortunately I am no longer in a position to attend to it. I would ask you to settle the matter, please. It is urgent, as Mrs Nordström is soon to give birth to her child, in Holland if possible.

   With best wishes for a happy time to you and your little band.

   Yours

   Einstein

I hope the 40 M have arrived—I sent it off in an ordinary letter.

The Finnish physicist Nordström had developed, almost simultaneously with Einstein's first publications about the general theory of relativity, a rival relativistic theory of gravitation, which contained only *one* scalar potential, as with Newton. According to Einstein, however, the ten components of a symmetrical tensor determine the gravitational field. Nordström's ideas were shrewd and ingenious. I found out later that he had been my strongest competitor for the Berlin Extraordinary Professorship.

Einstein's next letter, clearly from Ahrenshoop, and undated, shows that I did attempt to do something for Nordström. Whether I was successful I cannot remember; I also know nothing of Nordström's subsequent fate. In Einstein's letter the words 'must' and 'Frische' (holiday resort) were underlined. Presumably he was in some doubt as to whether he would 'refresh himself' in Ahrenshoop. He was clearly following the wishes of his second wife, his cousin Elsa, for she had nursed him during a serious illness and had probably saved him from death.

5

[*undated*]

Dear Born

It is very kind of you to look after the Nordströms. Just write to the General Staff that Nordström has already been granted a permit for the outward journey, at Haber's request. Then the return journey will be readily allowed. As I wrote to you before, he has to be back at the beginning of August.

It is wonderful here, no telephone, no duties, absolute peace. I simply can't imagine now how you can bear life in the big city. And the weather is wonderful too. I lie on the beach like a crocodile and let myself be roasted by the sun, I never see a newspaper and don't give a damn for what is called the world.

What you tell me about the inertia in a crystal lattice is very satisfactory. It can only be a matter of *electrical* energy, since the potential energy of the other assumed forces does not enter into the inertia, according to the fundamental laws of mechanics. I look forward very much to your explanation of this.

I am reading Kant's *Prolegomena* here, among other things, and am beginning to comprehend the enormous suggestive power that emanated from the fellow, and still does. Once you concede to him merely the existence of synthetic *a priori* judgements, you are trapped. I have to water down the '*a priori*' to 'conventional', so as not to have to contradict him, but even then the details do not fit. Anyway it is very nice to read, even if it is not as good as his predecessor Hume's work. Hume also had a far sounder instinct.

When I am back again, we will all sit down cosily together so that you can gently reintroduce me to the bustle of human activity, of which I take no notice at the moment. In the meantime, I hope that you and your wife are again in good health. We are well, and the small harem eat well and are thriving.

Best wishes

Yours

Einstein

So he liked Ahrenshoop after all, and it did him good. The remark about inertia in crystal lattices refers to the result of my investigations into electromagnetic fields in crystals, which I have published in several books and papers. These investigations were a further development of P. P. Ewald's fundamental work on dispersion in crystal lattices, but made use of a different method which Hilbert had suggested in one of his lectures. My result was new: it automatically followed that the electromagnetic reciprocal action of the lattice particle's charges contributed to the inertia (electromagnetic mass). Einstein's remark that only electrical energy would be involved was, however, absolutely correct.

The letter then contains Einstein's attitude towards the philosophy of Kant: it amounts to a rejection. In those days he was a complete empiricist and a follower of David Hume. Later on this changed. Speculation and guesswork without much empirical foundation played an increasingly important role in his thinking.

I have no idea what his closing remark about the 'small harem' (I cannot make it out as anything else) means. Probably it refers to his wife and stepdaughters.

A picture postcard from Ahrenshoop follows.

6

Dear Born

The closer our journey home approaches, the more I am plagued by conscience and the fear of a scolding for being lazy about writing. But what can a fellow write who lazes about all day, who sees no-one and who at the very most wanders about for half an hour in bare feet? If only we could introduce this last delightful habit (voluntarily) in Berlin! The clover leaf amused me very much. One can see that it represents three incorrigible hobby-horse riders in brotherly unity; two are introspective, one stares unconcernedly into space. The other day I read that the population of Europe has grown from 113 million to almost 400 million during the last century . . . a terrible thought, which could almost make one reconciled to war!

To a happy reunion!
Yours
Einstein

I can't remember what the clover leaves represented.
The observation about population increase and war is remarkable.

He added the following to a postcard from Arosa in Switzerland with a picture of the Silser Lake that Mrs Elsa Einstein sent.

7

19 January, 1919

Brilliant landscape and satisfied citizens, who have nothing to fear. This is how it looks. But God knows, I prefer people with anxieties, whose tomorrow is threatened by uncertainty. How will it all end? One cannot tear one's thoughts away from Berlin; so changed and still changing. I believe some good will come of it in another sense, once it is calm again. The young who have lived through it all will not quickly become philistines.

Hearty best wishes
Yours
Einstein

That trip abroad was probably Einstein's first after the war. His thoughts were still of a Berlin shaken by revolution. The card's brief message shows what hopes he had of the new regime, the Republic under Ebert. He deeply detested Prussianism with its arrogant militarism, and he believed it now to be finally defeated and that everything could improve. I believed the same at that time, and this was one bond in our friendship. We were completely wrong – it got very much worse. Subsequent letters contain reminders of this time of hope.

After a certain amount of to-ing and fro-ing, the exchange of chairs between myself and Laue was finally agreed. We succeeded in acquiring an attractive house with a garden in Frankfurt, in Cronstettenstrasse. Einstein's first letter addressed to us there follows.

8

Berlin
4 June, 1919

Dear Born

I already have a bad enough conscience because I have not answered your wife's extremely kind letter, and now your delightful letter arrives instead of a scolding. I am glad that you have made such a splendid nest for yourselves there, in your little house and garden. It is wicked of you, though, to take on such a burden of responsibility. Do you want to become a torment to your students and a reproach to your colleagues? Will you even keep your literary promises, e.g. to Sommerfeld? That is going too far. If Shakespeare had lived under present-day conditions he may well have altered his lines: 'At lovers' perjuries, They say, Jove laughs', which is a little hard, to: 'At the forgotten promise of a report'.

And then you tell me that, according to friend Oppenheim, I am supposed to have made heaven only knows what wonderful discovery. But there is no truth in it. The modest suggestion I made to him about this affair, which I told you about at Lake Grunewald, has become dangerously swollen in his exuberant imagination! The quantum theory gives me a feeling very much like yours. One really ought to be ashamed of its success, because it has been obtained in accordance with the Jesuit maxim: 'Let not thy left hand know what thy right hand doeth'. I do not see the political situation as pessimistically as you.

Conditions are hard, but they will never be enforced. They are more to satisfy the enemy's eye than his stomach. Ludendorf was undoubtedly much worse than the Parisians. The French are motivated by fear. Ludendorf, however, had the desires of a Napoleon. The hardships resulting from the errors of the French are alleviated by a slovenliness which never fails, as in my one-time fatherland, Austria.* Eventually, Germany's dangerousness will go up in smoke, together with the unity of her opponents, accompanied no doubt by a certain hysteresis. May a hard-bitten x-brother and determinist be allowed to say, with tears in his eyes, that he has lost his faith in humanity? The impulsive behaviour of contemporary man in political matters is enough to keep one's faith in determinism alive.

I am convinced that in the next few years things will be less hard than in those we have recently lived through.

With sincere regards to you and your wife, also from my wife.

Yours

Einstein

Haber's adaptation of your theory to monovalent metals is puzzling.

The literary promise concerned my promise to Sommerfeld (Professor of Theoretical Physics in Munich) to write an article about atomic theory of the solid state for the volume 'Physics' in the *Enzyklopädie der Mathematik*.[12] This lengthy treatise later appeared as a book.

Friend Oppenheim was the son of an important Frankfurt businessman (a jeweller), who had founded and endowed the Chair of Theoretical Physics occupied first by Laue and later by myself. Oppenheim junior was interested in philosophy, particularly the philosophical ideas contained in Einstein's theory of relativity. He was probably alluding to the beginnings of 'a unified field theory', which was intended to combine gravitation and electromagnetism and which occupied Einstein throughout his life.

The political remarks show that at that time I took a more pessimistic view of the situation than Einstein. The expression 'hard-bitten x-brother and determinist' (we used to say 'to x' when calculating with unknown values of x, as is normal in mathematics) was probably correct then, for my non-determinist views only arose some years later.

* Einstein probably meant his time in Prague as Professor at the German University; Bohemia was a part of Austria at that time.

I cannot remember now what Haber's application of my theory to mono-valent metals meant.

9

Sunday
1 September, 1919

Dear Mrs Born

I have a terribly bad conscience about both of you, but particularly you, because I so infrequently settle down to write to you. Let me say straight away, so that I won't forget, that I will do my best to squeeze some funds out of the K. W. Institute [Kaiser-Wilhelm Institute] for your husband, if possible, and if we ever have some to give away. I will visit you soon enough in your comfortable nest – provided you have no-one billeted on you – just you wait!

That business with Oppenheim has gone wrong. My academic remuneration does not depend on his purse but on that of Mr Koppel. I had no idea that your husband's chair was founded by Oppenheim – I only know of the observatory there. The relationship between Oppenheim (junior) (I have only seen old man O. on one single occasion) and us is of a strictly private nature and is due to Mr O. junior's philosophical hobby-horse. There is just one problem – I promised to come and stay both with you and with Mr O. junior, if I came to Frankfurt; the solution is beyond my powers, but no doubt it will turn out all right in the end. It is nothing like as bad as the answer Althoff gave to someone who had just been passed over for someone else for a professorship he had been promised. He said, cheerfully and rudely, 'Well, did you believe you were the only one to whom I have promised the professorship?'! Yesterday Stern came to see me. He is delighted with Frankfurt and with the Institute. I quite liked *Rausch*, though Strindberg's *Traumspiel* is incomparably better.

Mr Bieberach's love and veneration for himself and his Muse is quite delicious. May God preserve him, for it is the best way to be. Years ago, when people lived their lives in greater isolation, eccentrics like him were quite the rule amongst university professors, because they did not come into personal contact with anyone of their own stature in their subject, and apart from their subject nothing existed for them.

Politically, I am more on your husband's side than on yours. I believe in the growth potential of the League of Nations, and I believe further that the hardships connected with its formation will disappear after a while. Even now the conflict of interests of the Allies is so considerable that much is being modified (the constitutional incident concerning Austria; the intervention of the Allies in Silesia). In my opinion, the greatest danger to future development would be a withdrawal by the Americans; one can only hope that Wilson will be able to prevent it.

I don't believe that human beings as such can really change but I am convinced that it is possible, and indeed necessary, to put an end to anarchy in international relations, even if it were to mean sacrificing the independence of various countries.

Now to philosophy. What you call 'Max's materialism' is simply the causal way of looking at things. This way of looking at things always answers only the question 'Why?', but never the question 'To what end?'. No utility principle and no natural selection will make us get over that. However, if someone asks 'To what purpose should we help one another, make life easier for each other, make beautiful music or have inspired thoughts?', he would have to be told: 'If you don't feel it, no-one can explain it to you.' Without this primary feeling we are nothing and had better not live at all. If someone wanted to make a basic investigation to prove that these things help to preserve and further human existence, then the question 'To what end?' would loom even larger, and an answer on a 'scientific' basis would be an even more hopeless task. So if we want to proceed in a scientific manner at any cost, we can try to reduce our aims to as few as possible and derive the others from them. But this will leave you cold.

I do not agree with the pessimistic assessment of cognition. To have a clear view of relationships is one of the most beautiful things in life; you could only deny that in a very gloomy, nihilistic mood. But you should not quote the Bible to prove your point. In Luther's translation it says in many places: 'And he *knew* her; and she bore him a son; his name was. . . .' One can assume that the Tree of Knowledge refers to this. Therefore, it probably has very little in common with epistemology in our sense; or maybe the old fathers fancied themselves in this ambiguity? But that is not really like these lovers of speculation and argument.

Thank you very much for the lovely photographs. The one of your husband is wonderful: its subject is not so bad, either. He has not been here yet; I look forward greatly to seeing him. I have spent these last few days very pleasantly sailing, but unfortunately have contracted another ailment (stomach) on naval service, and I have to spend a few days in bed once more. Thus the indistinct writing.

With kindest regards to you both,
Yours
Einstein

Althoff was for many years an official concerned with university administration at the Ministry of Education, where he earned great merit in building up the universities. He was well known and feared for his lack of consideration and rudeness.

Otto Stern was a young physicist from Silesia who became my assistant. Our Institute possessed a workshop and an able technician called Schmidt. Stern made very good use of this to carry out his experiments, later to become famous, into a peculiar effect of the quantum, the so-called quantisation of direction. Up to that time, this effect had been only indirectly deduced from spectroscopic observations; Stern undertook to prove it directly by using atomic radiation in a high vacuum. He was supported in this by Walter Gerlach, assistant at the Institute of Experimental Physics (whose head was Prof. Wachsmuth). Stern later received the Nobel Prize for these investigations. At his suggestion I also experimented successfully at that time; with my assistant, Elisabeth Bormann, I made a direct measurement of the length of the free paths of atoms with the aid of atomic radiation.

I cannot remember what kind of play *Rausch* was.

The Bieberbach affair was as follows: The Faculty of Natural Sciences had a beautifully bound book, in which each new professor was required to write a short autobiographical note. When it was given to me by the Dean, the mathematician Schoenflies, I naturally read some of the cameo-biographies, and also showed them to my wife. She discovered a rather comic one – the young mathematician Bieberbach's, which was full of vanity. She copied some of the finest passages for Einstein.

Einstein's explanation to my wife of the nature of scientific research reveals the basis of his philosophy in a concise and clear way that is hard to find elsewhere. It led to a discussion of the Biblical concept 'cognition' which continued for some time between my wife and Einstein. In contrast to Einstein, who interpreted the tasting of the forbidden fruit from the tree of knowledge as sexual experience, she insisted that it meant spiritual enlightenment. For the first chapter of Genesis says: 'And God blessed them [man and wife], and God said unto them, Be fruitful, and multiply'. And later it says: 'And out of the ground made the Lord God to grow every tree . . . the Tree of Life also in the midst of the garden, and the Tree of Knowledge of good and evil . . . But of the fruit of the tree which is in the midst of the garden, God hath said Ye shall not eat of it.' In the third chapter the serpent says to Eve: 'For God doth know that in the day ye eat thereof, then your eyes shall be opened, and ye shall be as gods, knowing good and evil.'

The next letter shows that Einstein ceded this point to her, but not its consequences.

10

16 October, 1919

Dear Born

You are a splendid fellow! Have forwarded your pamphlet with expressions of agreement plus a few quibbles to the lucky recipient.

Your wife was right about the Tree of Knowledge. I clearly rated my ancestors more primitive than they were. But we won't allow her to reduce – 'cognition' like that. What better concept is there? Also, she should not grumble about loneliness in company when she has such a splendid fellow with her. It all comes from feeling cold. Perhaps the cold will also make you lose your temper about that business with the Ministry – that would be a good thing. The letters from your wife, incidentally, are masterpieces – and that is no flattery.

Best wishes to you both,
Yours
Einstein

In the original of the letter, the formal German 'Sie' (you) was crossed out and the more familiar 'Du' substituted. Several more similar alterations occur later, in each instance the more intimate form of 'you' being substituted.

I have forgotten which pamphlet earned me the epithet of a 'splendid fellow'. I only remember that I often supported him and his work.

On the 'cognition' question Einstein freely admits that my wife was right – but only in relation to the Tree of Knowledge in the Garden of Eden. He remained adamant about the value of 'cognition' in the sense of knowledge: 'What better concept is there?'

Although I knew that Einstein had a good opinion of me, the offer in the first few lines of the next letter, which acknowledged the 'Du' used previously, gave me great pleasure.

I I

9 November, 1919

Dear Born

From now on we shall use 'Du', if you agree. I have received your manuscript. But I cannot help thinking that it is too long for the Transactions according to the new rules. I will talk to Planck about it. Your application for the K. W. Institute will soon be dealt with; just have a little patience.

In regard to the Toeplitz affair, I can't make a noise again just yet, or my bark may prove ineffective in worse cases. Antisemitism must be seen as a real thing, based on true hereditary qualities, even if for us Jews it is often unpleasant. I could well imagine that *I* myself would choose a Jew as my companion, given the choice. On the other hand I would consider it reasonable for the Jews themselves to collect the money to support Jewish research workers outside the universities and to provide them with teaching opportunities.

We look forward very much to seeing your wife. Meanwhile I want to apologise to her because, as she has shown, I have not yet eaten enough of the fruit of the Tree of Knowledge, though in my profession I am obliged to feed regularly on it. Many thanks for the pears – your productiveness really extends to every imaginable delight.

I hope you are not too cold; we are amazingly well organised in this respect.

More soon. For the present, kind regards

Yours

Einstein

Although I was very conscious of Einstein's superiority to myself, it was quite easy to address him with the informal 'Du'. He was so simple and natural, so entirely without conceit, that the brotherly form of address seemed almost inevitable. Of course I was aware of the honour of being on such a familiar footing with him. Our friendship was never shaken, even though we had some sharp scientific arguments later on (some of which are in subsequent letters).

I cannot remember which manuscript was referred to.

The Toeplitz affair was probably a snub sustained by my old friend and fellow student, Otto Toeplitz, in connection with some appointment or other, which he put down to antisemitism.

Toeplitz was a brilliant mathematician; he made a considerable contribution to the theory of the square forms of an infinite number of variables (in the so-called Hilbert Space), which is currently used in quantum mechanics. An important contribution was a long article in *Enzyklopädie der Mathematik*, written in collaboration with another friend and fellow-student, Ernst Hellinger.

Einstein's remarks about antisemitism show that he was very conscious of the contrast between Jews and Northern Europeans, and that he took the existence of mutual antipathy very much for granted. He often argued the case in favour of the suggestion that Jews ought not to press their claims in an attempt to obtain the more desirable positions, particularly academic ones, but should create jobs for themselves, to be filled from their own ranks. I was, as far as I can remember, not altogether of the same opinion; my family was amongst those who strove for complete assimilation and who regarded antisemitic expressions and measures as unjustified humiliations. History has shown that Einstein was the more profound, although he was then still a long way from recognising the magnitude of the threat of antisemitism, and of the shocking crimes resulting from it.

12

Monday
9 December, 1919

Dear Born

Your excellent article in *Frankfurter Zeitung* gave me much pleasure. But now you, as well as I, will be persecuted by the press and other rabble, although you to a lesser extent. It is so bad for me that I can hardly come up for air, let alone work properly.

That article by Drill is comic, because he introduces into philosophy the democratic method of appealing to and haranguing the masses. Let the man continue to beat his drum; it would be a pity to waste time on a reply. Save your temper, and let the fellow run around and chatter. His proof of *a priori* causality is truly amazing.

During the few days I spent with Schlick in Rostock for the University's jubilee celebrations, I heard some vile political mischief-making and saw some really delightful examples of small-state politics. What made it so ludicrous was the fact that they all knew each other so thoroughly as human beings that, when one struck a lofty tone, it was always accompanied by ridiculous dissonances. The only hall available for the celebration was the theatre, which gave it an air of comedy. It was charming to see the representatives of the old and the new Government sitting together in the two proscenium boxes. The new government was, of course, treated to every conceivable jibe by the academic dignitaries, while the ex-Grand Duke was given a seemingly endless ovation. No revolution can help against such inbred servility. Schlick has a good head on him; we must try to get him a professorship. He is in desperate need of it because of the devaluation of property. However, it will be difficult, as he does not belong to the philosophical established church of the Kantians.

Planck's misfortune moves me very deeply. I could not hold back the tears when I visited him after my return from Rostock. He behaves remarkably bravely and properly, but one can see that he is eaten up by grief.

Your wife's letters are charming, so original and to the point. I hope that our friend Oppenheim will soon find the midwife he is looking for; if not, the happy event will have to be post-poned for a while. My friend Haber, who turned to me in his misery after you moved away, suffers from a similar kind of malignant pregnancy. He has such forceful methods for trying to wrest truth from nature. For material doubts, he falls back on his intuition. He is a kind of raving barbarian, but very interesting all the same.

Your confused Lorenz has ordered me categorically to attend an extremely superfluous lecture in Frankfurt; he is one of the quaintest birds occupying a professorial chair. Unfortun-ately I have other worries. My mother, who is mortally ill, is coming to stay with us – sooner or later I must try to accommo-date my children with my divorced wife in Germany. Difficulties and anxieties at every turn.

The behaviour of the Allies is beginning to appear disgusting even by my standards. It seems that my hopes for the League of Nations will not be realised. Nevertheless, France seems to be suffering severely in spite of the coal imports, as can be seen from its recent restrictions on railway passenger traffic. Here all fixed and movable property is being bought up by foreigners, to the point of our becoming an Anglo-American colony. Just as well that we do not have to sell our brains, or make an emergency sacrifice of them to the state. I hope you are all well and not suffering too much from the cold.

Best wishes
Yours
Einstein

I saw the article in the *Frankfurter* recently but now I am unable to find it again. I remember that after so many years I was still greatly amused by my peppery criticism of those hide-bound philosophers. I can only vaguely remember Drill, whose article Einstein found comic, as a typically rabid opponent of Einstein. Schlick, on the other hand, was an important philosopher. Later on he went to Vienna and was the founder of a school of philosophy known today as logical positivism.
Einstein's description of the celebrations at Rostock University is typical of him.
I assume that by Planck's misfortune he meant the death of his daughter shortly after the birth of her first child. She had a twin sister who was very like her, who took on the care of the child and later married her sister's

husband. Then a terrible thing happened, for she too died under identical circumstances after the birth of her first child.

Einstein's characterisation of Fritz Haber is quite accurate. During the war he and I broke off our relationship. He wanted me to join his war gas team, which I bluntly refused to do. Later on we became reconciled and I made more frequent visits to his institute in Dahlem to get experimental data from my friend Franck for my work on the calculation of chemical heat variations from lattice energies. Haber was keenly interested in this, and developed a way of representing my method of calculation graphically. This theory later entered the literature of physical chemistry as the Born-Haber cyclic process. Thus I had the opportunity to get to know the 'raving barbarian', as Einstein called him. On one occasion, for example, we were having a lively discussion in his room, but were constantly interrupted by assistants, post-graduate students or technicians who wanted something from the head of the institute. In the end, someone opened the door without having knocked first and the furious Haber seized a glass inkpot and flung it in the direction of the door, where it broke into pieces, spattering ink over the wall and the door. At the door, however, stood Haber's wife. She vanished, terrified, and we continued with our work as if nothing had happened.

The 'confused Lorenz' was Professor of Physical Chemistry at Frankfurt. He was indeed a little vague, but all the same very able in his field. I received much encouragement from him, in my attempt to explain the anomalies of ionic mobility of small ions with the help of dipolar experiments, for example, and in the experiments concerning the mechanical effects of dipoles carried out by my pupil Lertes.[5]

The final paragraph of this letter shows that Einstein was no longer able to maintain his political hopes, which he had so often set against my pessimism. But he tried hard to be fair about the difficulties of France. I believe that none of us at that time recognised the real danger resulting from the Allies' harsh treatment of Germany, namely, the injury to her national pride. This led to the development of the myth of 'the stab in the back', to secret rearmament, and ultimately to the rise of National Socialism.

13

Monday
27 January, 1920

Dear Born

First of all, the matter of our young colleague Dehlinger, whom you have written about to Berliner. We are now getting a lot of money for astronomical research which I have entirely under my own control. Would he like to work in astrophysics? I could appoint him for the time being at a salary of approximately 6,000 M a year, possibly more if the present adverse conditions require it. He would then work with Freundlich. Photometric investigations on star spectra. If, however, he prefers a post in technology, I have other connections who could try to find something for him. It is difficult nowadays to make a living by scientific work alone. Let me have further details as soon as possible.

We are also having a sad time just now, because my mother is at home in a hopeless condition and suffering unspeakably. It could be many months before she is released. Else is doing a great deal; it is not easy for her. All this has diminished still further my already faltering desire to achieve great things. Now you are quite different. Your little clan has its own difficulties to deal with, and you, dear Mrs Born, make yourself interesting in a most reprehensible way. (Whimsical poems and witty letters only are permitted.) And you, Max, are giving lectures on relativity to save the institute from penury, and writing papers as if you were a single young man living in splendid isolation in his own specially heated apartment, with none of the worries of a *paterfamilias* nagging you. How do you do it?

Haber is complaining bitterly about Fajans. You have described the latter* very well. He is quite unaware of the number of arbitrary assumptions he makes, and vastly overestimates the value of consistent results. You are right in sticking uncompromisingly to your sound method. I myself do not believe that the solution to the quanta has to be found by giving up the continuum. Similarly, it could be assumed that one could arrive at general relativity by giving up the coordinate system. In principle, the continuum could possibly be dispensed with. But how could the relative movement of n points be described without the continuum?

Pauli's objection is directed not only against Weyl's, but also against anyone else's continuum theory. Even against one which treated the electron as a singularity. I believe now, as before, that one has to look for redundancy in determination by using differential equations so that the *solutions* themselves no longer have the character of a continuum. But how?

The political situation is developing consistently in favour of

* Should be "former". See Bredig, Science 180, 1118 (1973), inside back cover.

the Bolsheviks. It seems that the Russians' considerable external achievements are gathering an irresistible momentum in relation to the increasingly untenable position of the West; particularly our position. But before this can happen, streams of blood will have to flow; the forces of reaction are also growing more violent all the time. Nicolai is being attacked and insulted so much that he is no longer able to lecture, not even in the Charité. Once again I have had to intercede for him in public (one could write a new *comédie* called: 'The *friend* against his will'). France is really playing a rather sorry role in all this (all the same it is to their credit that they have rid themselves of the Tiger [Georges Clemenceau]). Victory is very hard to bear. Erzberger's trial is comic; those with clean hands (and pockets) may stone him, if they exist! By the way, I must confess to you that the Bolsheviks do not seem so bad to me, however laughable their theories. It would be really interesting just to have a look at the thing at close quarters. At any rate, their message seems to be very effective, for the weapons the Allies used to destroy the German Army melt away in Russia like snow in the spring sun. Those fellows have gifted politicians at the top. I recently read a brochure by Radek – one has to hand it to him, the man knows his business.

You think I should let my voice be heard in England? I would do, if I really had something worthwhile to say. But I can see that the people there are deeply involved in their own problems. What could they possibly do to banish want? They, and the Americans, are sending emergency supplies. But little can be done in the face of this mass suffering.

The peace treaty certainly goes too far. But since its fulfilment is quite impossible, it is better that its demands are objectively impossible to fulfil, rather than just intolerable. One has to acknowledge that the citizens on the other side had to have something in black and white as a reward for the courage of the French. To rise against the treaty would only make sense if one believed in its real significance, which I do not. By the way, I am going to England in the spring, to have a medal pressed into my hand and to have a closer look at the other side of this tomfoolery. Spengler has not spared me either. Sometimes one agrees to his suggestions in the evening, and then smiles about them next morning. One can see that the whole of his monomania had its origin in schoolteacher mathematics. Euclid *versus* Descartes is brought into everything, although, one must admit, ingeniously. These things are amusing; if someone should say the exact opposite tomorrow with sufficient spirit, it is amusing once more, but the devil only knows what the *truth* is.

That business about causality causes me a lot of trouble, too. Can the quantum absorption and emission of light ever be understood in the sense of the complete causality requirement, or would a statistical residue remain? I must admit that there I lack the courage of my convictions. But I would be very unhappy to renounce *complete* causality. I do not understand Stern's interpretation because I cannot make real sense of his statement that nature is 'intelligible'. (The question whether strict causality exists or not has a definite meaning, even though there can probably never be a definite answer to it.) Sommerfeld's book is good, although I must say frankly that, for heaven only knows what subconscious reason, this person does not ring true to me.

I am pleased that your letters to the Ministry have served their purpose. That speaks well for those people; after all you did not mince your words. It has really got much better. Just imagine what would have happened before, had you written like that. Now the dictatorial omnipotence of you Ordinarii will be brought to a horrible end, or so I heard the other day. Just you wait!

For you, Mrs Born, I have an interesting suggestion. As soon as your children are up and about again, start learning how to experiment in the laboratory. This is such wonderful work if one has the time to devote oneself to it. I mean it quite seriously. Even assuming that a year or more would have to be spent in studying, it would be very much worth while. And once you are involved in it, it is a splendid way of working together. You do need something to stretch your mind. What do you think of it?

Best wishes to you all

Yours

Einstein

Dehlinger was a gifted young physicist from Vienna, who had developed a formula for the dispersion of light in the infrared for simple diatomic lattices, using my papers on the lattice theory of crystals as his point of departure. I know nothing of his subsequent fate. Arnold Berliner was then known to every natural scientist as the founder and editor of the journal *Die Naturwissenschaften* (The Natural Sciences). He was an electrical engineer by profession and occupied an important position at the A. E. G. (General Electric Co.). Through his journal he exerted considerable influence in scientific research circles. Extended correspondence with his authors gave him a deep insight into their psychology, which he summarised as 'Mimosa-like porcupines'. He lived to see the rise of Hitler, was unable to go abroad because of his age, and took his own life.

After his brief reference to the great suffering of his mother and to the small troubles in our house (my wife and children had gone down with measles), Einstein mentions my lectures on relativity in Frankfurt. In those days the inflation of the German currency had already gone so far that the Institute's budget was not sufficient. We needed money for the experiments into the quantisation of direction that Otto Stern, assisted by Walter Gerlach from the Institute for Experimental Physics under Wachsmuth, had just begun at the Institute. I myself was also doing some experimental work with beams of silver atoms. It occurred to me to exploit the popular interest in Einstein's theory of relativity for this purpose by organising lectures on the subject and charging an entrance fee for the benefit of the Institute. There was a wave of enthusiasm for Einstein's theory at the time, following Sir Arthur Eddington's announcement to the Royal Society that Einstein's prediction about the deflection by the sun of light beams from the stars had been confirmed by a British expedition under his leadership. The lectures were well patronised and I later wrote a book based on them.

The remarks concerning the physical chemists Fajans and Haber refer to problems which are no longer of interest.

Einstein's statements about the quanta are more important. They contain the early basis for his subsequent position on quantum mechanics. He insists unconditionally on retaining a continuum theory, that is, differential equations, and on obtaining quantum phenomena (discontinuities) by redundancy in determination (more equations than unknowns). In this letter Einstein's political views are particularly informative. He believed at that time, like many others, that the Bolshevik revolution would mean deliverance from the principal evils of our time: militarism, bureaucratic oppression, and plutocracy; and he hoped for an improvement in conditions from the Communists, 'however comic their theories'. I do not know if he had read much of Marx, Engels and Lenin's works. Similarly he was not very familiar with political and economic writers of a bourgeois leaning. At any rate, his hope for the Russian revolution was based on his dislike, one could almost say hatred, of the ruling powers in the West, than on a rational conviction of the correctness of Communist ideology. I emphasise this point because Communist writers often represent him as a supporter, or at least a precursor, of their doctrines.*

The theme of the Russian revolution frequently recurs in later letters. In any case, Einstein did not go to Russia but to America when he had to leave Germany. He also, as far as I know, never visited Russia.

My wife never took seriously his suggestion to learn to experiment. That kind of activity does not appeal to her.

The next letter must have been written in answer to the news from us that I had obtained a chair in Göttingen. Peter Debye had been there during the war as successor to my former teacher, Woldemar Voigt. During my time as a private lecturer there were two professors ordinarius in the department of physics, E. Riecke in experimental physics and W. Voigt in theoretical physics. To attract Debye to Göttingen, an additional extraordinariat was founded in 1914. Voigt took this so that Debye could become Professor Ordinarius. After Riecke's death a professorship extraordinarius was arranged for Robert Pohl. After the end of the war, Debye decided to accept an appointment in Zurich. I was offered his position in 1920. Einstein's reply to my question as to what we should do was as follows.

14

3 March, 1920

Dear Born

It is difficult to know what advice to give. Theoretical physics will flourish wherever *you* happen to be; there is no other Born to be found in Germany today. Therefore the question is really: where do you find it more pleasant? Now when I put myself in your position, I think I would rather remain in Frankfurt. For I would find it intolerable to be assigned to a small circle of self-important and, for the most part, unfeeling (and narrow-minded) academics (no other social intercourse available). Just remember what Hilbert had to endure with these people. Something else must be taken into consideration. If Max should be faced with the necessity of earning something on the side, a possibility one cannot altogether rule out under the present

* For example, in his book *Albert Einstein* (Berlin, 1953), Friedrich Herneck begins with the words: 'Albert Einstein, one of the greatest Germans after Karl Marx...'. Einstein would have found that laughable.

unstable economic conditions, it would be incomparably better to live in Frankfurt than Göttingen. On the other hand, life in Göttingen may well be more pleasant for the housewife than in Frankfurt, and better for the children; but this I cannot judge, as I do not know enough about conditions in Frankfurt.

And after all, it is not so important where one settles. The best thing is to follow your instinct without too much reflection. And besides, as a person without roots anywhere, I do not feel qualified to give advice. My father's ashes lie in Milan. I buried my mother here only a few days ago. I myself have journeyed to and fro continuously – a stranger everywhere. My children are in Switzerland under conditions which make it a troublesome undertaking for me when I want to see them. A person like me has as his ideal to be *at home* anywhere with his near and dear ones; he has no right to advise you in this matter.

I was very interested in your observations about ion mobility; I believe the concept is right. In my spare time I always brood about the problem of the quanta from the point of view of relativity. I do not think the theory can work without the continuum. But I do not seem to be able to give tangible form to my pet idea, which is to understand the structure of the quanta by redundancy in determination, using differential equations.

Hoping that this letter will find all four of you in good health and spirits, I remain, with best wishes

Yours

Einstein

We finally decided in favour of Göttingen. I went to Berlin to negotiate with the Ministry of Education, and explained to Ministerial Councillor Wende that I felt unable to take on both the theoretical and the experimental physics departments, but that I would be prepared to go to Göttingen if a second chair were to be given to an experimental physicist closely connected with me. Wende said that there was no position available, that the budget for the current year had already been allocated, and that it was extremely unlikely that a new professorship would be approved for the next financial year. To prove this, he gave me a great thick book which contained the budget estimates of the Ministry, and left the room. I studied the pages dealing with physics in Göttingen very carefully, and discovered the following: There were two professorships extraordinarius for experimental physics, one for Voigt, and the other for Pohl. One bore the remark: 'To be abolished on the death of the occupant'. Now Voigt had just died; but this remark was not placed, as it should have been, underneath the column dealing with his position, but below that of Pohl's – who was very much alive. This meant that Voigt's position was available. When Wende returned I gleefully pointed out the facts to him. But he shrugged his shoulders and said that it was obviously a clerical error: Voigt's position had only been provided for during his lifetime. However, I insisted so forcefully on the letter of the text, that Wende eventually said that he could not take the responsibility and would have to consult his superiors. The Minister, Professor Becker, and the Ministerial Director, Professor Richter, entered the room. When I had explained the position to them, they laughed, and Becker said: 'Well, as the revolution is still with us one can get away with that sort of thing. We will stand by the wording. Please give us some suggestions for the second professor.' So I accepted the chair; however, I did not become a full professor, but a professor extraordinarius, like the soon-to-be-appointed experimentalist. In the following year all three of us, Pohl, the new man and I, were promoted to full professorships.

The choice of the 'new one' caused me a few headaches. I followed my instinct for the essential requirements of the position, and proposed my old friend James Franck. I very much admired his experiments into the excitation of atomic line spectra by electronic collision carried out in collaboration with Gustav Hertz; they confirmed the fundamental and revolutionary assumptions of Bohr's atomic theory, and were therefore one of the foundations of quantum physics. That I had made the right choice was shown not only by the award of the Nobel Prize for 1925 to Franck and Hertz, but also by the flowering of experimental physics in Göttingen during the next twelve years (1921–1933). This was all therefore basically due to a clerical error.

The letter ends with two remarks about physics. The first of these refers to a paper of mine; the second, and more important, contains Einstein's ideas about the nature of the quanta. My work on ion mobility had been encouraged by the Frankfurt physical chemist R. Lorentz. This work was on the fact that ions in aqueous solution, particularly monovalent ones, exhibit a strange abnormality of movement: one would think that the small ions must be the fastest, the large ones the slowest, but the opposite is the case. The chemists explained this by the somewhat vague notion of hydration. I was able to define this idea more closely using Debye's theory, according to which the water molecules are dipoles. An ion moving about amongst them causes them to rotate, the more forcefully the smaller its radius. I developed this into a general theory which can be termed hydrodynamics, by analogy with the modern magneto-hydrodynamics. Also, one of my pupils, Lertes, was able to demonstrate experimentally one of the simple effects (the rotation of a sphere, filled with water, in a rotating electric field).

Einstein was occupied for many years with the idea of explaining quanta within the normal framework of differential equations supplemented in such a way as to contain a redundancy in determination. We frequently talked about it. Although nothing ever came of it, he believed so strongly in the value of the idea that he clung to it even after the discovery of quantum mechanics. His rejection of the latter was probably connected with this.

What makes this letter of special value to me is the light it throws upon Einstein's life and personality.

A postcard from Berlin follows.

15

[*Undated*]

Dear Born

By the same post I am sending you my last copy of the paper you asked for. It got smudged in Teubner's printing works. I am very pleased about your little book on relativity. Forgive me for not having written in spite of all your kind messages. That rogue of a postman is to blame. What is happening about Göttingen? Debye's paper is very good.

    Best wishes
     Yours
      Einstein

Best wishes to your wife. I will not be able to return to Frankfurt for some time. I hope we can meet here before that.

My book on relativity arose out of the lectures I mentioned before which I had delivered in Frankfurt. Einstein himself read the proofs and was satisfied with my method of presentation. Three editions were published, one after another. Now in 1962, after 44 years, it has been re-issued in a modernised English language paperback edition, and a similar German one appeared in 1964.

The following postcard from Kristiania is addressed to my wife, and contains condolences on the death of her mother. She died at our house in Frankfurt from the so-called 'Asian flu' which was raging all over Europe at the time. Underneath Einstein's message there are a few lines from his step-daughter Ilse.

16   *Kristiania*
                                                                18 April, 1920

Dear Mrs Born
    The news of the bitter experience you had to go through has touched me deeply. I know what it means to see one's mother suffer the agony of death and be unable to help. There is no consolation. All of us have this heavy burden to bear, for it is inseparably bound up with life. However, there is one thing: to unite in friendship, and to help one another to carry the burden. We do, after all, share so many happy experiences that we have no need to give way to pointless brooding. The old, who have died, live on in the young ones. Don't you feel this now in your bereavement when you look at your children? I am here with Ilse, giving a few lectures to the students – a lively, congenial crowd. Also the wonderful scenery and a truly formidable heatwave, which one would not have suspected up here.
                 Kindest regards to you and Max
                     Yours
                         Einstein

Dear Mrs Born, I want to tell you that I also feel with you in your grief, and think of you with warmest sympathy.
        Yours
            Ilse Einstein

The first of my letters to have been preserved is addressed not to Einstein himself but to his wife; it requires no commentary, nor does the letter from me to Einstein himself which follows it.

I7

Frankfurt a.M.
21 June, 1920

Dear Mrs Einstein

I have sent your kind letter on to my wife in Leipzig. She is staying there with her father. The last few weeks have been very sad; I cannot describe it all to you in detail. Hedi collapsed in the end, as a result of all the excitement, pain and over-exertion. In spite of this she went to Leipzig, but had to stay in bed and recuperate there. Apparently she is getting better now. Just now a card arrived from Albert in Kristiania with the sort of kind words only he can find; Miss Ilse also added a few words.

I want to ask a favour of you. You know that I have written a largish popular book about the theory of relativity. This will also contain a short description of Albert's life and personality. Could you possibly get the proofs from Dr Berliner, and read through the biographical summary? It was written with great sincerity, but I am not sure if the tone is right. There could also be some factual errors. I would be most grateful for your un-sparing criticism, and for any suggestions for alterations. I want, above all, to avoid any suggestion of burning incense before the idol. Albert does not need it anyway. Please let me have your opinion as soon as possible.

Yet another favour. The galley proofs, corrected for the second time, will be sent off to Albert within the next few days. I am or course very much concerned that he should read or at least look through the book before it is printed, and that he should make suggestions for alterations. He is probably hard to get at right now, and I will have to have the proofs back from him very soon, because the printing must not be delayed. Please make sure that he receives the proofs by the fastest possible means, that he reads them as quickly as possible and returns them to me by express post. I am most grateful to you for selecting and giving us a picture of Albert for the book.

My little ones are sweet, darling little things, and surround me with sunshine.

The question 'Göttingen, yes or no?' worries us a great deal.

We are still undecided. If you know what we should do, please let us into the secret.

 With kind regards, also to your daughter

 Yours

 M. Born

18

Dear Einstein

We will in all probability go to Göttingen, that is, if Franck is offered the chair and accepts; the faculty has put him forward. Now the question of my successor becomes urgent. Schönflies wanted to write to you and to ask for your expert opinion. I would, of course, like to have Stern. But Wachsmuth does not; he said to me, 'I think very highly of Stern, but he has such an analytical Jewish intellect.' At least it is open antisemitism. But Schönflies and Lorenz want to help me. Wachsmuth has proposed Kossel, which is very crafty of him; for nothing can be said against him, except perhaps that he knows no mathematics, but that is hardly a fault. Stern has raised the standard of our little Institute and really deserves recognition. I do not need to explain his value to you, of course. Then Lenz and Reiche are under consideration, and perhaps outsiders as well. *Embarras de richesse!* I have asked Laue to give his opinion; perhaps it would be best if you were to talk to him about it, so that your verdicts do not clash.

 I am being very lazy at the moment and hardly do any work; the only experiments I pursue with any eagerness are those on the free path lengths of silver atoms. My assistant is very good at her job. We have now constructed the apparatus, but the measurements will unfortunately not be started before the holidays. We depart for Sulden in the Southern Tyrol (Italy) on August 6th; I am looking forward impatiently to getting away from it all completely again, and seeing beautiful things. My wife has recovered a little from the hard time after the death of her mother. We often take trips out, which does her good. To-morrow we are going to the Rhine, where she has never been before. The children are well. Unfortunately the decision about Göttingen drags on endlessly; we have not yet found a flat there. My wife will go there next week and try to find accommodation. Are you coming to Southern Germany at all? We would so much like to see you and talk to you.

    With best wishes to your dear wife and to the young ladies
        Yours
            Max Born

The following letter, the first of my wife's to Einstein to be preserved, is particularly warm and profound and was perhaps the stimulus for his keeping our letters from that time onwards.

19   *Frankfurt*
                                                31 July, 1920

Dear Mr Einstein
    Max has asked me to thank you very much for your letter; your judgment is especially important to him, because Wachsmuth is agitating against Stern on antisemitic grounds. Epstein, as a Jew *and* a Pole, will therefore be even more strongly rejected. Max is working very hard; his experiment (atomic diameter of. . . . ?) is under way at last, and he stays at the Institute until eight o'clock at night making measurements. We are very happy that you will be coming to Nauheim, and I hope that you will stay with us for a few days. I am now – after my mother's death – so much in need of those true relationships of the spirit which are left to me. The further the hour of her death lies behind us, the stronger is my longing for the departed; the darker and more incomprehensible seems the enigma of death. The ending of such a strong personality and the sudden extinction of life is such a tormenting problem that one wonders how one is able to live without being constantly troubled by it. But it teaches one to live more consciously, to feel more deeply and strongly and to hold on to what one possesses. If one did not do this, one could sink without hope into the bitter and pessimistic attitude of mind of Widman's *Maikäfer-Komödie*; do you

know it? Its images constantly haunted my imagination in the first bitterness of my grief. One lives under the illusion that it is forever May, and that the whole world is constantly filled with young, juicy and delicious greenery, put there just for one's own use, and then all of a sudden and incredibly fast it happens, and one finds oneself lame and weary of life in the mud of a rain-soaked road. So I thought, well, I am now in the mud, but I can see that it is still May, after all, and I must not allow myself to be pulled down.

We have now decided for Göttingen, but we have as yet no prospect of accommodation there and may possibly remain here for the winter as the Ministry is still dawdling.

Something else: Max wants to stay in Nauheim for two days so that he will be able to spend the evenings with his colleagues. Would you like to do that as well? Or would you rather travel there from here each day (one hour's journey)? Shall we book a room for you in any case and, if so, for how many days? But you must stay with us before and afterwards, *whatever happens*. If you do not, God help you! We are going to Sulden, Sulden-hotel, Tyrol (Italy), on August 6th, *via* Munich, Merano and Bolzano, complete with passports and lire. Your wife was going to write to me when your are due to go to Southern Germany; how is she, and how are your daughters?

  With best wishes to you all
   Yours sincerely
    Max and Hedi Born

The next letter from my wife initiated a discussion between her and Einstein about 'publicity', his attitude to attack or glorification. The first of these letters shows that we, and Hedi particularly, were not in agreement with him about his reaction to that kind of irritation. We still believed in the 'secluded temple of science', as Hedi said. From this beginning a real conflict developed, as the following letters show.

20

Cronstettenstr. 9
8 September, 1920

Dear Mr Einstein

When are you coming to Nauheim, and on which days are we going to have you to ourselves? We will tell *no-one* of your presence and, if you prefer, you can remain incognito. Paulchen Oppenheimer seems to be away still. Please send us a postcard about your plans.

We are extremely sorry to hear about the unpleasant rows that are worrying you. You must have suffered very much from them, for otherwise you would not have allowed yourself to be goaded into that rather unfortunate reply in the newspapers. Those who know you are sad and suffer with you, because they can see that you have taken this infamous mischief-making *very* much to heart. Those who do not know you get a false picture of you. That hurts too. In the meanwhile I hope you are like old Diogenes again and smile about the beasts thrashing about in your barrel. That people can still disappoint and irritate you to the point where it affects your peace of mind just does not fit my image of you, which I keep on the private altar of my heart. You could not have withdrawn from the rough and tumble of ordinary life to the 'secluded temple of science' (see your talk to Planck) had you been able to find *the same* illusions, *the same* happiness and peace in your fellow-man as in your temple. So if the filthy waters of the world are now lapping at the steps of your temple, shut the door and laugh. Just say, 'After all, I have not entered the temple in vain.' Don't get angry. Go on being the holy one in the temple – and stay in Germany! There is filth everywhere – but not another female preacher as enthusiastic and *self-opinionated* as your affectionate friend
        Hedi Born

P.S. Now look here! If you or Elsa, to whom best wishes by the way, don't get in touch with us soon, I'll join the anti-relativity league, or set up in competition with you.

You simply *must* read *The Home and the World* by Rabindranath Tagore – the finest novel I've read for a long time.

21

9 September, 1920

Dear Borns

Don't be too hard on me. Everyone has to sacrifice at the altar of stupidity from time to time, to please the Deity and the human race. And this I have done thoroughly with my article. This is shown by the exceedingly appreciative letters from all my dear friends. A witty acquaintance said the other day: 'With Einstein all is for the sake of publicity; the Weyland G.m.b.H. is his latest and most cunning trick'. This is true, or at least partly so. Like the man in the fairytale who turned everything he touched into gold – so with me everything turns into a fuss in the news-papers: *suum cuique*.

In the first moment of attack I probably thought of flight. But soon my insight and the phlegm returned. Today I think only of buying a sailing boat and a country cottage close to water. Somewhere near Berlin.

I'll arrive at your place around the 18th, if you can put up with me. However, if I am expected to live in Nauheim for the duration of the scientific meeting, would you please see to it, dear Born, that we are staying close together. I shall not book any-thing from here, as you can judge better what is the best thing to do. But I would also like to stay with you for a little while, if possible, so that I can have a chat with my charming correspon-dent. Writing does not seem to be as effective, because of the annoying blotchiness of my ink. Else is also coming, but will stay with the Oppenheims.

We will have to be in Stuttgart on the 28th, where I am going to lecture in aid of a public observatory. Afterwards, we are going to Swabia, where my boys have been asked to meet me.

With kindest regards
Yours
Einstein

The important meeting of the Association of German doctors and natural scientists took place in Nauheim in September 1920. Einstein lived with us in our house on Cronstetterstrasse; we travelled to Nauheim each morning and returned in the evening. Nauheim was the scene of an angry encounter between Einstein and his opponents, whose motives were by no means purely scientific but strongly mixed with antisemitism.[15] In the physics section, Philipp Lenard directed some sharp, malicious attacks against Einstein, which were undisguisedly antisemitic. Einstein was provoked into making a caustic reply and I seem to remember that I supported him. Einstein returns to this incident in a later letter (26), where he regrets that he allowed himself to lose his temper and reply in anger. From then on Lenard carried out a systematic persecution of Einstein. He invented the difference between 'German' and 'Jewish' physics. He and another important physicist, Johannes Stark, who both later received the Nobel Prize, became leading scientific administrators under the Nazis and were responsible for the removal of all Jewish scholars. It was in Nauheim on this occasion that the outlines of the great danger of anti-semitism to German science first appeared.

22

Frankfurt a.M.
2 October, 1920

Dear Einstein

To judge by your card, Hechingen must be a charming, sleepy little place; just right to calm down the agitation which, to our regret, you were forced to endure here and in Nauheim. We do not want to disturb your slumbering consciousness with effusive letters; sometimes it is a good thing if one's friends are removed from one's consciousness, and I have the feeling that now is the time for us to disappear. After all, there is really nothing more obtrusive than 'suffering with someone'; it is an encroachment on a friend's life, a baring of the soul, of which one is ashamed afterwards.

But before we disappear from sight, like Punch, we have two other requests, and I would like to charge you, dear Mrs Elsa, to remind your husband of them from time to time. 1. That your husband should write to Mrs Hoff, Güntersburg Allee 57. This would not really be a waste of time, as there are few people like her. 2. My husband feels an inclination to slay the golden calf in America and to earn enough through lecturing to build a small house in Göttingen to his own requirements. Should you, by any chance, have the opportunity to recommend someone to lecture over there, please suggest Max. He would be able to go there in February, March and April, and appease his longing for Broadway at the same time (I can't understand this love of his, but forgive him for it.)

And now without further ado your Punch and Judy bow out,

Max and Hedi Born,

until you happen to remember them in their toy chest once again.

Why I am supposed to have 'longed for Broadway' is incomprehensible to me. Anyway, the journey to America did not materialise then.

The following letter concerns the problem of publicity that I have already referred to. In Nauheim, Einstein's enemies had reproached him with self-advertising, and with allowing his fame to be broadcast. We had already discussed this with Einstein during our talks every evening, after returning from Nauheim. We found that he was far too accommodating towards journalists, possibly because his wife was understandably pleased about his popularity.

Soon a new incident required urgent attention. An author and journalist, who had called on Einstein and had won his and especially Elsa's sympathy as a poor Jew, wanted to write and publish a book called *Conversations with Einstein*. We advised Einstein not to allow it, but without success. Following is my wife's spirited reaction to this piece of news; the letter was written in Leipzig, where she was visiting her parents, and thus without my knowledge. The letter is very long and detailed; I have abbreviated it considerably.

23 *Leipzig*
7 October, 1920

Dear Mr Einstein

Today, a friendly but serious word with you. I would much prefer not to have to disturb you during your week's holiday, but it is a matter of great consequence which has troubled your friends ever since Nauheim:

You *must withdraw* your permission to X for the publication of the book *Conversations with Einstein*, and what's more *at once*, and by *registered* letter. And, whatever happens, it must under no circumstances be published *abroad*. I wish I had the eloquence of an angel, so that I could make the consequences clear to you. Quite by chance . . . [a book by X] fell into my hands here; the level of this book disgusts me so much that I wrote the enclosed somewhat malicious comments, which I swear I am going to publish unless you withdraw your permission immediately. And I have a lot more to spill out, if it is a question of saving the honour and respect of a friend. I am not painting too black a picture.

[There follows a list of titles of the books by Mr X.]

That is good enough in itself. . . .

Now the *contents*. The man has no idea of the seriousness of your personality, of what is important and valuable to you and to us; otherwise he would neither have written the book nor exploited your kindheartedness to wrest your permission from you. Your 'conversations' will therefore be conducted at a very low level. The gutter press will get hold of it and paint a very unpleasant picture of you. And afterwards you will be quoted all over the place, and your own jokes will be smilingly thrown back at you, to show that people have read the book. Verses will be composed in your honour; a completely new and far worse wave of persecution will be unleashed, not only in Germany but *everywhere*, until the whole thing will make you sick with disgust.

And how could *we*, your good friends, then defend you? 'But look here – Mr Einstein, your " modest friend ", surely gave permission himself.' Then it would be useless for us to protest that you gave permission out of weakness and good nature *Nobody would believe it*. (This is confirmed by my father, who studied with X and has told me a great deal about him.) The *fact is simply that a man in his early forties, a comparatively early age, gave permission to an author to record his conversations*. If I did not know *you* well, I certainly would not concede innocent motives to any other human being given these circumstances. I would put it down to vanity. This book will constitute your moral death sentence for all but four or five of your friends. It could subsequently be the *best confirmation of the accusation of self-advertisement*.

We, your friends, are deeply shocked at this prospect. This book, if published *anywhere at all*, would be the end of your peace, everywhere and for all time. . . .

Please reassure us soon about this worry which pursues us day and night. Max has just written to me today: 'I have just had an express letter from Freundlich with X's answer, which is, of course, in the negative. I do not know what to do. I would so much like to discuss it with you; every day I have worries of this kind.'

Please, dear friend, quickly relieve our worries, and do not refuse our advice and request. I shall never talk to anyone about this business, for I have heard enough how much you dislike it when women meddle in your affairs. 'Women are there to cook and nothing else'; but it sometimes happens that they *boil over* [a play on words in German, where 'cooking' is 'Kochen', and 'boiling over', 'Ueber-kochen'].

Yours
Hedi Born

24   *Frankfurt a.M.*
                                                                    13 October, 1920

Dear Einstein

The enclosed pages from the bookseller's financial paper have come to me from various people. Comment is superfluous. It seems that you are less excited about it than your friends. My wife has already written to you saying what I think about this affair. (She is already regretting that she, too, has tried to turn your name into gold by sending me to America; women, poor creatures, carry the whole burden of existence, and grasp at any relief.) You will have to shake off X, otherwise Weyland will win all along the line, and Lenard and Gehrcke will triumph.

According to the advice of experts, the following is best: write strongly to X, saying that you can not, after all, agree to the publication of the conversations, because you have been accused of publicity seeking, and in view of the fact that the advertisement in the bookseller's financial paper has offered a useful new lever to your enemies. If X refuses, as is to be expected, you will obtain a provisional order from the Public Prosecutor's Office against the appearance of the book, and make sure that this is reported in the newspapers (or we could do this). I shall send you the details of where to apply soon. The experts have established that, just as one can no more print another person's photograph without his permission, thoughts expressed during conversation may not be published. This is a better method than having the proofs sent to you and reading them, for you would then have *no* responsibility for the book *whatever*. If, on the other hand, there were a statement in the introduction that you had read the proofs and approved of them, all the muck thrown up by the book would fall on you. I *implore* you, do as I say. If not: Farewell to Einstein! Your Jewish 'friends' will have achieved what that pack of antisemites have failed to do.

Forgive the officiousness of my letter, but it concerns everything dear to me (and Planck and Laue, etc.) You do not understand this, in these matters you are a little child. We all love you, and you must obey judicious people (not your wife).

Should you prefer to have nothing further to do with the whole business, give me *written* authority. If necessary, I will go to Berlin, or even to the North Pole.

    Yours
      Born

25

            11 October, 1920

Dear Born
Your wife has sent me an urgent letter about Mr X's book. She is objectively right, though not in her harsh verdict of X. *I have informed him by registered letter that his splendid work must not appear in print.*

    With kindest regards to you both
      Yours
        Einstein

I would like to thank your wife most sincerely.

Apparently my wife had succeeded after all in making clear to Einstein the danger threatening him if the book were to be published. A postcard which followed from Holland on 26 October confirms this.

26

[undated]

Dear Born

Have categorically forbidden publication of X's book. Ehrenfest and Lorentz advise against legal proceedings, as they would only serve to increase the scandal. The whole affair is a matter of indifference to me, as is all the commotion, and the opinion of *each and every* human being. Therefore nothing can happen to me. In any case, I have used the strongest means at my disposal, apart from legal ones, particularly the threat that I would break off our relationship. However, I still prefer X to Lenard and Wien. The latter two squabble because of a passion for squabbling, while the former does it only to earn money (which is, after all, better and more reasonable). I will live through all that is in store for me like an unconcerned spectator and will not allow myself to get excited again, as in Nauheim. It is quite inconceivable to me how I could have lost my sense of humour to such an extent through being in bad company. Lorentz yesterday mentioned your lattice equilibrium in his lecture; I was also mentioned! He is a man one can admire!

Kindest regards to you and your wife.

I am having a very pleasant time here in Leiden. Weiss and Langevin are also here.

H. A. Lorentz was Professor of Theoretical Physics in Leiden, and in those days was held to be the foremost man in his field. He had given the classical theory of electrons the form considered final at that time. Ehrenfest, who was born in Vienna and educated there in the school of theoretical physics (with Boltzmann and Hasenöhrl, *inter alia*) went to Russia and married an extremely gifted Russian woman physicist. He became widely known for his outstanding works of criticism, particularly in the field of statistical mechanics (partly in collaboration with his wife, Tatyana), his unusual talent for teaching and his sparkling wit. When Lorentz retired from his chair, he pushed through Ehrenfest's appointment as his successor. The two people mentioned at the end of the letter, Weiss and Langevin, were French physicists, the first one from Strasbourg, the second from Paris. Both carried out fundamental research into magnetism; Langevin had important achievements in other fields as well.

Einstein's clearly expressed indifference to the opinion of everyone else is as characteristic of him as the judgment that he thought more of the motives of the journalist than of those of two outstanding physicists.

With this card, the X affair is substantially at an end, though it is still mentioned from time to time in the letters which follow. It may well be asked whether there is any justification for giving so much space to it in this correspondence. In fact my wife's inflammatory letter (No. 23) was originally considerably longer. I have left out the second half, which contains some legal advice from my wife's father, as well as grotesque descriptions of the possible consequences of Einstein's compliance. What remains is sufficient to show why we, with all respect for Einstein's superior intellect, could presume to criticise his behaviour in every-day life.

The contemporary reader may well think 'much ado about nothing'. Nowadays the kind of publicity we fought against is commonplace, and spares no-one. Every one of us is interviewed and paraded before the general public in the papers, on radio and television, or written about in pamphlets and books. Nobody thinks anything of it.

In those days it was different. Only when great discoveries were made did brief, factual reports appear in the newspapers. I can remember the way in which Roentgen's discovery in 1896 was reported by the press; he himself was hardly mentioned. As far as I am concerned, I myself committed a minor offence against the rules in my book *Einstein's Theory of Relativity*. The first edition of 1920 contains a photo facing the title page, and at the end a short biography of Einstein in which I described not only his scientific achievements but also his personality. Immediately after publication I received a letter from Max v. Laue, in which he wrote that he and many other of my colleagues objected to the photo and biography. Such things did not belong in a scientific book, even when addressed to a wider audience. Impressed by this, I left out both these personal details from the new editions published soon afterwards. I was possibly particularly sensitive about Mr X's plan to compile a book from interviews with Einstein about all kinds of topics, not only scientific ones, because my own much more harmless attempt to describe the person of the author in my book on relativity had been rejected by my colleagues.

But what chiefly caused me and my wife to object to this business was its connection with antisemitism. Einstein's theories had been stamped as 'Jewish physics' by colleagues who did not understand them. And now a

Jewish author, who had already published several books with frivolous titles, came along and wanted to write a similar book about Einstein. It is understandable that this upset us greatly. Einstein probably did not consider any of this to begin with. He wanted to show his gratitude towards X, who had helped him while he was ill in Berlin during the period of wartime deprivation. But he saw our point of view and did everything to prevent publication of the book. He did not succeed. A copy of it lies in front of me. I have browsed through it a little, and find it not quite as bad as I had expected. The scientific part is primitive and contains frequent misunderstandings. Otherwise, however, it contains many rather amusing stories and anecdotes which are characteristic of Einstein. It is quoted in more recent books about Einstein.

Our agitated correspondence about this affair was thus pointless in the end. Large-scale movements such as antisemitism and the prevalence of publicity, etc., necessarily run down in accordance with the law of determinism so often quoted by Einstein in this connection.

27

Frankfurt a.M.
28 October, 1920

Dear Einstein

I am very glad that you have taken energetic steps against the book by X. Only the future will show whether they are enough to prevent any trouble. The main thing is that you are determined not to have your peace disturbed in future. However, when all is said and done, you are not the only person involved, as we, who venture to call ourselves your friends, would also be affected by the stench and, I fear, would be unable just to hold our noses as you have done before. You can simply flee to Holland, but we are settled in the territory of Weyland, Wien and company.

I am writing to you quickly in Holland, as I want Mr Fokker's address. He has sent me a fine paper in which he expiates one of the sins of my youth. The address was actually on the envelope but, as I was ill in bed with asthma and unable to be on my guard, my children destroyed the envelope. I would very much like to thank Fokker; Ehrenfest will know where he lives.

Get Ehrenfest to show you a copy of Boguslavski's letter which I sent to him, and think how the poor fellow can be saved. Planck said that he was willing to help, but thought that nothing could be done officially in Berlin. Now I am negotiating with Hilbert for him to invite Boguslavski through the Wolfskehl Foundation.

I am glad that things are going so well for you in Holland. But you must not be angry with me if as a result of recent events I doubt you as a judge of human nature to the extent that I do not share your admiration for Lorentz. In Lenard and Wien you see devils, in Lorentz an angel. Neither is quite right. The first two are suffering from a political illness, very common in our starving country, which is not altogether based on inborn wickedness. When I was in Göttingen just recently I saw Runge, reduced to a skeleton and correspondingly changed and embittered. It became clear to me then what is going on around here. On the other hand, Lorentz: he even refused to write anything for Planck's sixtieth birthday. I take that *very much* amiss. You can tell him so quietly. One can disagree with Planck, but one could only doubt the honesty and nobility of his character if one had none oneself. Lorentz is apparently more afraid of losing his well-fed friends amongst the Allies than he cares about justice. I am not taken in by his using my lattice calculations in his lectures. This is not the only thing I hold against him, but then I am not writing just to slander someone. However, I must confess that I find your association with Lorentz, Ehrenfest, Weiss and Langevin far happier than the intercourse with the author of '..................'.

You will also have met Chulanovski from Russia there; please ask him for information about G. Krutkov, who has sent me a paper of his about adiabatic invariants, which I thought excellent. He must be an outstanding theoretician; I had never heard of him before.

My wife sends her best regards. She is driving herself very hard, as our cook had to be dismissed a few weeks ago for thieving and deceit (countless times). Also, miserable creature that I am, I was confined to bed with asthma until yesterday, and had to be nursed. The children are well.

    With kindest regards
        Yours
          Max Born

Boguslavski was a Russian pupil of mine, extremely talented and an attractive and worthwhile person. He suffered from tuberculosis of the lungs, and as he came from a titled family he suffered great hardships during the revolution. Eventually he turned to me for assistance, and I tried to do something for him with the help of Planck, Einstein and others.

28

Institute for Theoretical Physics
of the University of Frankfurt a.M.
Robert Mayer St. 2
8 December, 1920

Dear Einstein

Enclosed is the circular of the *Mathematische Annalen*. As I have never received any paper intended for this publication, and know nothing about it, I have not added any remarks.

I also enclose a copy of a letter from Russia, from my pupil and friend Boguslavski. The letter arrived some time ago. The contents may interest you. It can be seen that an attempt should be made to invite the poor man (who has TB as well) to Germany, to prevent him from starving to death. I have already tried everything possible, first Planck, then Klein and Hilbert in Göttingen, whom I asked to get the Academy to send an invitation of some sort to B. But they all refused; to use Hilbert's expression, they want nothing to do with 'foreign politics'. Perhaps you can think of a way. Some of what Boguslavski writes about his work is clearly nonsense, but this is probably due to his piteous condition; he is a fine intelligent man. By the way, a mutual friend, Dr Bolza from Würzburg, has tried to send a few things to Boguslavski through the Red Cross; with what success I do not know.

While on this subject: some time ago I sent you a letter from Epstein, who was asking for help. In the meantime I have received an answer from G. N. Lewis in America, to whom I had written about this matter. He has created a position for Epstein at the University of California, Berkeley, and offered it to him. But I have not heard from Epstein whether he intends to accept or not; perhaps the Swiss are keeping him. An attempt to bring him here as my successor has been wrecked by the opposition of the faculty. I did not succeed in having Stern made first choice either, because Wachsmuth wanted Madelung. Stern is now second choice, Kossel third.

As regards science, I have tried a number of things without getting enthusiastic about anything. What attracts me most is a proper theory for the irreversible processes in crystals, once suggested by Debye. But I cannot find reasonable general formulations. The measurements in the Institute on free path lengths are going quite well; the main thing was to keep the gas pressure constant for the thirty-minute vaporisation of the silver; we are now doing it to 5 per cent. However, we have not yet completed an exact measurement of the thickness of the silver deposit, as we had to get together the optical equipment bit by bit. Landé, who was recently at the conference in Heidelberg, told me yesterday that Ramsauer (*alias* Lenard) had severely criticised my book on relativity because I had given the impression that Maxwell's proposal (for determining the absolute movement of the solar system from the eclipse of Jupiter's satellites) had in fact been carried out with a negative result. I can see that the criticism is not unjustified, and there-fore expect vociferous attack by Lenard or one of his associates.

Healthwise I have been bad for several weeks, as may have been apparent from the bilious tone of my last letter to Holland. But I am now fairly well again, although the political situation depresses me more than I like to admit to myself.

With kindest regards
Yours
Born

Saratov
18 August, 1920

Dear Born

At last I have the opportunity to send letters out of the country, and I am using it to write to you. For almost two years now I have been professor in Saratov at the local University. Although I accepted a chair in Moscow as much as a year and a half ago, I dare not return there for fear of starving to death. But this year even we, here in the South-East, are going to have a bad time, as the harvest has been extremely poor. Now I dream of being able to go abroad once again; my scientific interests, as well as my state of health, demand it. Life in the socialist Eden does not seem to be meant for me. I have been feeling ill for almost six months now, and am staying in a kind of sanatorium.

Scientific life has almost ceased to exist here. No journals are being published, neither are there opportunities to have anything printed. A mimimum of scientific work is being done; anyone wanting to do it would soon starve. Furthermore, for the last three years we have not received any foreign journals. Therefore I now have very little idea of what is currently being thought about in scientific circles. I myself have, of course, done much during these last few years, and would like to be able to talk about it. As recently as last spring I was still working, and had just started to write a small book. However, now I feel so ill that for the time being I am obliged to give it all up. In my book I intended to give a fairly comprehensive description of the movement of electrons in different kinds of electromagnetic fields. The second part of the book was to contain an outline of the theory of atoms. I have investigated several types of movement presumably for the first time.

Some time ago I had the following idea which I have not yet been able to verify. The nucleus of heavy atoms need not be a charged point. By developing the potential of the nucleus as powers of $1/r$ and retaining only the term with $1/r$ one can treat the nucleus as a positive point charge and a dipole. The problem of the movement of the electron in the field of this nucleus can be rigorously solved. The projection of the electron path on the unit sphere is then the orbit of a spherical pendulum, where gravity acts parallel to the dipole axis. The elliptical integral representing the action (quantum integral) can be developed as a series of powers of the dipole moment, and one can thus determine the position of the spectral lines in the presence of this dipole. The solution can be most easily written with the help of the partial differential equation of Jacobi; the variables can be separated for polar coordinates.

Lately I have been much interested by the following train of thought; I still regard it as important, although I have not yet obtained positive results. Thermodynamics and electrodynamics alone are insufficient for developing a radiation formula, because radiation pressure ought to be used only integrally (for all frequencies) to obtain the work done. Now we have substances which absorb (and reflect) selectively, and one can probably use as an ideal limiting conception a piston which completely reflects the radiation of a certain spectral range but allows all others to pass through. Such a piston would separate the radiation of different frequencies in the same way as a semi-permeable membrane separates molecules of different kinds. This concept certainly contains nothing to contradict the fundamental laws of electrodynamics and thermodynamics. But with the help of such a piston and a Planck coal dust particle it is easy to construct a *perpetuum mobile* of the second order. And this can be done for any radiation law. Now a radiation law can be regarded as a definition of the temperature concept, since the temperature can be derived from it as a function of the mechanical quantities 'energy' and 'frequency'. How is temperature to be defined so that the contradiction of the second law of thermodynamics can be avoided? The answer is: the temperature is a monotonically increasing function of frequency only (independent of the energy). For instance, $T = \alpha \gamma$. All this is absurd but very attractive.

I cannot write much. I only wish I could talk to you in person. Do try to get me an official invitation to Berlin to give a few lectures there. The invitation will have to look as official as possible, so that I can attempt to obtain a passport for leaving the country with it. You would be rendering me a great service, as I am in urgent need of a few months recuperation. Einstein can help you forward the invitation to Russia. It should be sent either to my Moscow address, Pokrova, Little Uspanki 8, or here (University of Saratov).

It is difficult to describe our living conditions. As a Professor I earn approximately 1.5×10^4 roubles per month. With this one can buy approximately one pound of bread per day. Everyone is allowed to buy only 150 g of bread at the controlled price. This is, moreover, practically the only thing one does get. Everything else has to be bought at 'speculative' prices. Trading in the normal sense, as is well known, does not exist here. There are only secret 'dealings' whereby one must procure all the necessities. One pound of butter costs approximately 2×10^3 roubles, sugar somewhat more. A pair of boots costs $3–6 \times 10^4$

roubles, etc. One frequently meets people who spend their entire month's salary in a single day. How this squares with the continuity equation of money is extremely puzzling. One must assume, however, that the money in circulation is confined to the official issue, as the forging of paper currency would hardly be a paying proposition. Firewood costs about 100 roubles per kilogram! But very few people are able to pay that much. Therefore everybody has to cut their own wood. Generally speaking, life for the majority of people is quite unbearable. Winter will soon be here again, and we can look forward to enjoying room temperatures of 4–5°.

A congress of physicists is due to begin in Moscow in ten days' time. Unfortunately I will be unable to make the journey because of the state of my health.

If you see any of my Göttingen friends, please give them my regards. I would particularly like to see Bolza and Karman again. Please write to Debye and tell him that I am still alive, and ask him please to continue to look after my cases of books at the Physics Institute. I am not writing to him myself, as I cannot at present send more than two letters out of the country.

Give my regards to your wife. You are all fortunate people. You cannot imagine the amount of misery which surrounds one here. Look after yourself.

Yours

S. Boguslavski

(Reply through Prof. Dr M. Vasmer, Dorpat, Estland, Teichstr. 19)

Gilbert N. Lewis was a distinguished physical chemist in Los Angeles, whom I got to know through Fritz Haber. When I later visited California (1926), both Lewis and Epstein gave me a very friendly reception.

The following letter from Einstein begins with a return to the formal ('Sie') mode of address. This may be connected with the morally presumptuous tone of my previous letter (which I later attributed to my illness). Einstein's reference to 'burying the hatchet' had nothing to do with this, but with an exchange of letters between my wife and his, of which I knew virtually nothing. Einstein chivalrously defended his wife. More of this in my next letter.

29

30 January, 1921

Dear Born

Today I write principally because I want solemnly to bury the hatchet. I have had a tiff with your wife for the sake of mine, mainly because of a rather exaggerated letter which she wrote to her. But a lot has happened since and it is wrong for men like us to lose contact over such a trifle. X's unfortunate opus has appeared without any earth tremors (so far) and without my having read any of it.

I do not know of anything I could do for Boguslavski, much as I pity him; what he says about the theory of radiation is curious. It seems to be based on a misunderstanding of what can be done with partially reflecting screens.

I have only thought up some trivialities lately. The best of these is an experimental query regarding the radiation field. The statistical laws of radiation make one doubt whether Maxwell's field really exists in radiation. The mean field strength in high temperature radiation is of the order of 100 volts/cm; where such a field exists, it must produce a perceptible Stark effect on emitting and absorbing atoms. But if the other distribution of the field's effect according to the statistical laws of radiation holds, then the effect should occur only on a few molecules, but very strongly so that one would observe a quite weak diffuse effect next to a sharp line. I shall investigate this with Pringsheim; it is not easy. Have a look at the short paper by Byk on the law of corresponding states and quanta in the *Phys. Zeitschrift* – it is a nice piece of work. Your little book on relativity has enabled many people to understand the subject. E.g. half the Foreign Office are said to have pored over it (now nothing can go wrong with it).

You need not be so depressed by the political situation. The huge reparation payments and the threats are only a kind of moral nutrition for the dear public in France, to make the situation appear rosier to them. The more impossible the conditions, the more certain it is that they are not going to be put into practice. I hope you are in good health. With kind regards to you and your wife
Yours *Einstein*

This letter contains several scientific observations. Above all, there are doubts about Maxwell's radiation field, which cannot be reconciled with the statistical laws of radiation. In one of his earliest papers, Einstein had shown that, according to one of Lorentz's calculations, the wave theory of radiation implies that the mean square fluctuation of radiation energy is proportional to the square of the mean energy density. Einstein's quantum theory of light, which represents radiation as a kind of gas consisting of photons, shows that in an ideal gas the mean square fluctuation is proportional to the mean energy density itself. According to Planck's empirically obtained radiation law, however, the mean square fluctuation is exactly the sum of these two terms. This means that radiation consists of neither waves alone nor particles alone but of both at the same time. This was the famous and notorious 'duality' which always worried Einstein from then on, and of which much will be said in these letters. He was never willing to allow that this, his own result, was final. Here he wants to remove Maxwell's field with the consideration that the Stark effect of the temperature radiation field is large enough to enable one to decide between the particle theory and the wave theory. Whether he ever really carried out the experiments planned with Pringsheim, I do not know. The remark suggesting that half the Foreign Office had pored over my relativity book must have caused me a great deal of amusement at the time.

30

Frankfurt a.M.
12 February, 1921

Dear Einstein

I should have liked to reply to your kind letter at once, but I had to go to Göttingen suddenly, as there was some hope of accommodation there (a hope which may, by the way, be fulfilled). I know about only part of the unpleasant correspondence between our wives, as my wife decided one day not to take me into her confidence any longer. All the same, I feel guilty, as I did not prevent her from writing sharp and hard words. I have taken the matter very much to heart, more so than anything else I can remember. For everything connected with you affects me deeply. Believe me, if it were not so, I would not have been so agitated about the X affair. The earth, as it happened, was not exactly shaken; but it is not very pleasant to see the advertisements on every hoarding. Well, no more of this. I will probably get upset again over these relationships with the world, as my own time scales do not seem to apply (they are too short); but you will notice in future.

If even you, in Berlin, are unable to do anything for Boguslavski, I know of no way of helping him. One could at most send him an invitation privately, containing our signatures; he might get a passport on the strength of it. If he once got here, I could soon provide the means to enable him to exist for a few months. His theoretical speculations are not worth much; in his observations about radiation he clearly forgets that compression by reflecting pistons alters the frequency. I have given quite a lot of thought to this in the past, and know that semi-permeable screens do not offer a solution. Your bold idea of using the Stark effect of the fields in thermal radiation in order to determine their statistical character is very good; I hope you will have some success with it. I have read Byk's paper, and discussed it with Stern. We were not, however, particularly enthusiastic about it; after all, it is only the beginning of the beginning of a theory.

We are all very busy, for we have to complete all research in the Institute before the end of the present term. Then comes the new master, Madelung. Unfortunately I did not succeed in arranging Stern's chair. He is very unhappy about it, for his prospects are poor under the current antisemitic conditions. He is thinking of going into industry, which I consider a crazy idea. He intends to take a few weeks' leave this summer, and to come to Göttingen – Bohr will be there from the beginning of June. Can you come as well?

My path-length measurements are still unsatisfactory. Although I now have the knack of keeping the pressure constant to within a few per cent with the silver radiation, and can also measure the layer thickness of the deposits to within a few per cent, the technique is not yet perfect. I make the thickness measurement using an interference method developed by Wiener for the optics of telescopes; but I do it in the microscope, and that works much better. The thickness of a layer (of about 1μ) can be measured almost point by point (in visual fields of 0.01 mm²). I want to use this method to measure the bending constants of very small pieces of crystals – perhaps I shall succeed in doing this with diamond. Paul Oppenheim has managed to get me a piece ½ cm long. As Voigt's successor I am bound to try something like this.

I have done little theoretical work. I have recently written an account of Carathéodory's thermodynamics, which will appear shortly in the *Physikalische Zeitung*. I am very curious to know what you will say about it. Carathéodory himself, to whom I sent the proofs in Smyrna, thought that I had interpreted him correctly. I have also proved the following proposition, which had me considerably puzzled: if the positive and negative ions in an NaCl type lattice are somehow interchanged, the electrostatic lattice energy always increases. The NaCl lattice therefore has a minimum energy with respect to such exchanges and this may also (partly) explain its frequent occurrence. I need this proposition for a theory for the melting of salts I have in mind, in which I visualise the ions as tumbling about through one another during melting. But that is difficult! As you can see, it is not a very profound piece of research.

I am also working on my article for the Encyclopaedia, with Dr Brody as my private assistant. He is a very clever man. (Unfortunately he knows very little German, and is rather hard of hearing.) He found a new general quantisation method using Poincaré's integral invariants; he says that he has told you about it. Maybe there is some truth in it. We now have Gerlach with us, who really is splendid: energetic, well-informed, ingenious and helpful. He has just received an offer from the Chilean Government to take over physics and electrotechnology there (in Santiago); I wonder if it is the sensible thing to do? I think that he has good prospects here, too, but he is an enterprising fellow and well suited to an overseas appointment of this kind. Franck has now settled in Göttingen (although for the time being he is with Bohr in Copenhagen); he must have enough freedom there, and so I am busily collecting money for him. So far I've got 68,000 M. It is not at all easy to inspire laymen with some interest in our work. I must have more money. Wien got a whole million for re-equipping his Institute in Munich. I believe that what Wien has, Franck should also get.

I must revise my book on relativity, as Springer intends to issue a second edition; but I will not get round to it this term. If you have spotted any mistakes or omissions, I should be grateful for the information. Pauli's article for the Encyclopaedia is apparently finished, and the weight of the paper is said to be 2½ kilos. This should give some indication of its intellectual weight. The little chap is not only clever but industrious as well.

I have had some fun here recently, in the form of a substantial burglary. The rogues broke in at night through a cellar window after breaking the bars, and got away with a lot of silver, linen, both bicycles, and even my suit and shoes from the first floor. Since then I have slept badly and feel insecure in my own house. The police have failed completely.

I cannot share your optimism in political matters, although I do not believe that things are quite as black as they are painted. We are not going to pay as much as is asked for. But I can see the effect of this power politics on the minds of the people; it is a wholly irreversible accumulation of ugly feelings of anger, revenge, and hatred. In small towns such as Göttingen, this is very noticeable. I can, of course, understand it. My reason tells me that it is stupid to react in this way; but my emotional reaction is still the same. It seems to me that new catastrophes will inevitably result from all this. The world is not ruled by reason; even less by love. But I hope that the harmony between us will not be disrupted again.

With sincere regards, also from my wife

Yours

Max Born

Madelung was an old friend of mine, and a physicist of outstanding merit. Quite recently, during a congress in Copenhagen in 1963, I suggested that one of his papers should be acknowledged as the origin of the dynamic theory of crystal lattices.[8] Stern has become a great physicist, as I had predicted. The method of molecular radiation which he introduced into atomic physics has become one of the main instruments of present-day research; his teaching has spread all over the world, and has produced numerous discoveries of the first rank as well as a significant number of Nobel prizewinners.

The micro-interferometer, which Mrs Bormann and I used to measure thin layers of silver deposit, was built by Carl Zeiss of Jena and was listed in their catalogue for a number of years. I did not manage to measure the elasticity constants of the diamond. About thirty years later the Indian physicist Bhagavantam was the first to succeed in doing this, using a completely different method (ultrasonics). Thus, a generation later, one of my old formulae was finally proved correct.

My interpretation of Carathéodory's thermodynamics did not have the effect I had hoped for of displacing the classical method which, in my opinion, is both clumsy and mathematically opaque. Only in recent years have textbooks appeared which make use of it.

As for the financial assistance for Franck, the greater part of the sum of 68,000 M came from the Recklinghausen industrialist Carl Still. Courant had got to know him first and had introduced us to him. Still was the son of a Westphalian peasant. He had started off as a lowly mechanic, and built up a large firm through his own industry and ideas. The firm built coke ovens and installations recovering all kinds of coal by-products. He was profoundly interested in science and may even have hoped for help from us with his distillation processes. He frequently invited all of us, together with the mathematicians Hilbert and Runge and all our wives, to hunt hares on his large country estate, Rogätz, on the Elbe, near Magdeburg. Although we did no shooting I can still see Hilbert, dressed in rubber boots, standing in front of me on the edge of a field. But all the same we were all presented with a hare or a fat goose when we left. We introduced Max Planck to Still; this was a good thing, for when Planck was bombed out of his house in Grunewald (Berlin) during the war, he and his wife found refuge in Rogätz. They stayed there until the Russians got close, and then the Americans evacuated them to Göttingen. We saw Carl Still once more, on our first visit to Germany after the end of the war. He was already seriously ill and died shortly afterwards. Our friendship with his wife, who is approximately the same age as I, still continues, and is now being carried on by our children. Today the firm is flourishing again under his son Karl Friedrich Still. Both father and son have been awarded honorary doctorates by the Aachen Technische Hochschule.

Still's gift was one of the few instances when I received financial assistance from a private source. It was, of course, meant for Franck's research and not for mine, but I was quite in favour of this. Like Einstein, I have always held that a theoretician needs only pen and paper and a few books. Though I had initially been offered the post of chief of the whole Göttingen Institute, I actually occupied only a very small room there. Later on in Edinburgh it was much the same, but that was as it should be.

The letter ends with some political reflections. When I read through them again, I was amazed how accurately I evaluated the situation even then. I experienced the growing bitterness of the German people and felt that renewed warmongering would result, leading to catastrophe. The catastrophe was not avoided.

31

Dear Einstein

A small boy, Gustav Born, came into the world on July 29th. My wife is quite well and sends her regards. I shall remain here for another few weeks and then go somewhere to recuperate.

Unfortunately I have to attend the Physics Congress at Jena because of the journals, etc. And I have sworn never to attend another congress. Auerbach has invited me to stay with him and wrote to tell me that you ought to be there as well. That would be nice. Franck is going to visit Bohr in Copenhagen in September. I am now working with Brody on the equation of state of solid bodies for which we are now developing a rigorous theory for crystals – a difficult business. It is, however, coming on nicely.

Warm regards to you and your family,
Max Born

32

Dear Born

Many thanks for the detailed report you sent me. The K. W. I. [Kaiser Wilhelm Institute] is rather slow, because I have to summon all my dear colleagues for grants. What you want would devour the greater part of all our worldy goods, but a good case can be made out for it, and I hope to be able to arrange it. Just a little patience.

I have thought of a very interesting and fairly simple experiment on the nature of the emission of light. I hope to be able to carry it out soon. Meanwhile I am again the slave of the damned postman, who inundates me mercilessly. I have spent a happy month at the lake with my boys. Congratulations to you and your wife, and best regards,

Yours
Einstein

33

Dear Einstein

In writing to you today I address the mighty Director of the Institute of Physics of the Kaiser Wilhelm Society about the X-ray equipment we applied for. Franck has already told you how things are. In the meantime, however, something has happened. About ten days ago a representative of the Veifa-Werke was here and he made the following offer: if we order at once, the firm will supply the equipment we want at the current price. We could, however, cancel the order before October 31st (3 weeks' grace) should no decision have arrived from the Kaiser Wilhelm Society by then. If the order were placed later, we would be subject to the full price increase caused by the currency devaluation, which would amount to about 50 per cent (!!!). We have accepted this proposal and placed our order in the hope that confirmation of the grant will arrive from the Kaiser Wilhelm Society within three weeks. The deadline, October 31st is approaching and we are still waiting. Pohl and Franck have asked me to write to you and ask what the position really is and whether we should cancel the order on October 31st or whether the grant is certain enough for us to let the order stand. It would be a great pity if we received 100,000 M, but so late that the cost of the equipment had increased to 150,000 M. Maybe the decision could be speeded up a little. In the meantime, we have, by a complicated transfer of equipment, collections, toilets etc. cleared out two adjoining rooms and we will use them for X-ray research, one room for each department. Meanwhile, Dr Kuestner is working under very difficult conditions at the medical clinic, where there is some Veifa equipment, so that he can familiarise himself with it. We have lots of problems and would be glad to receive the equipment.

After this official business, some private matters. My health was not too good during the holidays; towards the end of July I got catarrh and still have not got rid of it completely, even though I spent three weeks in Ehrwald in the Tyrol. Catarrh is not serious in itself, but I always get asthma with it and that affects me a great deal. For months I have had disturbed nights because of asthma. But it is getting very much better now, and I hope to be quite free from it in a few weeks' time. It is high time too, for the university term begins shortly, and there is always a good deal going on here. W. Pauli is now my assistant; he is amazingly intelligent, and very able. At the same time, he is very human for a 21 year old – normal, gay and childlike. Unfortunately he wants to go away again in the summer, to Lenz in Hamburg, as he had already promised. Brody is still with me as well; he is a very clever and stimulating man. An attempt will have to be made to find a post for him with a living wage; I can only pay him a pittance (from a fund collected by Franck, Courant and myself). Polanyi intends to discuss this with you.

Scientifically there is nothing special to report. A large paper of mine about thermodynamics is at the printers, but already I wish it could be unprinted because the basic arguments seem shaky to me. The result (which incidentally I consider to be correct in spite of its shaky basis) is curious: Grüneisen's idea of the proportionality of energy and thermal expansion is not true at low temperatures; the latter is satisfied by a T^2-law instead of a T^4-law. This should be tested experimentally (Nernst?). Then another paper of mine about lattice potentials, which is quite nice mathematically, is at the printers. Pauli and I are tackling some quantum calculations of atoms, using the approximation method which Brody and I recently developed in the *Zeitschrift für Physik* with the example of the oscillator system. Perhaps something will come of it. Apart from this I am thinking about a number of things, but mostly without success. The quanta really are a hopeless mess.

My wife and children are well; Göttingen agrees with them splendidly. Our little son is flourishing.

The political situation is once more worrying me a great deal. In spite of my good intentions to be objective, my aversion towards the Allies grows because they are so disgustingly hypocritical. The Germans, it is true, have also robbed and stolen when they could, but they have not talked any nonsense about 'saving civilisation', etc. But I can't even write about it without getting excited so I had better stop.

Is it true that the Mount Wilson people have now confirmed the red shift? Has this already been published, and if so, where?

I received (as editor of the *Physikalische Zeitschrift*) a letter from Glaser asking me to accept the enclosed manuscript. Debye also recommended its acceptance. I read it and found that it contains a crude attack on Grebe and Bachmann and some mudslinging at you. I have returned it with a request for changes and for permission to bring it to Grebe's notice. It would be rather nice if the announcement from Mt Wilson about the confirmation could appear in the same issue, for Glaser bases his argument mainly on the negative result obtained at St Johns. Could you write to them for a brief report for publication? But I must stop now.

With kindest regards to your family; also from my wife (with all due respect, and modesty).

Yours

Born

The last letter touches on a matter of supreme importance – the announcement of a confirmation of the general theory of relativity by the spectral red-shift in the gravitational field.

The financial matters mentioned are practically incomprehensible today. One has to remember that the inflation of the German currency was beginning. A drop of one half in the value of money may have taken about two to three months at that time. Later on it took only as many days. Hence our troubles with the purchase of the X-ray equipment. Officialdom and public corporations did not understand the situation. The courts supported the currency catastrophe by rigid judgments. I myself lost the greater part of my inheritance. A man who owed me money on a mortgage sent me the entire nominal value of the mortgage (50,000 M, I believe) in one single note of the inflated currency which was actually worth 1 M at the time. This was held to be legal. The High Court had decided that a *mark is a mark*. After such experiences as these, my faith in the wisdom of financial and legal experts, instilled into me during my upbringing as the son of middle-class parents, was very much weakened. However, at the time when Franck and I moved to Göttingen, things were not quite as bad as that – yet. Even so, we had to expend a considerable amount of time and energy in order to keep the institute going. It was even worse for our wives; they were forced to convert our salaries into food, clothing and other necessities immediately. But I am digressing.

Of the scientific comments, my remarks about calculations of atomic structures done in collaboration with my young assistant Pauli are most interesting. The aim was to see whether the Bohr-Sommerfeld rules for the application of the quantum hypothesis to mechanical systems would lead to correct results. We used appropriate approximation methods based on Poincaré's astronomical perturbation calculation. The results were negative, and so it seemed that the quanta were a 'hopeless mess'.

Soon afterwards, however, I saw it differently. Was it possible that the success of Bohr's theory in the case of the hydrogen atom and other similar simple systems was a sort of accident? Could there perhaps be another, better, theory? This became our programme, especially when Heisenberg succeeded Pauli. We began to look systematically for cases where Bohr's theory failed, and soon found one with the helium atom. (Other cases had already turned up in the dynamics of crystal lattices; atomic lattices built of Bohr's atoms with plane electron orbits led to completely wrong compressibilities.)

The red-shift remained a dubious phenomenon for a long time. Only very recently has anyone succeeded in verifying Einstein's result. It became possible after a thorough study of the sun's atmosphere, whose ascending and descending streams veil the gravitational effect by the normal Doppler effect; clouds of sodium vapour were found which hovered comparatively quietly over the atmosphere of the sun, and showed the gravitational effect in purity. Finally, the red shift has also been verified directly on the earth, by γ-rays, by means of the Mössbauer effect. This, however, is too far from the subject.

A postcard from Hedi follows with a photograph of her holding our little son in her arms; the few words are meant as an apology for her previous abruptness.

34

1 November, 1921

With this card, Gustav Born begs to introduce himself to you, and begs you (1) for your goodwill and affection and (2) not to bear a grudge to his mother for whom he is, after all, not responsible.

    X X X   Signed: *Gustav*

35

Dear Einstein

The authorities cannot decide whether you are still tarrying in the warm countryside of Italy or are already in Berlin. However, in the former case, it is probably correct to assume that you will soon return. Therefore I am writing and I hope you will get my letter soon.

First of all, I must thank you most sincerely for the magnificent gift of the X-ray equipment. Franck, Pohl and I are delighted with it, for it should be part of any decent institute nowadays, and problems frequently arise which can only be solved with the help of X-rays. Pohl will write you an official letter of thanks, but I must add a few words of my own. This valuable gift shows that you people in Berlin have confidence in our ability to produce something worth while, and this is very gratifying. Pohl is chiefly responsible for purchasing the equipment, and a great many difficulties have been encountered, such as lack of space and unreliability on the part of the firms. The Veifa works in particular have dealt with us in such a manner as to make it unlikely that we shall buy from them. Pohl is shortly going to Berlin to negotiate with Siemens. We do not want to buy any of the sets that are ready-made for medical use; we would rather, if possible, assemble a carefully planned unit of our own, using the best available components.

Apart from this, there is not much pleasant news to report, for I am almost constantly ill. My summer trip to the Tyrol did not help much, for after my return I had asthma almost every night and became very run down. About three weeks ago I had a very severe attack, accompanied by bronchitis, and had to keep to my bed for a long time. I had some treatment from our medical specialists (especially E. Meyer) which succeeded in curing the asthma. But I still have severe catarrh and am unable to lecture. Pauli is deputising for me, and seems to be doing quite well in spite of his mere twenty-one years. It is a pity that I am so shaky, for in every other way things are good here. To be working with Franck is a joy. I'm on good terms with Pohl, too. Young Pauli is very stimulating – I shall never get another assistant as good. Unfortunately, he wants to go to Lenz in Hamburg in the summer. I have been unable to do any serious work lately, but I now understand perturbation theory rather better and have some inkling of what Bohr is really doing. I am also systematically continuing with my work on crystals; several papers written during the summer have recently appeared in *Zeitschrift für Physik*.

I would like to know what you think of Polanyi's papers on rates of reactions; he maintains that these could not be explained without an as yet unknown kind of energy-transmission (the transmission of quanta of energy from one molecule to another without mechanical reciprocation, simply hopping through space). Franck and I do not believe it. Langmuir was here recently; he thinks on similar lines, but we still do not believe any of it. Incidentally, we liked Langmuir very much; he knows lots of physics. Polanyi's paper about tensile strength is also quite crazy and yet it contains a grain of truth. We would so much like to talk to you about it!

A pupil of mine (a nephew of Minkowski with the same first name) is working out an exact theory for streams of slow electrons (speed below the smallest $h\nu$) in gases. This is based on the following idea of Franck's. In an extreme vacuum, the Child-Langmuir equation gives the current as a function of the voltage ($J \propto V^{3/2}$, I think). If one now adds the gas, the electrons are thrown about so that the space charge density is increased and the J/V law altered. The free path length of the electron in the gas should follow from this change, according to the existing theory. This is of interest, however, in view of Ramsauer's quite crazy assertion (in Jena) that in argon the path length of the electrons tends to infinity with decreasing velocity (slow electrons pass freely through atoms!). This we would like to refute. My theoretical ideas are: I start with the Maxwell-Boltzmann collision equation

$$\frac{\partial F}{\partial t} + \zeta \frac{\partial F}{\partial x} + \dots + \frac{X}{m} \frac{\partial F}{\partial \xi} + \dots = \iint \text{collision integral.}$$

This equation is usually integrated so that the left hand side is equated to zero and in the first approximation the integral vanishes because of Maxwell's distribution function. In the second approximation this distribution is then inserted into the left hand side. I then proceed the other way round. In the first approximation, ignoring all collisions and with normal space charge distribution, it is necessary to put

$$X = -e\frac{\partial \psi}{\partial X}$$

and to use the second equation $\Delta \psi = -e\int F \mathrm{d}\xi \mathrm{d}\eta \mathrm{d}\zeta$. In the second approximation, one collision is taken into account, and so on. This project seems to be going well. Minkowski intends to carry out some experiments, together with Miss Sponer, but these are sure to be very difficult.

We were greatly amused by Lenard's Soldner article. I do not know if you saw the report on it which appeared in *Frankfurter Zeitung*, as well as Laue's reply on the one hand, and Hilbert's and mine on the other?

I am reading Laue's second volume; I must say I like it very much after all. All the same, Pauli's article for the Encyclopaedia was an even greater achievement.

My wife is very well; she is breast-feeding the little boy, and this agrees with both of them. At the moment, though, she is confined to bed with a large and painful boil. The two little girls are also well.

Please give my regards to your wife and the young ladies, and to all our friends and acquaintances in Berlin.

With best wishes
Yours
M. Born

My report about 'young Pauli' is not quite complete. I seem to remember that he liked to sleep in, and more than once missed his 11 a.m. lecture. We used to send our maid over to him at half past ten, to make sure that he had got up. He was undoubtedly a genius of the highest order, but my fear that I would never get an assistant as good proved unjustified. His successor, Heisenberg, was just as gifted, and also more conscientious: there was never any need to have him woken up, or to remind him of his duties in any other way.

The comments about the physical chemist Polanyi are too dated to be of any interest today. I should just add that later, during the Hitler regime, Polanyi went to England and obtained a chair at Manchester – not for chemistry, but for philosophy and sociology; he was a versatile, imaginative man.

Ramsauer's assertion that the free path length of the electron in argon increases with decreasing velocity was bound to seem crazy at the time. But it was nevertheless right. It was first explained by means of de Broglie's wave mechanics: the matter waves of the electrons have a wavelength proportional to the velocity. If their collisions with atoms are regarded as diffraction phenomena, it becomes clear immediately that slow electrons, that is, those with long wavelengths, are less influenced by atomic obstacles. At the time I had no inkling of all this, and thus called these important experiments 'crazy'. Did Einstein already have a deeper insight then? I do not know.

Soldner, a German mathematician and geodesist, had predicted the deflection of light by the sun as early as 1801. He had actually dealt with the beam of light as if it were a comet, moving according to Newton's law. (This makes sense, because the path of a small object attracted by a central body does not depend on its mass.) He ended up with the same formula as Einstein did in his first paper dealing with this problem; but this differed by a factor of two from Einstein's final formula, which took into account the change in the gravitational field near the sun as required by the general theory of relativity. Naturally, Soldner's work was exploited to the full by Einstein's enemies.

36

30 December, 1921

Dear Borns

Today I wish you a happy new year. We were all delighted with the photo of the youngest Born. The fight of the Amazons is now forgotten. I am very sorry to hear that you, dear Born, have had so much trouble with your health. I hope that you are all fit and well again.

Pauli is a splendid fellow for his 21 years; he can be proud of his article for the Encyclopaedia. Polyani's ideas make me shudder. But he has discovered difficulties for which I know no remedies as yet. In particular I am racking my brains over a numerical analysis in connection with radiation-molecular balance. There is probably a lot of truth in Polanyi's ideas about the strength of crystals, but their extension to gases seems wide of the mark to me. Your investigation of electron currents sounds interesting. I liked your reply about Soldner in *Frankfurter Zeitung* very much.

The experiment on light emission has now been completed, thanks to Geiger and Bothe's splendid cooperation. The result: the light emitted by moving particles of canal rays is strictly monochromatic while, according to the wave theory, the colour of the elementary emission should be different in the different directions. It is thus clearly proved that the wave field does not really exist, and that the Bohr emission is an instantaneous process in the true sense. This has been my most impressive scientific experience in years. Ehrenfest writes enthusiastically about Bohr's theory of atoms; he is visiting him. If Ehrenfest is convinced, there must be something in it, for he is a sceptical fellow.

Regards to the little ones, and all good wishes to you both for the New Year.

Yours

Einstein

Pauli's article for the Encyclopaedia dealt with the theory of relativity. Sommerfeld was originally supposed to write it. He got Pauli to help him with it, but Pauli made such a good job of it that Sommerfeld handed the whole thing over to him. It is truly remarkable that a young student of 21 was capable of writing so fundamental an article, which in profundity and thoroughness surpassed all other presentations of the theory written during the next thirty years – even, in my opinion, the famous work by Sir Arthur Eddington.

The investigation into the emission of light by positive rays, which Einstein carried out in conjunction with Bothe and Geiger, is mentioned again in subsequent letters. It was a great disappointment in the end.

37

Göttingen
1 January, 1922

Dear Einstein

We have been very much shaken by the contents of your letter, though in our stupidity we are unable to reconstruct the set-up of the positive-ray experiment for ourselves. We have a thousand questions in our minds and all sorts of reflections for which we need you as a sedative. As this letter cannot run to 50 pages, and as we can hardly expect a 100-page reply, we conceived the brilliant idea of having you officially invited to visit us in Göttingen, at the expense of the Wolfskehl Foundation, to give an informal lecture. This means you would also be here for Hilbert's 60th birthday, an idea which has delighted the old man. His birthday is on January 23rd; the lecture could be held on Tuesday, 24th, and we hope that you will devote at least Sunday, the 22nd, to us. Maybe your wife would like to accompany you. It would be wonderful if you could manage that, and we look forward to it so much that you must not refuse under any circumstances. Sincere regards and best wishes for the New Year.

  Born and Franck

38

Jan. '22

Dear Born

I shall gladly come and visit you, partly in order to congratulate Hilbert in person, and partly to tell you about the experiment, and how simple it is. The joke is this: the positive ray particle, according to the wave theory, continuously emits variable colours in different directions. Such a wave travels in dispersive media with a velocity which is a function of position. Thus the wave surfaces should be bent as in terrestrial refraction. But the experimental result is reliably negative. Kindest regards, also to Franck and to your family.

  Yours
   Einstein

39

7 January, 1922

Dear Mr Einstein

First of all I want to thank you and your wife most sincerely for your new year greeting, which showed the warmth of your friendship. May all your own dearest wishes come true many times over. I hurried over to Hilbert with your card. He could hardly believe at first that you are really coming, and was then tremendously pleased. He wants me to ask you to make sure to be there on his birthday, Monday, 23rd, and to put in an appearance at the large gathering in the evening. The lecture can be held on *Tuesday*, at any time you like. I hope you will not just streak past us like a meteorite, but will be able to stay for a few days as our guest. You will see how well we live here, and we shall feed you on easily digestible dishes. If your wife would like to come with you, she is cordially invited and will be very welcome. Max is with Blaschke today and tomorrow. He is unfortunately in a very bad state. Perhaps you could give him pleasure by visiting him once more? It must not look too deliberate. With kindest regards to you and your family.

Yours
Hedi Born

40

18 January, 1922

Dear Born and dear Franck

I must, with a heavy heart, decline after all. But it really cannot be helped. I am so much behind with my writing and other obligations that I just cannot afford an escapade into the Eldorado of erudition. So I will have to pay homage to Hilbert by letter. Please let Courant know as well; he wanted to engage me as a musician.

Laue is violently opposing my experiment, or rather my interpretation of it. He maintains that the wave theory does not involve any deflection of rays whatever. He suggested a nice experiment to investigate the supposed wave bending of the rays by means of capillary waves which exhibit considerable dispersion, as a substitute for a theory which it is so hard to develop with the required rigour.

Today there was a great dispute at the colloqium, to be

continued next time. Do not be angry – to postpone is not to abandon.

   With warmest regards, also to your wives

      Yours

         A. Einstein

   Many thanks to Mrs Born for the charming picture. The other evening I read to Laue and Vegard all the poems she dedicated to us. They found them delightful and all saw in her a serious competitor to Master Busch. In view of the tussle we had with one another, I want to send her my special greetings.

This letter contains, for the first time, some doubts about the ideas on which the positive-ray experiments were based, raised by Max von Laue, then unquestionably an expert in all optical matters. Franck and I were delighted at Einstein's news of the experiment, not because of our own reflections on it but because of our pleasure in Einstein's success in taking another important step forward.

4I

Göttingen,
30 April, 1922

Dear Einstein

   Laue was here recently – we very much enjoyed his stay. He told us that you are going to Holland. I hope this letter will reach you in time.

   First of all I have to ask for your help again, this time for Brody. When I talked to you last Christmas in Berlin, you said it might be possible to secure a post for him in Kowno. I have recently discussed this with I. Schur in Berlin (you were in Paris at the time), who has all kinds of contacts with Kowno. He was going to attend to it. It is now a matter of urgency that something should be done. My wife, who is looking after Brody's family (his wife and small child have been here for some time), reports that they live under miserable conditions. I give him something from our private fund (about 2000 M per month), but that is very little for a family. Apart from that we give what help we can. But the man must get out of this humiliating situation. I value him very highly as a physicist; if he had more energy and was in better circumstances, I am sure he would achieve a great deal. A pretty piece of work he did is about to appear in *Physikalische Zeitschrift*, and he is also working with me on thermal expansion. Hilbert thinks very highly of him, particularly because he speaks extremely well in seminars. I could, if I wished, secure a lectureship for him here without much difficulty; but I consider it senseless because, as a Hungarian Jew and with his decidedly Eastern ways, he would never be offered a chair. I already have enough worries and responsibilities with Paul Hertz, who is also on the point of starving.

Could you perhaps find some modest post for Brody in Holland? Or in some other part of the world? I have applied to the Academic Assistance Council for a grant for him, but they have not yet replied. Could you put in a good word for him there? Or is there some other way?

Now to other things. I am spending a good deal of time writing the article about lattice theory for the Encyclopaedia. I hope to have it finished by May. It is a rather laborious task. Unfortunately it now turns out that there is a mistake in my recently published theory of the equation of state of crystals. I had claimed that Gruneisen's law of the proportionality of energy and expansion does not hold throughout but that, at low temperatures, the former is proportional to T^4 and the latter to T^2. This was nonsense, though. It was based on a bad blunder. That this could happen to someone of my ripe old age is somewhat depressing. But as long as one discovers the mistake oneself it is not quite so bad, and I console myself with the knowledge of what a tricky business it is. Moreover, both Pauli and Brody read the paper thoroughly without spotting the mistake.

Pauli has unfortunately gone to Lenz in Hamburg. We recently started work on a joint paper, a continuation of the one published in collaboration with Brody about the quantisation of non-harmonic oscillators. The approximation method developed there can be applied to all systems where the unperturbed system is quasi-periodic and the flow function can be developed in powers of a parameter. The case when the unperturbed system is degenerate can also be included and leads precisely to Bohr's method of secular perturbations. As a matter of fact we now really understand Bohr's ideas, at least in part. We have also started to do calculations for ortho-helium (two coplanar electrons) and were able to confirm Bohr's old claim that the inner electron moves around fast on an elliptical orbit whose major axis always points towards the slowly moving

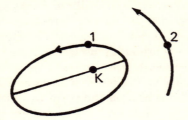

outer electron. Pauli took the paper to Hamburg with him and wants to finish it there. I cannot find the time because of the Encyclopaedia article. Then, too, the damned term is just starting again, an unwelcome interruption of my serene contemplation.

Franck's Institute is full of doctoral students who do nice work under his guidance. Hilbert is in Switzerland and will not be back for another 8 days.

My family are well in spite of the continually frightful weather. My wife sends warmest greetings. Please give my regards to my colleages in Holland and Berlin.

> Yours
> *Born*

The plight of younger people like Brody who had to depend on small, fixed, constantly devalued salaries was indeed miserable.

The report of the blunder I made in my article on solids was by way of a prelude to the major blunder which Einstein reports in his next letter.

42

Berlin

Dear Born

It is extremely difficult at the moment to find posts for theoreticians. Holland suffers from overproduction. Should there be any chance of doing something for Brody here, it would be because of the extraordinary significance of his achievements. There are some excellent theoreticians there (such as Fokker) in modest teaching posts in Gymnasia. A few months ago I wrote about Brody to Millikan and Epstein in Pasadena, but have not yet received a reply. I will talk to Laue who, unless I'm very much mistaken, has some influence with the *Not-gemeinschaft*. I got to know your perturbation method through Becker's thesis [for a lecturer's qualification] and enjoyed it.

I too committed a monumental blunder some time ago (my experiment on the emission of light with positive rays), but one must not take it too seriously. Death alone can save one from making blunders. I greatly admire the sure instinct which guides all of Bohr's work. It is good that you should be working on helium. The most interesting thing at the moment is Gerlach's and Stern's experiment. The orientation of atoms without collisions cannot be explained by means of radiation, according to current reasoning; an orientation should, by rights, last more than a hundred years. I made a little calculation about it with Ehrenfest. Rubens considers the experimental result to be absolutely reliable.

Make sure you use the money for the purchase of the X-ray apparatus quite soon. Why is it taking so long?

Kindest regards to you all

Yours

Einstein

Here Einstein admits that the considerations which led him to the positive-ray experiments were wrong: 'a monumental blunder'. I should add that now (1965), when I read through the old letters again, I could not understand Einstein's observation at all and found it untenable before I had finished reading. This is, of course, quite simply because we have learned a good many things about the propagation of light during the intervening forty-odd years. The same is true of the idea that the laws of the propagation of light in transparent media have nothing to do with quanta but are correctly described by the wave theory (Maxwell's equations and their relativistic generalisations for moving bodies). It is quite possible that Laue had already realised this at that time, and used it in argument against Einstein's ideas.

Now I can hear all Einstein's opponents, the anti-relativists, cry: 'What did we tell you? Einstein, too, makes mistakes – why should we believe in his crazy theory of relativity?' The answer to this is that we all make mistakes. 'Death alone can save us from making blunders.' At first there were quite a number of serious scientists who did not want to know anything about the theory of relativity; conservative individuals, who were unable to free their minds from the prevailing philosophical principles. As long as such people conduct their polemics decently, there is no reason why one should object to them.

Einstein himself belonged to this group in later years; he could no longer take in certain new ideas in physics which contradicted his own firmly-held philosophical convictions. But Einstein never engaged in polemics, subjectively or maliciously. There are always real, disinterested scientists who are so ruled by prejudices outside science and philosophy that they reject any new ideas suggested by people of whose background, ancestry, religion, etc., they disapprove. These included the antisemitic physicists at whose hands Einstein, and later many other people including myself, suffered.

Finally, there are the pure cranks, outsiders who can point to no positive scientific achievements themselves but who believe that they have found defects in some new doctrine such as Einstein's theory of relativity. One would think that there would be fewer of these as time goes on. But this is not so. Over the years a large number of first-class physicists and mathematicians have thoroughly investigated the theory of relativity and none has found fault with it. It is hard, therefore, today to take seriously anyone who believes he has discovered a mistake. I have frequently taken the trouble to uncover the errors in papers written by cranks of this type, but never in all my experience has any of them admitted that he had made a mistake, as Einstein did.

H. Rubens, professor of experimental physics at the University of Berlin, was particularly known for his investigations of infra-red radiation and its application to Planck's radiation formula.

It is strange that Einstein referred me to Stern's and Gerlach's experiment as the most interesting. He had forgotten that it had been carried out in my Institute in Frankfurt under my very eyes, as a result of discussions with me, and that it had been financed with money I myself had raised with the aid of my relativity lectures.

If my memory does not deceive me, Stern also made the little calculation which Einstein had made with Ehrenfest, namely that the orientation of atoms in the magnetic field, predicted by Sommerfeld and experimentally demonstrated by the Stern-Gerlach experiment, cannot be interpreted classically.

43

Göttingen
6 August, 1922

Dear Einstein

We recently had a visit from a woman physicist who now lives in Holland; she mentioned that Michelson's experiment had been repeated in America, with positive success. H. A. Lorentz is supposed to have brought the news with him. Do you know anything about it? The Michelson experiment is one of those which seem definitely *a priori*. I do not believe a word of the rumour. But all of us here would be most grateful if you could find time to write a postcard.

Franck and Courant have spoken to me about you. We have a lot of worries about professional appointments. Pohl has decided to stay on in Göttingen. This relieves us of the worry of selection. But now I fear that Franck may go to Berlin. I sincerely want him to be offered the chair, but he would be foolish to accept. Courant says that you are of the same opinion.

Scientifically there is nothing of any importance. My assistant Hückel and I are having a lot of trouble with the quantisation of polyatomic molecules in calculations of the infra-red bands (in H_2O, for example). We have the right approximation method, but the calculations are very complicated. I expect to finish my Encyclopaedia article this month; I am completely fed up with it. I have given a good deal of thought to the quantum theory of molecule formation. A short notice in *Die Naturwissenschaften* about the H_2 molecule contains some results of interest to connoisseurs. But the more unequivocal these turn out to be, the crazier the whole system seems. I am not yet on the right track as far as questions of principle go.

My wife and children are well. The girls are staying in the country with a former maid of ours; they are due to return soon. We shall stay here until the middle of September, when we are going to Leipzig and from there to Italy. We received £22 sterling for the translation of my book, and have turned it into lire. This will not take us very far, but we greatly look forward to our little journey to the South. With warmest greetings, also from my wife, to you and your family.

Yours

M. Born

The Michelson experiments were made by the American physicist Miller, first in flat country and later on top of Mount Wilson, a high mountain. To begin with, he claimed to have discovered, using his Michelson interferometer, the so-called aether wind. Some time later he withdrew the claim; the shift of the interference fringes, on which he had based his claim, had been too small. I believe he then attributed it to the movement of the solar system. When I was in the United States in 1925/26, Miller's measurements were still frequently being discussed. I therefore went to Pasadena to see a demonstration of the apparatus on top of Mt. Wilson. Miller was a modest little man who very readily allowed me to operate the enormous interferometer. I found it very shaky and unreliable; a tiny movement of one's hand or a slight cough made the interference fringes so unstable that no readings were possible. From then on I completely lost faith in Miller's results. I knew from my visit to Chicago in 1912 that Michelson's own apparatus was very reliable and his measurements accurate. My scepticism has been substantiated by later developments. Michelson's result that the aether wind does not in fact exist is universally accepted today.

Then follows a brief report about my work on special problems of the quantum theory, which is no longer of any interest today.

44

23 December, 1922

Dear Borns

Splendid sunshine at Christmas. A happy, beautiful country, with a delicate, sensitive people. We start for home again on the 29th, over the great waters, *via* Java, Palestine and Spain; it will probably be April before we get there.

In the meantime, warmest greetings

Yours

Einstein

This postcard from Japan was the only message we received from Einstein during his world trip, which took him and his wife to China, Japan, Palestine and many other countries. On his way out there he received the news that he had been awarded the Nobel Prize; not for his theory of relativity, but for his explanation of the photoelectric effect by means of his photon theory. Further details of this can be found in any of the numerous biographies of Einstein, such as the one by Carl Seelig.[17]

45

Göttingen
7 April, 1923

Dear Einstein

They say you are back. I had intended to write you a welcome-home letter, but now it is too late. The most important thing is for us to congratulate you heartily, if somewhat belatedly, on the Nobel Prize. Two more deserving recipients than you and Bohr could not be found, and we were as pleased as Punch. We also want to thank you sincerely for the beautiful card from Japan. We did not know your address, and so were unable to reply. But now I would like to re-establish the exchange of views between us, if I may lay claim to your time. I would like to hear about your experiences during your great trip. I may possibly come to Berlin for a few days towards the end of the month, in order to visit an American friend and benefactor of mine, who helps me to support my students. I hope to see you then. We have been living very peacefully and quietly here. The only external event of any importance has been a visit by Lord Haldane. He seems to be rather confused; all the same, the breadth of his education and his qualities as a European made a deep impression on us (i.e. Hilbert, Franck, Courant and myself).

If you happen to glance through the last six months' issues of scientific journals, you will see that I have been fairly industrious, and have kept quite a large number of students going. But they are only minor problems that I am struggling with. I don't seem to get any closer to the great mystery of the quanta, in spite of all my efforts. We have been looking at perturbation theory (Poincaré's) to determine whether it is possible to obtain the observed term values from Bohr's models by exact calculation. But it is *quite* certainly *not* the case, as was demonstrated with helium, where we found any number of multiple periodic orbits (to a sufficient approximation). I had Heisenberg here during the winter (as Sommerfeld was in America); he is easily as gifted as Pauli, but has a more pleasing personality. He also plays the piano very well. Apart from the work on helium, we examined together some questions of principle in connection with Bohr's atomic theory – particularly with regard to the phase relations in atomic models (*Zeitschrift für Physik*). I have at long last finished my great Encyclopaedia article on the lattice theory ; it has grown to about 250 pages, and will be published as the second edition of my old book. I hope it will come out in May. Then I am going to put this subject into cold storage until the question of homeopolar binding forces between atoms has been solved from Bohr's point of view. Unfortunately every attempt to clarify the concept fails. I am fairly sure though that in reality it must all be very different from what we think now. But one can draw plenty of qualitative conclusions from Bohr's ideas; Franck does that magnificently, and is doing some nice experiments again. I live in dread of Franck getting the position in Berlin. It would be better for him, for physics, and also for Berlin if he were to remain here. To say nothing of myself. At the moment he has gone to Hertz in Holland.

I hear that you have a new theory about the connection between gravitational and electromagnetic fields, which allegedly points to a relationship between gravitation and the earth's magnetic field. I am very curious. Most of what is published about relativistic problems leaves me cold. I find Mie's pulpy effusions horrible. Hilbert follows all this half-heartedly, as he is completely preoccupied with his new basic theory of logic and mathematics. What I know of it seems to me the greatest step forward imaginable in this field. But for the time being most mathematicians refuse to recognise it.

The papers report that you have turned your back on the League of Nations. I would like to know if this is true. It is, indeed, almost impossible to arrive at any rational opinion about political matters, as the truth is systematically being distorted just as in wartime. The follies of the French sadden me, because they strengthen our nationalism, and weaken the Republic. I give a lot of thought to what I could do to spare my own son the fate of participating in a war of revenge. But I am too old for America and, moreover, the war hysteria seems to have been even worse there than here. The other day I read a little essay by Coudenhove-Kalergi: 'Apology for the Technical Age', which contained some enlightening arguments. If you do not know it, you should certainly try to get hold of it.

We were in Berlin last March. I talked to Planck, and his

company gave me much pleasure. On the other hand, the German Physical Society, where I gave a lecture, was like a waste-land – no trace of participation or discussion. Rubens is much missed there; for all his coolness and caution, he was full of interest and life as far as science went. My family are well and send warmest regards to you all.

Yours

Max Born

My American friend and benefactor was Henry Goldman, who was senior partner of the great banking house Goldman, Sachs & Co. in New York. I got to know him when an old friend went to New York after the war to marry his American fiancée. Partly as a joke I said that he ought to try to find me a rich German-American, who would be prepared to give some financial support to my Institute, which had been severely handicapped by the inflation. A few weeks later, I received a postcard from New York: I have your man, his name is Henry Goldman, and he lives at. . . . With my wife's help I drafted a nice letter to Mr Goldman, and a few weeks later received a very charming reply, together with a cheque for a few hundred dollars, quite a considerable sum by German standards. I went to Berlin to get to know my benefactor. I should like to recount briefly how things went with Goldman after that.

Goldman was a portly, Jewish-looking gentleman; his grandfather had emigrated to the U.S.A. from Hessen without a penny, because the Jews were treated particularly badly there. In America, he started off as a door-to-door salesman, and ended up as the owner of a small bank. His sons and grandsons developed this into a giant concern, which amongst other things had financed the Woolworth Co. The family's German memories meant much to my Henry Goldman and, when the war broke out in 1914, he did not believe that the Germans alone were to blame. He even fell out with his family over this issue. Later, he did everything he could to help Germans in those difficult times. I introduced Goldman to Einstein, and both of them later visited us in Göttingen, and stayed in our house. During our American journey in 1926, my wife and I visited the Goldmans and spent Christmas Eve with them in their elegant flat on Fifth Avenue in New York. Hitler's seizure of power was, of course, a terrible blow to Henry Goldman. All his life he had defended the Germans against American accusations, and helped them. Now he lived to see antisemitism made into one of the main points in the programme of a criminal government. I saw Henry Goldman once more (in 1934 or 1935), in his London hotel. He was a broken man and died soon afterwards.

The story of Lord Haldane's visit is as follows: Years ago he had studied in

Göttingen, and he liked the German culture and language. This must have been why he resigned from his post as British War Minister in 1914, when his country aligned itself with France and Russia. Soon after the end of the 1914–18 war he visited Göttingen to look up a certain old lady, Miss Schlote, in whose house he had lived during his student days. My wife knew her, and in this way Haldane found out that we lived in Göttingen. He had great admiration for Einstein and had read my relativity book. He himself had written a large book, *The Reign of Relativity*,[18] which, however, had virtually nothing to do with Einstein's theory but merely enlarged upon the trivial proposition that 'everything is relative'. His visit helped to enliven our usually very quiet existence in Göttingen.

Later I met Haldane again. I had been invited to the opening of a new physics laboratory at the University of Bristol, donated by the cigarette-manufacturing firm of H. O. Wills. There I was to receive an honorary doctorate, my first, together with a number of famous physicists, Lord Rutherford, Sir William Bragg, Sir Arthur Eddington, Langevin (from Paris) and others. To my surprise the Vice Chancellor, who conducted the ceremony in the festive, but cold hall, was none other than Lord Haldane. He welcomed me like an old friend. As it happened he, like myself, was suffering from a bad cold. This prevented us from attending the banquet that evening in that same cold hall, and we had our dinner served to us in a small room, where a coal fire gave at least the illusion of warmth. I remember that he talked almost the whole time, mainly about the negotiations he had conducted in Berlin (known as the Haldane Mission) to end the naval arms race between Germany and Great Britian. This foundered because of the stubborn attitude of von Tirpitz and the Kaiser, which Haldane described vividly. Many historians believe that the first world war might well have been prevented by such a pact, and European history would have taken an entirely different course.

As regards perturbation theory: astronomers normally use simple, well proven techniques, and they do not take much notice of the considerable developments, systematically made by Henri Poincaré. But the perturbation problems involved in the theory of electron orbits in the atom make the general rigorous theory indispensable. We therefore made ourselves familiar with it, as did Niels Bohr in Copenhagen, who used it as the basis for an interpretation of the periodic system of the elements. Heisenberg and I, however, pursued a different objective. We had reason to doubt that Bohr's ingenious but basically incomprehensible combination of quantum rules with classical mechanics was correct. We therefore intended to carry out a thorough calculation of the two-body problem of the helium atom (nucleus with two electrons), and thus needed to use Poincaré's rigorous approximation technique. The result was quite negative, and that led us finally to turn our backs on classical mechanics and establish a new quantum mechanics.

The rumour about Einstein's new investigation, in which he attempted the unification of his theory of gravity with Maxwell's theory of the electromagnetic field, proved to be correct. At that time he began his often repeated, although unavailing, attempts to develop a unified field theory along these lines.

Hilbert's efforts to find a new basis for mathematics enthralled and fascinated me to begin with. Later, I was no longer able to follow. I had some correspondence with Einstein about these problems, when they became the cause of a dispute between Hilbert and the Dutch mathematician Brouwer (letter No. 58).

Einstein repudiated the League of Nations when he resigned his membership of the Commission for Intellectual Collaboration under the chairmanship of the philosopher Henri Bergson. The reason for this step was probably hardly political at all, but mainly the lack of time and his dislike of travelling. If I am not mistaken, it was Madame Curie who replaced Einstein on the committee.

46

22 *July, 1923*

Dear Borns

Neither my bad conscience, nor even my wife's, was strong enough to stir my lazy flesh at last to answer your extremely kind letters. But your card, dear Mrs Born, has really stung me into action. However, the abortive twinges of a bad conscience are the only unpleasant emotions I have when I think of you. For not only have you always been so good and kind, but your contributions in physics, music, poetry and prose, as well as in cosy conviviality, have done much to enrich this curious existence of ours. All is well with us.

Scientifically, I have at present a most interesting question, connected with the affine field theory. There are prospects now of understanding the earth's magnetic field and the electrostatic economy of the earth, and examining the concept experimentally. But we will have to wait for the experiment.

Both my wife and I thank you most sincerely for your kind invitation. But I must stay here for a while in this overcrowded

place, where one is driven almost to distraction by visitors, correspondence and telephone calls. Langevin is making his way here for a pacifist demonstration; a splendid fellow. However ineffective the good and the just may be, they alone make life worth living. With warmest wishes for a happy holiday to you both, and the dear children,
Yours
A. *Einstein*

Kindest regards from my wife, who is very busy and intends to write to you herself another time. Franck, who has just been here, told me that according to the results of measurements of ionised gases already made, the effect I am looking for cannot exist. There is to be no understanding the earth's magnetic field. I am sending this letter to you, to make sure that it arrives safely. But please write and tell your wife that we both think of her with affection, and not to be angry about our laziness.

47

Institute for Theoretical Physics
of the University
Göttingen
Bunsenstrasse 9
25 August, 1923

Dear Einstein

Your kind letter gave us much pleasure. Thank you very much. Today I should like to ask you something (and would appreciate a *prompt* reply) : one is constantly bombarded with official communications from the Helmholtz Society, the German Physical Society, etc., asking one to attend the congress of physicists in Bonn. If this were to be somewhere else, I would not even consider going. But in Bonn, because of the French occupation, great importance seems to be attached to receiving large numbers of visitors, and Franck is of the opinion that we should go for the sake of good form. In my opinion it would have been more sensible not to hold the congress in occupied territory; for it is a mistake to mix up scientific meetings with politics in any way whatever. But now the folly has already been committed, and the question is only whether it is necessary to take part.

There could easily be considerable difficulties from an embargo on travel and so on. I myself have no desire at all for a high concentration of physicists, but would much rather live and work quietly by myself, particularly as I have only just returned from the North Sea. I would like you to tell me what you Berlin physicists are doing (particularly Planck, Laue, Haber, Meitner, etc.) and whether you think this journey would be desirable. Please reply straight away, as one would have to try and get a passport quite soon.

My wife was in Langeoog with the children for more than five weeks, and I was there as well for the last three. We have all recovered well; the children in particular have gained strength and are looking very well. We bathed a lot but otherwise did nothing except lie on the beach and laze about. Although I was acclimatised, I came down with bad catarrh almost straight away. I had imagined that the vacations in Göttingen would be quiet and peaceful; but in the first three days after our return we have already had two foreign visitors, an Englishman from Oxford and Mr Grimm from Munich. But as from tomorrow I am going to feign death and refuse to see anyone. It is not really that I have anything special on. As always, I am thinking hopelessly about the quantum theory, trying to find a recipe for calculating helium and the other atoms; but I am not succeeding in this either. My Encyclopaedia article has been published and I will send you a copy soon. Otherwise I spend my time reading, going for walks, playing music and occupying myself with the children. I am practising systematically and have, I think, made some progress. Unfortunately it is very difficult here to get a trio or quartet together.

In the latest issue of the *Annalen*, containing the nice paper by Grüneisen and Goens which verifies your theory of dissociation velocity, there is a paper by Gerold v. Gleich about the perihelion of Mercury. I do not like its tone at all. Are you going to reply to it? It is odd that so many people have no feeling for the intrinsic probability of a theory. Have you made any progress with your affine world?

Kindest regards to your wife from both of us.

Yours

Born

81

48

29 April, 1924

Dear Borns

Your letter, dear Mrs Born, was really excellent. Indeed, what causes the sense of well-being inspired by Japanese society and art is that the individual is so harmoniously integrated into his wider environment that he derives his experiences, not from the self, but mainly from the community. Each of us longed for this when we were young, but we had to resign ourselves to its impossibility. For of all the communities available to us there is not one I would want to devote myself to, except for the society of the true searchers, which has very few living members at any time.

I called off my visit to Naples; I was pleased that a minor indisposition gave me the opportunity. I am going to Kiel for a while instead. Bohr's opinion about radiation is of great interest. But I should not want to be forced into abandoning strict causality without defending it more strongly than I have so far. I find the idea quite intolerable that an electron exposed to radiation should choose *of its own free will*, not only its moment to jump off, but also its direction. In that case, I would rather be a cobbler, or even an employee in a gaming-house, than a physicist. Certainly my attempts to give tangible form to the quanta have foundered again and again, but I am far from giving up hope. And even if it never works there is always that consolation that this lack of success is entirely mine.

Enjoy the beauty of the sunny land, with best wishes.

Yours
Einstein

The remark about the advertising agencies was quite unconscious, the result of a good mood, and I had no idea that you were wedded to it in some way. Your pretty remark makes me want to stroke your head, if that is at all permissible in the case of a married lady.

The letter from my wife to which Einstein replied is missing.
The basic reason for the dispute between us on the validity of statistical

laws was as follows. Einstein was firmly convinced that physics can supply us with knowledge of the objectively existing world. Together with many other physicists I have been gradually converted, as a result of experiences in the field of atomic quantum phenomena, to the point of view that this is not so. At any given moment, our knowledge of the objective world is only a crude approximation from which, by applying certain rules such as the probability laws of quantum mechanics, we can predict unknown (e.g. future) conditions.

49

Göttingen
15 July, 1925

Dear Einstein

Your kind letter gave us much pleasure. My wife left with the children for Silvaplana in the Engadine the day before yesterday, and I expect she will write to you from there. In the meantime, I want to give you some of our news.

As regards physics, first of all, your kind remarks about my activities spring from the kindness of your heart. I am fully aware, however, that what I am doing is very ordinary stuff compared with your ideas and Bohr's. My thinking box is very shaky – there is not much in it, and what there is rattles to and fro, has no definite form, and gets more and more complicated. Your brain, heaven knows, looks much neater; its products are clear, simple, and to the point. With luck, we may come to understand them in a few years' time. This is what happened in the case of your and Bose's gas degeneracy statistics. Fortunately, Ehrenfest turned up here and cast some light on it. Then I read Louis de Broglie's paper, and gradually saw what they were up to. I now believe that the wave theory of matter could be of very great importance. Our Mr Elsasser's reflections are not yet in proper order. To begin with, it transpired that he had made a considerable error in his calculations, but I still believe that the essence of his remarks, particularly on the reflection of electrons, can be salvaged. I am also speculating a little about de Broglie's waves. It seems to me that a connection of a completely formal kind exists between these and that other mystical explanation of reflection, diffraction and interference using 'spatial' quantisation which Compton and Duane proposed and which has been more closely studied by Epstein and Ehrenfest.

But my principal interest is the rather mysterious differential calculus on which the quantum theory of atomic structure seems to be based. Jordan and I are systematically (though with the minimum of mental effort) examining every imaginable correspondence relationship between classical, multiple-periodic systems and quantum atoms. A paper on this subject in which we examine the effect of non-periodic fields on atoms will appear soon. This is a preliminary study for an investigation of the processes occurring in atomic collisions (quenching of fluorescence, sensitised fluorescence *à la* Franck, etc.); one can understand, I think, the essential characteristics of what goes on. The different behaviour of atoms depends mainly on whether they have an (average) dipole moment, a quadrupole moment, or even higher electric symmetry still. As regards your objections to Jordan's paper. I still feel very unsure of myself; but as I am now coming to grips with these things from my own somewhat complicated point of view, I will understand them one of these days. On the whole, you are certainly right; though Jordan's opinion is based on a somewhat different consideration, as he allows coherent bundles of rays, whereas you only mention incoherent ones.

Even if Jordan is mistaken in this, as I now think is highly probable, he is still exceptionally intelligent and astute and can think far more swiftly and confidently than I. On the whole my young people, Heisenberg, Jordan and Hund, are brilliant. I find that merely to keep up with their thoughts demands at times a considerable effort on my part. Their mastery of the so-called 'term zoology' is marvellous. Heisenberg's latest paper, soon to be published, appears rather mystifying but is certainly true and profound; it enabled Hund to bring into order the whole of the periodic system with all its complicated multiplets. This paper, too, is soon to be published. In addition, I am busy calculating the lattice theory over and over again with some of my other, less independent, pupils. We have just finished a paper by Bollnow which calculates the relationship between the crystallographic axes of two crystals of the tetragonal system, rutile and anatase, two forms of TiO_2, based on the requirement that the lattice should be in electrostatic equilibrium. The result is quite good.

I am tremendously pleased with your view that the unification of gravitation with electrodynamics has at long last been successful; the action principle you give looks so simple. As we have time, Jordan and I are going to try some variations of it. But we would be most grateful if you could send us your paper on this subject as soon as possible. This kind of thing is much deeper than our petty efforts. I would never dare tackle it.

We have had many visitors again this term. Kramers was here for eight days, as I mentioned before, and Ehrenfest, with whom both of us, particularly my wife, are now on very friendly terms. Last week Kapitza from Cambridge was here, and Joffé from Leningrad. He made a tremendous impression on us: he does such beautiful work, and yet has published hardly anything at all. Philipp Frank is now here with his wife, and many other people as well. For us this is very stimulating, but it is often too much for our wives. So they simply run away; my wife and Mrs Courant have already left, and Mrs Frank is due to leave in two days' time. But do not conclude from that that your visit is going to be unwelcome! We are greatly looking forward to it! But it ought to be at a quieter time. In July, most of the foreigners are already on holiday, and they descend on us in droves. But you know all this business. There is going to be another rumpus tomorrow; it is the inauguration of Prandtl's new hydrodynamics institute, with guided tour, official dinner and gala concert. It will cost me almost an entire working day.

But I, too, am about to escape. On July 30th I am giving a lecture in Tübingen for Gerlach and Landé, and then I am going to join my family in the Engadine. In October I am supposed to go to Cambridge, at Kapitza's invitation; we are also all supposed to be going to the Russian Physicists' Congress in Moscow next winter; Joffé is going to pay our travelling expenses. As you see, we too get around, though not as far as Japan and the Argentine. One more thing: in today's astronomy colloquium, Kienle reported a beautiful new piece of work (from Mt Wilson, I think); the satellite of Sirius is one of those minute, mysterious dwarfs of enormous mass – a density of 28,000 – and, according to Eddington, is a conglomeration of naked nuclei and electrons. The red shift (of approximately 20 km/s) has now been determined, and is exactly proportional to the enormous density (and small radius). But I must stop now.

Kindest regards to your wife and daughters,

Yours *Born*

This letter is the most significant so far, and (to me) the most important. The theory of gas degeneracy, proposed by the Indian physicist Bose, had immediately been taken up by Einstein and developed further in a momentous treatise of his. He transferred the statistical behaviour of radiation from a 'photon gas', whose statistical characteristics differ from the normal (Boltzmann distribution), to ordinary gases, which should then exhibit variations from normal behaviour (degeneracy) at low temperatures. But the most important thing about it was its connection with de Broglie's wave theory of matter. At Einstein's instigation I studied de Broglie's theory, which had been published a few years earlier. By a strange coincidence, a letter arrived just then from the American physicist Davisson, who had obtained puzzling results with the reflection of electrons from metal surfaces. The results were supported by graphs and tables. While I was discussing this letter with Franck, it occurred to us that the curious maxima of Davisson's curves could perhaps be explained by the diffraction of the electronic matter waves in the crystal lattice. A rough calculation with de Broglie's formulae resulted in a wavelength of the correct order of magnitude. We handed over the development of this idea to our pupil Elsasser, who had done experimental work with Franck to begin with but who now wanted to change over to theory. In spite of the difficulties mentioned in this letter, Elsasser did eventually succeed. His paper must be acknowledged as the first confirmation of de Broglie's wave mechanics.

The connection I suggested with Duane's and Compton's 'spatial quantisation' does indeed exist: de Broglie's spin quantum condition is exactly the same thing, but differently and more intuitively expressed. While Duane speaks of conceptual decomposition of a radiation process into harmonic components, de Broglie regards these as real, material waves, which are supposed to replace the particles. Later on I showed the relationship between particle and waves in another way, which today is fairly generally accepted: the waves represent the spread of probability for the presence of particles. But this is not the place to pursue these matters in detail. Nor will I go into the 'mysterious' differential calculus here, which is the basis of the quantum theory of atoms.[19] I would like to draw attention to the book by van der Waerden, which contains all the more important treatises on the origins of quantum mechanics as well as a thorough introduction to the relationship between them.[20]

My praise of my young collaborators, Heisenberg, Jordan and Hund, was well deserved. They all rank among today's leading physicists. We used the expression 'term zoology' to describe the compilation of experimental data about spectral lines and their dissection into 'terms' which, according to Bohr, indicate steps of energy in the excitation of the atom. No satisfactory theory existed for the regularities found in this way, and they had to be accepted as empirical facts, rather like the distinguishing characteristics of zoological species.

Then comes the most important matter: a few lines about Heisenberg's new paper, which seems to have appeared 'mystifying' but nevertheless true. This must have been the treatise in which he formulates the basic concepts of quantum mechanics and explains them by using simple examples. As my recollection of this time, which marked the beginning of a revolution in physical thinking, is a little hazy, I wrote to Prof. van der Waerden, who confirmed my assumption. His book will enable the reader to look up the sequence of events in complete detail. I shall just mention those matters which have a direct bearing on Einstein's letter.

Heisenberg gave me his manuscript on the 11th or 12th of July, asking me to decide whether it should be published and whether I had some use for it, as he was unable to get any further. Although I did not read it straight away, because I was tired, I had certainly read it before I wrote to Einstein on July 15th. The certainty with which I maintained that it was correct, in spite of its mystifying appearance, seems to show that I had already discovered that Heisenberg's extraordinary calculus was really nothing other than the well-known matrix calculation; moreover, I already knew that Heisenberg's reformulation of the conventional quantum condition represents the diagonal elements of the matrix equation

$$pq - qp = \frac{h}{2\pi i}$$

and that therefore the remaining elements of the quantity $pq - qp$ must be zero. If this is the case I was cautious enough not to mention any of this to Einstein, since the disappearance of the non-diagonal elements had first to be proved. Van der Waerden's book describes how he succeeded in this with Jordan's help, and how the paper by Heisenberg, Jordan and myself came into being. The paper by Hund which I mention follows another, slightly earlier, investigation of Heisenberg's. I have gone into these matters in so much detail, even though they are not directly connected with Einstein, because I am rather proud of the fact that I was the first to write a quantum mechanical formula in 'non-commuting' symbols. Two further scientific matters of importance are mentioned in this letter: Einstein's field theory, which was intended to unify electrodynamics and gravitation, and the satellite of Sirius. I think that my enthusiasm about the success of Einstein's idea was quite genuine. In those days we all thought that his objective, which he pursued right to the end of his life, was attainable and also very important. Many of us became more doubtful when other types of fields emerged in physics, in addition to these; the first was Yukawa's meson field, which is a direct generalisation of the electromagnetic field and describes nuclear forces, and then there were the fields which belong to the other elementary particles. After that we were inclined to regard Einstein's ceaseless efforts as a tragic error.

A few remarks on the list of the visitors to Göttingen. Kramers was a Dutchman, a pupil of Bohr's, extremely gifted, and a likeable person. Kapitza was a Russian physicist, who had escaped to England from the Bolshevik revolution when he was young and had studied in Cambridge. He had a very successful career, working at the Cavendish Laboratory and becoming a Fellow of Trinity College. His visits to Göttingen took place during this period. Later he returned to Russia, made his peace with the Communists, and achieved great distinction. Joffé, older by a generation, had remained in Russia and was held to be the leading physicist in the Soviet Union. Philipp Frank was a theoretical physicist at the German University of Prague, and afterwards went to America. While in Prague he made friends with Einstein and later wrote a captivating biography of him. Kienle was professor of astronomy at Göttingen. The lecture I mentioned concerns an astronomical observation which can be regarded as a confirmation of Bose and Einstein's theory of gas degeneracy. But as the letter does not mention this relationship, I rather think that it had not been clear to Kienle or to us.

50

7 March, 1926

Dear Mrs Born

Your short letter was truly delightful. Stomach aching but head held high; only the strong are able to manage that. Even so, it must have been a splendid experience to accompany your husband on his travels, for he had a great deal to give; and to receive is also very pleasant, when it is balanced with the giving. The Heisenberg-Born concepts leave us all breathless, and have made a deep impression on all theoretically oriented people. Instead of dull resignation, there is now a singular tension in us sluggish people. You experience only the psychological aspect of all this, but no doubt in a purer form than someone with a more materialistic outlook. The most important thing at the moment is for you to make a complete recovery, so that you will be able to run about in the sun again and live your life freely. I know from experience how to get well: to exist like a plant for a while, and to vegetate quietly and contentedly. Unlike most of your sex you have not got the knack of this; I imagine that lively little head of yours does not want to be put out of action. Remember the past of Asia; then you will experience the comforting haziness of all living things, and get well.

     Meanwhile best wishes

        Yours

           A. Einstein

Apart from Einstein's amiable words about my wife's illness in America and how to get well, this letter is remarkable for his attitude to quantum mechanics. Heisenberg and I felt pleased, but it was not long before the cooling off set in (letter No. 53).

The following letter is from my wife again.

During the winter of 1925–26 we were at the Massachusetts Institute of Technology (MIT) in Cambridge, near Boston. I gave lectures there on two subjects: crystal-lattice dynamics and quantum mechanics. These have appeared as a booklet, published by MIT in English and by Springer in German; it is probably the first book on quantum mechanics. In this book I gave so much prominence to Heisenberg that my own contribution to quantum mechanics has received very little attention until quite recently. When my course ended at the beginning of 1926, we wanted to set out on a journey across the continent, taking in the Grand Canyon in Arizona and ending up in California. But my wife fell ill and was sent back to Europe. So I had to travel by myself, and proclaimed the new quantum doctrine at many universities. The result was that hordes of Americans, and soon many other foreigners as well, visited Göttingen during the next few years. My wife went back to Germany and entered Prof. v. Noorden's well-known sanatorium in Frankfurt to take the 'cure'.

5<small>1</small>

11 April, 1926

Dear Einstein

My thanks for your kind letters are rather late, but the last three weeks in Frankfurt were anything but enjoyable (wholesale dentistry with 5 gold crowns, three extractions, two jawbone operations, etc.), so that I was really unable to think of anything but teeth. This led to an amusing incident, for one day when I was on my way to an extraction, quite absorbed, a gentleman whispered in my ear: 'dreaming of spring'. Whereupon I replied drily: 'no, dentist'. And we both grinned and went our separate ways.

I have just asked my friend Elli Rosenberg (*née* Husserl, of philosophical descent) to send you copies of my American reports. You may be able to spare the odd hour or so one day to glance through them. Max, too, has now returned to this country; his letters from Boston and San Francisco contained a lot of physics. I am hoping that we may be able to make a short trip to Berlin about the beginning of May, and will be able to tell you more then. For example, Max saw Miller's experiments on Mt Wilson, and was aghast at the slipshod way they were carried out.

My head is too tired tonight to produce even the slightest of thoughts. I find it rather annoying to realise that the output of one's brain is proportional to the increase or decrease of the amount of fat on one's body. As I have not yet regained any of the twenty or so pounds I lost, you can well imagine how short of ideas I am. I have never been so sure of Heaven as I am at present (see the Sermon on the Mount: and blessed are the poor in spirit . . .).

Look after yourselves. With warm wishes
Yours
Hedi Born

52

4 December, *1926*

Dear Born

You will have to be a little patient. My son-in-law is certain to read the play, and will write to you. But the poor man has to economise with his strength, as his heart is in poor condition. I have reminded him again to give an opinion on the play as soon as possible. I liked the beginning of the play very much, and I think its impact will not be lost on him.

Quantum mechanics is certainly imposing. But an inner voice tells me that it is not yet the real thing. The theory says a lot, but does not really bring us any closer to the secret of the 'old one'. I, at any rate, am convinced that *He* is not playing at dice. Waves in 3-dimensional space, whose velocity is regulated by potential energy (for example, rubber bands). . . I am working very hard at deducing the equations of motion of material points regarded as singularities, given the differential equation of general relativity.

With best wishes

Yours

A. Einstein

Hedi had sent her play *A Child of America* to Einstein, asking for his opinion. Einstein's son-in-law, who had married the eldest of his step-daughters, Ilse, was the then well-known and respected author and critic, Rudolf Kayser.

Einstein's verdict on quantum mechanics came as a hard blow to me: he rejected it not for any definite reason, but rather by referring to an 'inner voice'. This rejection plays an important part in later letters. It was based on a basic difference of philosophical attitude, which separated Einstein from the younger generation to which I felt that I belonged, although I was only a few years younger than Einstein.

53

14 December, 1926

Dear Mr Einstein

Today my 'Bill' arrives with his 'new nose', as you so aptly called it. I hope you will laugh at the three further acts as much as you did at the first one. I am tremendously pleased and encouraged to know that you enjoyed it so much. For one cannot gain sufficient distance from one's own creation oneself; one lived with it so intensely and only parts from it with great trepidation.

At the moment, when I am not planning any work, I feel dull and without aim and purpose, and anaesthetise myself by attending some fine lectures on the history of art. When one has begun even so modest a work of art, one looks at the creations of the masters with very different eyes.

It would be nice if you could drop me a few lines when you have read Bill. Why don't you take him on to the sofa with you after lunch?

Margot wrote to tell me that your wife is ill. I wish her a speedy recovery, and all of you a restful Christmas.

With kindest regards to you all from Max and myself

Yours

Hedi Born

54

6 January, 1927

Dear Mrs Born

I have very much enjoyed reading your play, and I think it could be quite successful as a satire on the contemporary scene. It is witty and amusing throughout, though it seems to me that as a work of art it does not do much to confirm the well-documented truth that the centre of gravity for creative activity is located in different parts of the body in men and women. You make your characters dance like marionettes; they are nothing but puppets in your hands, whose purpose is to demonstrate your opinion to the child of our times; that is all. They are not permitted to have any lives of their own. They are rather transparent, like ghosts, more or less abstract. But your *wit* saves the day. Bernard Shaw has often done something similar, and his fireworks are enjoyed by everyone. I do not know whether Rudi has read it yet; the poor man lives constantly under a deluge of paper, while conditions have improved quite considerably in this respect where I am concerned.

I am going to give the play to Mr Jessner, and tell him that I consider it witty, amusing and up-to-date, and will give him some idea of the contents. I hope it will make its mark.

Kind regards to you and your husband

Yours

A. Einstein

Jessner was then manager at the State Theatre in Berlin.

55

Dear Mr Einstein

Thank you very much for your criticism, which has occupied my mind a great deal. I have by now had all sorts of criticisms, frequently diametrically opposed, e.g., as to the relative value of the various acts, but I am, of course, particularly interested in a *fundamental* criticism such as yours. There, too, I have already heard quite different opinions, for example from Hilbert, who approved of Bill as a character. But I am by now sufficiently detached from this child of mine to know myself what is wrong with him. I expect you are right in saying that my characters are too cerebral. (I am not sure that this is not inevitable in any satire, unless one allows Mephistopheles himself to appear in person.) For me, the idea, when I have one, is the most important thing, not the human being and its fate. At best, an idea is closely bound up with a certain person. It is not that the idea has to be extracted from my brain with pincers and forceps; it arrives of its own accord after a particularly powerful emotional experience. I once wrote to Margot: If I had not felt such a tremendous disgust with our times (i.e. with what I want to attack), I would never have found the strength for creative expression. Why I experience this so overpoweringly I cannot say. The serious purpose which provoked the play may now be difficult to detect. It is one of the crazy contradictions of my nature, though probably lucky for me, that all tension and suffering is resolved in a smile.

I am fully aware that satire on the contemporary scene is, by definition, condemned to be of temporary interest only. I still hope that if one day I can give shape to more timeless problems (which directly influence and control fate) I will find the proper note to sound. I *hope*, but I certainly have no illusions about myself. As you were kind enough to call me 'witty', you would hardly expect me to be blind to my own nature.

There is no need to tell you that *I* myself am able to see, and really get to know, my characters in my mind's eye. I was 'possessed' by them, for otherwise I would not have been able to make them speak as they should. But what interests me most in people is their *spiritual attitude* to life, rather than just their fate; most of the so-called tragic destinies are nothing more than the brutal vicissitudes of life, which are linked by pure chance to one particular individual. When I think of you, for example, I do not think of individual talents and achievements, but I marvel at your supreme mastery of life itself. I remember something you once said, which for me is the key to your personality and way of thinking: when you lay gravely ill you said: 'I have such a feeling of solidarity with every living being, that it does not matter to me where the individual begins and ends'. You probably put it much more beautifully, but this is what you meant. Individual *acts* mean nothing to me: they are just a momentary flash of light.

Now to your droll pronouncement about creativity: 'the centre of gravity for creative activity is situated in different parts of the body in men and women.' Here the usual interpretation of '*head*' and '*heart*' does not apply, as, of all things, you have conceded me '*wit*'. And as to the still cruder, purely geometrical interpretation? I would not put it past you. But even in this case the contradiction above still applies, for wit is in the head. And is the effort of imagination needed for a play that grows from nothing, and for its dramatic composition, not really a creative activity? Please do not misunderstand me: I am not just trying to defend myself, but I cannot quite understand what you mean. You could not really mean that women are incapable of creating rounded characters. Do you know 'Kristin Lavranstochter' by Sigrid Undset? (particularly the first volume). I believe that every creative person shows in his characters what is most important to him personally; where his own struggles lie. The passionate person over-emphasises passion, the ecstatic ectasy, the split personality the split, etc. A Shakespeare, who combines everything, is surely unique.

I am most grateful to you for offering to pass the play on. I do hope you do not find it embarrassing. At the special request of the children, I enclose the result of a writing game we played yesterday. They are sketches which are made up as follows: one person draws the head, a second the trunk, a third the lower part of the body, and none of them knows what has been done by the others before him. Finally, a name is written underneath at random. You are going to be very pleased with your portrait.

   Kind regards to you all from Max and myself,
    Yours
     Hedi Born

56

            15 January, 1927

Dear Mrs Born

A few days ago I gave your manuscript to Jessner, who has already promised to examine it. You should not take my little joke too literally, nor as an 'either-or'. It is not meant too seriously, nor does it claim that the following assertion is unambiguous: one smiles, and goes on to the business of the day. What applies to jokes, I suppose, also applies to pictures and to plays. I think they should not smell of a logical scheme, but of a delicious fragment of life, scintillating with various colours according to the position of the beholder. If one wants to get away from this vagueness one must take up mathematics. And even then one reaches one's aim only by becoming completely insubstantial under the dissecting knife of clarity. Living matter and clarity are opposites – they run away from one another. We are now experiencing this rather tragically in physics.

By the way, there is no need for you to defend your work to me, for I have every respect for it and enjoy it. It is rarely that one finds someone like you who has such a wealth of ideas allied with charm.

The best of luck for your endeavour, for yourself and for your family.

    Yours sincerely
     A. Einstein

Many thanks for the lovely combined photo.

57

[undated]

Dear Born

I have just noticed that in my slovenliness I forgot to send you the enclosed paper. You were therefore unable to understand the rest. Please forgive me.

Last week I handed in a short paper to the Academy, in which I show that one can attribute quite *definite movements* to Schrödinger's wave mechanics, without any statistical interpretation. This will shortly be published in the minutes of the meetings.

Kindest regards
Yours
A. Einstein

These lines had been added to a letter of Ehrenfest's to Einstein. They concern some professional appointment, no longer of interest today.
The note shows that Einstein rejected the statistical interpretation of quantum mechanics not just because of his 'inner voice'. He had tried a different, non-statistical interpretation of Schroedinger's wave mechanics and was submitting a paper about it to the Academy. I cannot remember it now; like so many similar attempts by other authors, it has disappeared without trace.
At this point there is an interval of a year and a half in the correspondence. Whether letters have been lost, or whether silence really reigned, I do not know.

58

Institute for Theoretical Physics
of the University
Göttingen
Bunsenstr. 9
20 February, 1928

Dear Einstein

After consultation with Harald Bohr, who is in Göttingen this term, I want to write to you about a matter which is, strictly speaking, none of my business, but which nevertheless has caused me alarm and uneasiness on many occasions. I am

Plate 1. MAX BORN, MID 1950's

(*Photograph by Tita Binz*)

Plate 2. INTERNATIONAL SOLVAY CONFERENCE, BRUSSELS, 23–29 OCTOBER, 1927

A. PICCARD   E. HENRIOT   ED. HERZEN   TH. DE DONDER   E. SCHROEDINGER   E. VERSCHAFFELT   W. PAULI   W. HEISENBERG   R. H. FOWLER   L. BRILLOUIN

P. DEBYE   M. KNUDSEN   W. L. BRAGG   H. A. KRAMERS   P. A. M. DIRAC   A. H. COMPTON   L. V. DE BROGLIE   M. BORN   N. BOHR

I. LANGMEIR   M. PLANCK   MADAME CURIE   H. A. LORENTZ   A. EINSTEIN   P. LANGEVIN   CH. E. GUYE   C. T. R. WILSON   O. W. RICHARDSON

© Karsch
Ottawa

Max und Hedi Born mit besten Grüssen
A. Einstein.

(*Photograph by Karsch*)

Plate 3.   ALBERT EINSTEIN, LATE 1940'S

Plate 4.   MAX AND HEDWIG BORN, 1955

referring to the Hilbert and Brouwer affair. Up to now I have merely followed it from a distance, and have only recently been initiated into all the details by Bohr and Courant. In this way I learnt that you remained neutral with regard to Hilbert's letter to Brouwer, on the grounds that one should permit people to be as foolish as they wish. I find this quite reasonable, of course, but you seem not to be quite in the picture on some points, and so I want to write briefly and tell you about it. There will probably be a conference soon at Springer's about this matter, and Bohr told me that he considered it very important for the inner editorial staff to present a united front. I would therefore ask you please to maintain your present neutrality, and not to take any action against Hilbert and his friends. It would help to restore my peace of mind, as well as Bohr's and that of many other people, if you could write a few words to me about this.

I would like to tell you briefly why this business interests me. It only matters to me because I am worried and concerned about Hilbert. Hilbert is very seriously ill, and has probably not very long to live. Any excitement is dangerous for him, and means losing some of the few hours left to him in which to live and to work. He still has, however, a powerful will to live, and considers it his duty to complete his new basis for mathematics with whatever strength is left to him. His mind is clearer than ever, and it is an act of extreme callousness on Brouwer's part to spread the rumour that Hilbert is no longer responsible. Courant and other friends of Hilbert's have frequently said that the sick man should be protected against any excitement, and Brouwer has misrepresented this to mean that one should no longer take Hilbert's actions and opinions seriously. Hilbert is quite in earnest about his proposed action against Brouwer. He talked to me about it a few weeks ago, but only in quite general terms and without going into any detail. In his opinion Brouwer is an eccentric and maladjusted person to whom he did not wish to entrust the management of *Mathematische Annalen*. I think Hilbert's evaluation of Brouwer has been shown to be correct in view of Brouwer's most recent actions. In my experience, Hilbert's judgment is almost always clear and to the point in human affairs.

I have followed the previous history of the whole business, including the quarrel about the visit to the Congress in Bologna, from a distance only. But I do know that the visit to this Congress was a heavy burden for Hilbert; anything of this kind meant a tremendous exertion for him because of his illness. Hilbert is not politically very left-wing; on the contrary, for my taste and even more for yours, he is rather reactionary. But when it comes to the question of the intercourse between scientists of different countries, he has a very sharp eye for detecting what is best for the whole. Hilbert considered, as we all did, that Brouwer's behaviour in this affair, where he was even more nationalistic than the Germans themselves, was utterly foolish.

But the worst of it all was that the Berlin mathematicians were completely taken in by Brouwer's nonsense. I would like to add that the Bologna business was not the decisive factor — only the occasion for Hilbert's decision to remove Brouwer. I can understand this in Erhard Schmidt's case, for he always did lean to the right in politics, as a result of his basic emotions. For Mises and Bieberbach, however, it is a rather deplorable symptom. I talked to Mises about it in August, during our journey to Russia, and he said right at the beginning of our discussion that the people in Göttingen were blindly following Hilbert, and that he was probably no longer responsible.

Thus the allegation about Hilbert's weakened mental powers was made even then. I then immediately broke off my discussion with Mises, for I do not consider him significant enough to allow himself the liberty of passing judgment on Hilbert. I also enclose a paper which Ferdinand Springer sent to Bohr and Courant. This shows that Brouwer and Bieberbach have threatened to denounce Springer as lacking in national feeling, and that they would do him harm if he remained loyal to Hilbert. I need not tell you what I think of such behaviour. Forgive me for bothering you with so long a letter. My only desire is to see that Hilbert's earnest intentions are put into effect without causing him any unnecessary excitement. I would have no objection to your showing this letter, or part of it, to Schmidt, if you consider it correct. As an old friend of Schmidt's I believe that it is possible to negotiate successfully with him even if he is of a different opinion. I hope that you yourself are feeling much better now. I get news of you from time to time in Margot's letters to my wife. Those two are very close friends indeed, and suit each other. I myself am busy completing a book on quantum mechanics, which I have been writing for the last year. Unfortunately I have overtaxed my strength a little in doing this, and will probably have to go on leave for a time during January. It is really not at all easy to find the time and strength for that kind of work, on top of all the lectures and other professional duties.

With kindest regards, also from my wife to yours

Yours

Max Born

Harald Bohr, a brother of the physicist Niels Bohr, was a notable mathematician who frequently visited us in Göttingen.

David Hilbert, my revered teacher and friend, was then (and still is) considered to be the foremost mathematician of his time. At that time he was busy trying to find sounder logical foundations for mathematics, in order to eliminate the intrinsic contradictions found by Bertrand Russell and others in the theory of infinite sets, without sacrificing any previous mathematical knowledge. This led him to consider true mathematics as a kind of logical game with symbols, for which arbitrary axioms are found. The latter, however, should be *applied* by a 'metamathematics' based on evident, real conclusions. Brouwer rejected this concept of mathematics, and suggested another, termed intuitionism. The two ways of thinking differed in one essential result. Hilbert's concept justified the so-called existence proofs, whereby the existence of a certain number or a mathematical truth is deduced from the fact that to assume the contrary would lead to a contradiction. Brouwer, however, postulated that the existence of a mathematical structure could only be taken for granted if a method could be found that would actually construct it. As it happened, many of Hilbert's greatest mathematical achievements were precisely such abstract proofs of existence, which for some time had not only been accepted by the mathematical world, but had been celebrated as great feats.

It is therefore no wonder that Brouwer's behaviour greatly upset Hilbert, and that he expressed his opposition in no uncertain terms; whereupon Brouwer replied with even greater rudeness. To make matters worse, a political quarrel broke out on top of the scientific one. After the 1914–18 war, 'International Unions' had been founded for all the principal branches of science; the Germans, however, had been excluded from them. The hatred directed against Germany gradually diminished, and at the time this letter was written (1928) the German mathematicians were about to be admitted to the 'International Union for Mathematics', on the occasion of a large mathematical congress in Bologna. But a group of 'national' German mathematicians protested against this; they felt that it would not be right to join the Union without further ado after having been excluded for such a long time, and that one should protest against it in Bologna. Three important Berlin mathematicians were amongst the leaders of this movement: Bieberbach, who was a good analyst; von Mises, a research worker of some significance, who was also concerned with theoretical physics; and Erhard Schmidt, the most outstanding of the three. Schmidt and I had been friends ever since my student days and, although politically we were poles apart, we always remained on the best of terms. But the Dutchman Brouwer was more nationalistic than all these proved to be. Hilbert went to Bologna, despite his grave illness, and faced his adversaries. As far as I can remember, he got his way and the Germans joined the Union. But the whole business had annoyed him so much that he expelled Brouwer from the management of the Mathematische Annalen. This started a new storm amongst German mathematicians. But Hilbert finally got the upper hand.

The whole affair was, strictly speaking, no concern of mine. But, as I said in the letter, I was moved to intervene by my anxiety about the state of Hilbert's health. Hilbert suffered from pernicious anaemia, and would no doubt have died within a short time had not Minot in the United States discovered the specific remedy, a liver extract, just in time. This was not yet commercially available, but the wife of the Göttingen mathematician Edmund Landau was a daughter of Paul Ehrlich, the founder of chemotherapy and discoverer of Salvarsan. It was due to his good offices that Hilbert was able to receive regular supplies of the extract and so to live for many more years.

I doubt whether my letter to Einstein had any influence on the course of the great mathematical quarrel.

As for the further development of the fundamental problems of mathematics, Brouwer had many supporters to begin with, including some important ones such as Hermann Weyl. But gradually Hilbert's abstract interpretation was, after all, realised to be by far the more profound. Things took a new turn when Gödel discovered the existence of mathematical theorems which can be proved to be incapable of proof. Today, mathematics is more abstract than ever, and exactly the same is true of theoretical physics.

The journey to Russia I mention was a kind of wandering physicists' congress, organised in Leningrad by Joffé, who has been mentioned before. It began in Leningrad, and was continued first in Moscow and then in Nizhni-Novgorod; there the participants boarded a Volga steamer and travelled down river, stopping at all the large towns *en route* to continue the congress. The whole thing was very fascinating and stimulating, but extremely fatiguing. I went as far as Saratov, and from there returned to Germany by train.

The book about quantum mechanics I mentioned at the end of the letter was written in collaboration with Jordan over a period of several years.

59

Dear Einstein

A young Russian turned up here some time ago with a six-dimensional theory of relativity. Since I was already uneasy about the various five-dimensional theories, and as I was not at all convinced that it could lead to anything worthwhile, I was very sceptical. But he talked very intelligently and soon convinced me that there is something to his ideas.

Although I understand less than ϵ of this matter, I have submitted his paper to the Academy of Göttingen, and enclose a copy of it and *urgently* request you to read it and evaluate it. The man, whose name is Rumer, left Russia because relativists are badly treated there (truly!). The theory of relativity is thought to contradict the official 'materialist' philosophy and, as I have already been told by Joffé, its adherents are persecuted. Rumer came to Germany, and has somehow managed to study at the technical school in Oldenburg, where he is now going to sit for the technical exam. Afterwards he intends to try and make a living here as best he can, and if he fails, to emigrate to South America.

If the paper makes a *good* impression on you, I would ask you please to do something for this man. He is familiar with the literature of mathematics, from Riemann's geometry right up to the very latest publications, and may well be the ideal assistant for you. He has a pleasant personality, and gives the impression of being extremely intelligent. I do not know whether he is really Russian, or Jewish; but I think the latter the more likely. His address is: Georg Rumer, Oldenburg, Am Festungs-graben 8.

I am still not feeling particularly well. I spent eight days in Waldeck with my children, but it was noisy and restless. My nerves are in a bad state. Next week I travel alone to the Vierwaldstätter See, where an acquaintance (a Swiss solicitor) has a cottage and a motorboat in Kehrsiten-Bürgenstock (my address there is: Hotel Schiller). I saw your picture in the last issue of the *Illustrierte* in a sailing boat, looking sunburnt.

Hedi is suffering from colitis, and is undergoing a strict dietary cure.

With kindest regards, also to you wife and to Margot.

Yours

Max Born

I enclose an outline of the contents of a book Rumer intends to write.

I continued to find Rumer's six-dimensional theory of relativity alarming. Later on we wrote a short paper together on nuclei; its purely speculative nature was more representative of his mentality than of mine.

The hostile attitude of official Communist philosophy towards the theory of relativity continued for a long time. Perhaps Rumer's fate was connected with this. When I flew to Moscow as a member of the English delegation to the 25th Jubilee celebrations of the Soviet Academy in June 1945, soon after the end of the war, and enquired after Rumer, it was hinted that he was in disgrace and had disappeared. I heard nothing from him until he sent me congratulations on my 75th birthday, from Novosibirsk. I wrote asking what had happened to him, and he replied with a long letter saying that he had been deported and had lived for many years in one of the terrible camps near the Arctic Ocean. He had managed to survive only because of the help of a kindly nurse, who was now his wife. After the death of Stalin he received a telegram, which not only gave him back his freedom but also recalled him to Moscow, where he was appointed head of the Institute of Physics at the new scientific centre in Novosibirsk. He is now one of the most important men in Soviet science.

The strange thing is that his long period of suffering in northern Siberia had aroused no bitterness, no hostility towards the regime. On the contrary, he wrote me long letters in which he tried to convince me that the Soviet system is superior to Western institutions, not only politically and economically, but also morally.

60

Institute for Theoretical Physics
Göttingen
Bunsenstr. 9
13 January, 1929

Dear Einstein

The upheavals of the beginning of the university term have prevented me from answering your good long letter until now. I also wanted to discuss your remarks with Jordan and he has only recently arrived here. We are very grateful to you for your criticism, and have altered the relevant passage in our book accordingly. You are, of course, absolutely right that an assertion about the possible future acceptance or rejection of determinism cannot be logically justified. For there can always be an interpretation which lies one layer deeper than the one we know (as your example of the kinetic theory as against the macroscopic theory shows). Jordan and I are not much inclined to believe in anything like that, but of course we should not claim anything for which we have no rigorous proof, and therefore we have altered the passage in question accordingly.

I am now reading the theory of relativity, not only because I have to teach it to my students, but also to feel at home again in this field. I hope to progress as far as your most recent papers, and will then study them carefully and let you know my opinion.

Rumer is staying here in Göttingen. He has obtained a grant from Warburg in Hamburg, which enables him to study here a little longer.

My wife is now quite well again; but she would very much like Margot to come here for a visit. I would like to enter into a conspiracy with you. Hedi's birthday is on December 14th, and I wonder if it would be possible for Margot to pay us a surprise visit on that day? That would give us a lot of pleasure.

With kindest regards to your wife and to Margot.

Yours
Max Born

The letter in which Einstein criticises a passage in our book seems unfortunately to have been lost. But the gist of his remarks is clear from my letter. At this point I would like to say a few words about that book. Shortly before the discovery of quantum mechanics, I had published a book in collaboration with Friedrich Hund (then my assistant).[22] This book was still based on the Bohr-Sommerfeld theory, which grafts 'quantum conditions' on to the classical laws of mechanics; it has recently been re-issued in America in an English version by Fisher and Hartree. In the introduction it says: 'I have called this book Volume One; the second volume is to contain a closer approximation to the "ultimate" atomic mechanics. I realise that it is rash to promise such a second volume, as for the time being there are only a few vague indications as to the nature of the changes which must be made to the classical laws in order to explain the properties of the atoms.' But before the end of that same year, papers by Heisenberg, Jordan and myself were published, laying the foundations for the new mechanics. Thus I was soon able, with Jordan's assistance, to tackle the writing of the promised second volume. In the introduction to this volume it says: 'My hope that the veil then still obscuring the essential structure of the atomic laws would soon fall has been realised with surprising speed and thoroughness'. It took several years to write the second volume. In the meantime, Schroedinger's wave mechanics appeared, and won the approbation of theoretical physicists to such an extent that our own matrix method was completely pushed into the background, particularly after Schroedinger himself had shown the mathematical equivalence of wave and matrix mechanics.

Jordan and I, however, were convinced that our method was the better one, and that Schroedinger's wave equation was preferred because it took as its point of departure traditional ideas of mathematical physics (eigenvalue problems of oscillating systems). Schroedinger himself even claimed, and maintained throughout his lifetime, to have eliminated quantum theoretical peculiarities such as quantum jumps by his theory. In our opinion Heisenberg's method was more deeply penetrating. Wave equations in more than three dimensions are no 'return to classical concepts'. It is true that I had supported my statistical interpretation of quantum mechanics (1926) by the argument, *inter alia*, that I considered the collision of particles with other particles as a scattering of waves. But this was only a simple borderline case, where the three-dimensional, intuitive description could be used. Jordan and I regarded quantum mechanics, as developed by us in Göttingen and independently by Dirac in Cambridge, as the implementation of Bohr's correspondence principle; that is why our book is dedicated to Niels Bohr. We planned a third volume which was to put wave mechanics into its rightful place, but we did not get that far. The completion of the second volume took much longer than we had expected, and then our ways parted. Because of the general predisposition in favour of Schroedinger, our second volume was not favourably received. I recall in particular a review published by Pauli, which was utterly destructive.

Now the situation seems to be changing. At the conference of Nobel prizewinners for physics in Lindau in the summer of 1965, Dirac said in a lecture that he believed the reason for the great difficulties with the quantum field theory, which were leading to almost grotesque tricks such as infinite renormalisation, to lie partly in the fact that Schroedinger's ideas, and not those of Heisenberg, were used as a starting point. He went so far as to say, 'For the purpose of setting up quantum electro-dynamics, Schroedinger's is a bad theory, Heisenberg's a good one.' I believe that Dirac is right, and that the preference for Schroedinger is based only on the fact that he works with familiar thought processes. Our old book may thus enjoy a renaissance. Almost all the textbooks published in the meantime deal principally with wave mechanics.

After this digression into physics, I return to Einstein's letter. Jordan and I had apparently sent him the proofs of our book, possibly in the hope of changing his negative attitude towards quantum mechanics. But it did not succeed. He particularly objected to a passage in the book (presumably in the introduction) in which we called the statistical interpretation of physics the final one. We gave in to his request to alter this passage, although we did not change our opinion. Today this view is probably shared by the vast majority of physicists.

61

14 December, 1929

Dear Born

Your lucid letter gave me much pleasure. The complete person is revealed by both important and unimportant actions.

I liked Rumer very much. His idea of using a multidimensional treatment is original, and formally well developed. Its weakness lies in the fact that the known laws are incomplete, and there seems no logical way of completing them.

In any case, it would be gratifying if one could make it possible for him to do scientific work, and this could, of course, best be done by giving him some routine job which would leave him enough spare time for independent work. Unfortunately, such opportunities do not exist. Would it really be impossible to create grammar school teaching posts or similar official appointments for this kind of case, with a reduced number of teaching hours and pay? This would be definitely more satisfactory than grants for a limited period, for the stork is Bohemian when it comes to intellectual births, and refuses to accept a fixed delivery date.

      Kind regards,
        Yours
        [no signature]

62
                Institute for Theoretical Physics
                          Göttingen
                       Bunsenstrasse 9
                    19 December, 1929

Dear Einstein

I am very pleased that you want to take Rumer under your wing. The idea of giving him some sort of routine job which would leave him enough spare time for his scientific work is, of course, good in theory but extremely difficult to implement in practice. The establishment of grammar school teaching posts with reduced hours of teaching and lower pay is desirable, but would of course be very difficult to achieve, and then probably only after years of preparatory work. My own relations with the Ministry are far too tenuous for me to be able to effect anything in this direction. But perhaps your influence would be successful. This seems to me a practical problem where you could well use the full weight of your name to benefit young people. Would it be possible for you to make an appointment with Richter, the permanent head of the ministerial department, and put the case to him?

But such wild hopes as these will not help Rumer at this moment. Incidentally, he has completed a technical training course at the Technical School in Oldenburg, and passed his finals there. He could therefore look for a job in practice, but while there is so much unemployment a foreigner has practically no chance of finding a job in Germany. In my opinion we can do nothing else now but get him a grant, for at least one year. My wife told me that you and Ehrenfest had offered to do this, and to obtain it from the Rockefeller Foundation. I do not want to approach them under any circumstances just now, as they have treated me rather badly. Tisdale was here last spring, and when he saw how badly my nerves were playing me up he suggested that he would have me sent to California for a few months, at the expense of the Rockefeller Foundation. At the time I declined his offer because I hoped to recover sufficiently during the holidays. But when I was not very much better after the long vacation, I wrote to Tisdale again and reminded him of his proposal. Thereupon he refused rather brusquely to support my application at Head Office. I can really only think of one explanation for this, and that is that the Rockefeller people have something against Göttingen. Maybe something I don't know about happened when the Mathematical Institute was being established. Therefore I should not like to put a proposal to him just at the moment.

Please, therefore, be kind enough to write to Tisdale (The Rockefeller Foundation, 20 rue de la Baume, Paris), and apply for a grant for Rumer for a year's stay with you, or with me perhaps, or someone else, and please add that Ehrenfest and I would wholeheartedly support it. But I will not conceal the difficulties from you: generally the Rockefeller people strictly obey the rule to hand out stipends only to those who can prove that they have a definite salaried position in their own country. This does not apply in Rumer's case. But it is just possible that your name may be enough to have an exception made in this case.

Laue has sent me an attractive invitation to lecture to the Physical Society [*Physikalische Gesellschaft*] in Berlin in January. I accepted with pleasure, as I have not seen any of you for such a very long time. I'm afraid I have no very special news for you as regards physics.

Hedi sends her best wishes to you all, and particularly to Margot.

Yours

Max Born

Einstein expressed over and over again the thought that one should not couple the quest for knowledge with a bread-and-butter profession, but that research should be done as a private spare-time occupation. He himself wrote the first of his great treatises while earning his living as an employee of the Swiss Patent Office in Berne. He believed that only in this way could one preserve one's independence. His proposal to create a part-time grammar school teaching post for Rumer was in accordance with this. What he did not consider, however, was the organisational rigidity of almost all professions, and the importance which individual members of a profession attach to their work. No professional pride could develop without it. To be able successfully to practice science as a hobby, one has to be an Einstein.

63

Pasadena
5 February, 1931

For the last five weeks we have been loafing in this paradise without, however, forgetting our friends.
> Kind regards
> Yours
> *A. E.*

64

Göttingen
Wilhelm Weberstrasse 42
22 February, 1931

Dear Einstein
When Hedi saw your entry into California on film, she thought of you as completely caught up in the hectic turmoil of American life. We were all the more pleased to receive your card, which arrived today. It is nice to feel that you think of us from time to time. I expect you are brooding on *cosmology*, expansion of the universe, and similar matters. We were lectured on these questions in the astronomy seminar, where Weyl intervened with explanatory comments. Weyl is altogether a most valuable addition to our circle. He often attends the physics colloquium, regularly visits my theoretical seminar, frequently takes part in the discussion, and everything he has to say is, as a rule, tremendously lively, intelligent and ingenious. My young people have learned a great deal from him, but then the seminar has inspired him to write two short papers about the application

of group theory to molecules and valencies for the *Göttinger Nachrichten*. Our personal relationship with the Weyls is also very pleasant, as both of them have a variety of literary interests, and this brings them into contact with Hedi.

I am glad that the term will soon be at an end, for I have been working extremely hard. I worry about quantum electrodynamics; I feel I have made a promising start, but it is abominably difficult. The problem is to eliminate the infinite self energy of the electron and everything connected with it. In addition I have been writing up my optics lectures, which I want to publish some day in order to earn some money. Apart from that, there is little to report from Göttingen. Occasionally we go to the cinema to see how beautiful it is elsewhere, and your card with the orange trees has reawakened our longing for faraway places. A few years ago, in Como, I think, Millikan asked me if I would like to go to Pasadena for six months. At that time I replied that I did not want to be separated from my children for such a long time when they were so young. Now the girls are almost grown-up, and we could get away easily in a few years' time. Could you please ask Millikan, when the opportunity arises, whether he could perhaps use me in eighteen months' or two years' time? I could not do it earlier than that for other reasons; from next October I have to be Dean for a year. For all of ten years I have shirked this office by my partly genuine, partly feigned blockheadedness in official business matters, but it will not do any longer. Well, I hope to get through this year, too. My collaborator Rumer, on whose behalf I once wrote to you, will now be able to remain with me for another year as my assistant. Heitler is going to America this summer to Columbus, Ohio, and Rumer is going to replace him. I have scrounged some money for the winter.

At Christmas I spent twelve days in Switzerland as the guest of an industrialist friend of mine, and visted Zürich on the way back. I gave a lecture there at the invitation of the student body, and afterwards, when we continued our session in a local pub, I met your son. I liked him very much; he is a fine, intelligent fellow and laughs in exactly the same wonderful way as you do. Well, what else is there to tell you? Things in Europe do not look pleasant, either politically or economically. We also have personal worries, like so many other people about 'displaced' relatives. But things must surely improve in spite of Hitler and his consorts. I know all sorts of things about California, as I am just reading Ehrenfest's wonderfully vivid, descriptive letters about his travels which he has sent to Hedi. How well that fellow observes and describes his experiences. While reading I can quite clearly see the Californian landscape in front of me, as well as the dear people there; particularly the Tolmans, Epstein and the Millikans. Please give them all my warmest regards. I expect Hedi will want to add a few words of her own. This letter is meant to be a birthday greeting, so will have to reach you at approximately the right time.

Best wishes to your wife. From Margot, the young wife, we hear little.

Yours
Max Born

Dear Einsteins

I just want to add my loyal good wishes. Keep well, both of you. I am always very amused to see and hear you in the weekly newsreel – being presented with a floral float containing lovely sea-nymphs in San Diego, and that sort of thing. The world has, after all, its amusing side. However crazy such things may look from the outside, I always have the feeeling that the dear Lord knows very well what he is up to. In the same way as Gretchen sensed the Devil in Faust, so he makes people sense in you – well, just the Einstein. For none of them will ever be able to really *know* you – however thoroughly they may have studied the theory of relativity.

God bless you all. Our little Margot remains silent – silent – silent.

In warmest friendship,
Yours
Hedi Born

I do envy you the orange trees and the blue skies.

The allusion to cosmology and expansion of the universe refers to the discovery by the American astronomer Hubble, which created a sensation in those days. He showed that the more distant star systems, called galaxies, which all resemble our own Milky Way, are moving apart with a velocity which is greater the further away they already are. It was as a result of this discovery that the renewed interest in cosmology initiated by Einstein's theory of relativity, gained further momentum.

Hermann Weyl, who had been a student and private lecturer in Göttingen at the same time as I was, became Hilbert's successor. Weyl was one of the last of the great mathematicians to concern himself with theoretical physics and astronomy. He made important contributions to both. When Hitler came to power he went to Princeton, to the 'Institute for Advanced Study', where Einstein too had gone.

The year I was Dean was one of the worst of my academic life. The German Cabinet, under Chancellor Brüning, was forced to take extreme economic measures as a result of the crisis in Europe caused by the collapse of the American financial system. An order thus went out to the universities to dismiss immediately a large proportion of the younger assistants and other paid staff. Many members of our scientific faculty found this shocking: firstly, because it was cruel to single out the young, struggling ones, many of whom were married, for dismissal, and to deprive them of their already meagre incomes; furthermore, it would paralyse the activities of the institutes, practically bringing them to a standstill. We formed a committee and decided to propose to the faculty that we would pay most of the people affected out of our own pockets by offering to make a voluntary contribution which amounted to less than 10 per cent of our salaries. The battles this caused within the faculty still make me shudder. In the course of an interminable meeting we won with a considerable majority. But those who were outvoted displayed an animosity we had never before experienced; amongst them were some historians, but most of them were agriculturalists and forestry people. Six months later we knew what they really were: disguised Nazis, who considered solicitude for the individual just as superfluous as the existence of scientific institutes. The only bright spot occurred when I personally told the Curator of the University, Geheimrat Valentiner, the faculty's decision. He was so moved that tears came to his eyes; he said something like, 'if all corporate bodies acted as unselfishly as your faculty, our country would soon be rid of its problems.'

Walter Heitler was my assistant for many years, together with Lothar Nordheim. While the latter went to America (California) during the Hitler period, Heitler first went to England, and later became Professor at the Institute for Advanced Studies in Dublin. He eventually became professor in Zürich as a result of his significant work with F. London on the quantum theory of chemical components and on cosmic radiation, as well as his splendid book about the quantum theory of radiation.

The industrialist friend mentioned in the letter was Carl Still, from

Recklinghausen, whom I mentioned before (commentary to letter No. 30). As regards my optimism about the political situation, this letter must have been written during one of my momentary spells of hopefulness. But I remember very well that I was just as prone to moments of complete despair. The poor condition of my nerves, frequently mentioned in these letters, was due not only to overwork but also to other worries, mainly political ones. At the beginning of the year 1929, I think, I was sent to a sanatorium at Constance on Lake Constance; there I was kept in bed at first, but was later allowed to sit in the lounge and talk to people. But the conversation of the patients, who were manufacturers, doctors, lawyers, or at any rate all people from the upper middle classes, was almost wholly about Hitler and the high hopes they had of him, interspersed with virulent attacks on the Jews. This drove me back to my room again. I was only able to recover completely when I escaped from the sanatorium and went to Königsfeld in the Black Forest. During lone treks on skis I got the better of my worries, and towards the end of my stay I got to know Albert Schweitzer. While walking past a church I heard wonderful organ music, and went inside. There at the organ I found Dr Schweitzer, well-known to me from photographs. I spoke to him during an interval in his playing. In the course of several long walks he told me about his life and his work in Lambarene. This helped me to recover my equilibrium. The political optimism displayed in my letter may well have been connected with this. The American friends mentioned in connection with Ehrenfest's letters from the United States are all high-ranking physicists: Tolman, who was mainly known for his work on the theory of relativity and cosmology; Epstein, through his contributions to Bohr's theory of atomic structure; Millikan, for his final confirmation of the corpuscular structure of electricity and his exact measurement of the charge of the electron.

Institute for Theoretical Physics
Göttingen
Bunsenstr. 9
6 October, 1931

65

Dear Einstein

By the same post I am sending you a new paper by Rumer, which shows, it seems to me, real progress in the direction he has pursued for many years. I am well aware that you are occupied with an entirely different range of ideas, but perhaps you will find time to have a look at Rumer's paper. I think his statement is quite correct; the assumption of a Riemann space leads inevitably to certain assumptions about the matter tensor and fairly necessarily to a curious new kind of field theory of matter. The question is, should one continue in this direction and elaborate this field theory, or should one – as you are trying to do – change over to a wholly new geometry? I have no opinion on this. However, I think that every avenue should be explored.

With kind regards, also from my wife.

Yours

M. Born

There are about eighteen months between this letter and the next, during which time so much happened that scientific matters receded into the background. Several elections for the Reichstag were held, which increased the number of Nazi delegates, and Hitler's power grew accordingly. His brown hordes terrorised the country. Then came Hitler's seizure of power. And one day (at the end of April, 1933), I found my name in the paper amongst a list of those who were considered unsuitable to be civil servants, according to the new 'Laws'. Franck was not amongst them; as a front-line warrior during the first world war he was excused for the time being.

Einstein was in the United States during this period. He returned to Europe in the spring of 1933, but went to Belgium and England and not to Germany, where his life could have been in danger.

After I had been given 'leave of absence', we decided to leave Germany at once. We had rented an apartment for the summer vacation in Wolkenstein in the Grödner valley (Selva, Val Gardena in Italian), from a farmer by the name of Peratoner. He was willing to take us immediately. Thus we left for the South Tyrol at the beginning of May (1933); we took our twelve-year old son, Gustav, with us, but left our adolescent daughters behind at their German schools. From Selva I apparently wrote to Einstein *via* Ehrenfest in Holland, and this is his reply:

66

Oxford
30 May, 1933

Dear Born

Ehrenfest sent me your letter. I am glad that you have resigned your positions (you and Franck). Thank God there is no risk involved for either of you. But my heart aches at the thought of the young ones. Lindemann has gone to Göttingen and Berlin (for one week). Maybe you could write to him here about Teller. I heard that the establishment of a good Institute of Physics in Palestine (Jerusalem) is at present being considered. There has been a nasty mess there up to now, complete charlatanism. But if I get the impression that this business could be taken seriously, I shall write to you at once with further details. For it would be splendid if something good were to be created there; it could develop into an institute of international renown. But for the time being I have not much faith in it.

Two years ago I tried to appeal to Rockefeller's conscience about the absurd method of allocating grants, unfortunately without success. Bohr has now gone to see him, in an attempt to persuade him to take some action on behalf of the exiled German scientists. It is to be hoped that he'll achieve something. Lindemann has considered London and Heitler for Oxford. He has set up an organisation of his own for this purpose, taking in all the English universities. I am firmly convinced that all those who have made a name already will be taken care of. But the others, the young ones, will not have the chance to develop.

You know, I think, that I have never had a particularly favourable opinion of the Germans (morally and politically speaking). But I must confess that the degree of their brutality and cowardice came as something of a surprise to me.

I originally intended to create a university for exiles. But it soon became apparent that there were insurmountable obstacles, and that any efforts in this direction would impede the exertions of individual countries.

I do hope I shall soon be able to write to you with more concrete news. Meanwhile I wish you and your family a peaceful time in the mountains.

  Yours

  Einstein

I've been promoted to an 'evil monster' in Germany, and all my money has been taken away from me. But I console myself with the thought that the latter would soon be gone anyway.

Lindemann, a thorough-going Englishman despite his German name, was well known to me, almost a friend, since my days as a lecturer. He studied with Nernst in Berlin, and often came to Göttingen. His work was so good that he rose quickly: Fellow of Christ Church College, Oxford, Professor of Experimental Philosophy and Head of the Clarendon Laboratory. In the second world war he was Churchill's most influential scientific adviser. It was his idea to break the fighting spirit of the German people by air attacks on the centres of the large cities. In 1933 he came to Germany to get the dismissed German scholars for England. He was especially keen on promoting physics in Oxford. Oxford was traditionally given over to the humanities, while at Cambridge, Newton's university, the sciences blossomed. And so Lindemann travelled all over Germany trying to obtain physicists of note for Oxford. In July he even came to Selva (Gardena) to negotiate with me. I had, however, just accepted an invitation to go to Cambridge. Einstein's letter also says that Lindemann had considered Heitler and London for Oxford. Heitler had, as already mentioned, been my assistant in Göttingen for many years. London, the son of one of my mathematics professors from my student days in Breslau, had studied mainly with Sommerfeld in Munich. London and Heitler jointly published a fundamental work in which the chemical (non-polar) valency forces were for the first time explained in physical terms by means of quantum mechanics. This theory has since been successfully developed by the American chemist Linus Pauling; he was awarded the Nobel Prize for chemistry for this, but Heitler and London did not get the prize for physics. Neither went to Oxford. Instead, Lindemann got Franz Simon, Professor of Physical Chemistry at Breslau, and some younger research workers, Mendelssohn, Kurti and Kuhn *inter alia*. They soon brought the Clarendon Laboratory to full bloom. In the end Simon became Lindemann's successor, was knighted and so became Sir Francis. The main research effort at his institute was in low temperature studies.

It is evident from Einstein's letter that at that time I was trying to do something for Edward Teller, but I cannot remember it. He had been in Göttingen for some time and had helped me to write one of the chapters in my book on optics (the theory of the Raman effect). He later became famous in America as the 'father of the hydrogen bomb' and has always tried passionately to influence public opinion in favour of power politics and against any compromise between East and West.

Einstein's severe judgment of the Germans would no doubt have been subscribed to by all of us who had been expelled by Hitler, as well as our friends in other countries. But what we experienced then was child's play in comparison with what happened later. And yet I am now living in

Germany again. These pages will show how this came about. Einstein himself never again set foot on German soil.

One of Einstein's letters appears to have been lost between this letter and the one that follows.

67

Selva-Gardena
Villa Blazzola
2 June, 1933

Dear Einstein

Many thanks for your kind letter. I wish I could help you to look after the young exiled physicists and others like them, but I am in the same position myself. I spend my time trying to improve my rather run-down nerves (sleep is still a problem), and thinking about physics a little. I do have, after all, one advantage: for quite some time now I have had plenty of time at my disposal. But it is not too easy without a library. One of my pupils, an Englishman, has come here and I do a little work with him.

Many thanks for your concern about my – or rather our – future. I see my task as being more to make my children's lives worth living, rather than to spend the rest of my days in pleasure and comfort. I have not given up, by any means, but I share Ehrenfest's opinion that those who are younger have a better chance of achieving something. It is all the more sad that their prospects in life are so poor. As regards my wife and children, they have only become conscious of being Jews or 'non-Aryans' (to use the delightful technical term) during the last few months, and I myself have never felt particularly Jewish. Now, of course, I am extremely conscious of it, not only because we are considered to be so, but because oppression and injustice provoke me to anger and resistance. I would like my children to become citizens of a Western country, preferably England, for the English seem to be accepting the refugees most nobly and generously. Also, I studied in England 26 years ago, know the language, and have many friends there. But I do not know whether it will be possible for anything as good as that to happen. You seem to have it in mind to recommend me (or Franck?) to the Institute of Physics to be created in Palestine.

In the interests of my wife and children I would rather not do that, though I admit that I know next to nothing about life and conditions in Palestine.

Meanwhile I have already received several invitations for the immediate future: one to go for a few months to Columbus, Ohio, where Landé is, and one to go to Paris for a whole year, free from teaching obligations. The latter, of course, would appeal to me greatly, and even more to Hedi; but the salary offered is too small to live on with a wife and three children for a whole year. Once I got to Paris, I expect the same thing would happen to my money as has happened to yours: you would then be the big monster, I the small monster. But if it could be arranged, we would be very pleased: just imagine, Paris after ten years in Göttingen! There is yet another possibility: I have been informed that I have received (or am going to receive) a post in Belgrade (Yugoslavia); however, the letter was not official. Hedi is attracted to anything adventurous and strange. I am put off by the scientific wasteland which probably still exists there, and the language. I have absolutely no talent for languages, and to learn a Slav language seems almost impossible to me. But if nothing else comes along, I would undertake it. But younger people should really be picked for such posts, people who would find it easier to adapt themselves.

I am going to write to Lindemann about the Teller business, and will also ask him to take care of this letter, as you did not give any address. I received direct news from Göttingen through my English pupil the other day about Franck, Weyl and my daughter Irene, who is staying with the Weyls there and is enjoying her life, without taking much notice of current events. Happy youth that makes that possible! And yet she is not at all superficial in her emotions. Courant spent a few days with H. Bohr in Copenhagen and his condition seems to have improved a little. Franck is resolutely determined not to go abroad while he has the slightest prospect of finding work in Germany (though not as a civil servant). Although there is, of course, no chance of this, he remains in Göttingen and waits. I would not have the nerve to do it, nor can I see the point of it. But both he and Courant are, in spite of their Jewishness which is far more pronounced than in my case, Germans at heart.

Hedi sends her kind regards to you and yours. I am most deeply grateful to you for all you are doing on our behalf.
Yours
M. Born

The pupil who looked me up in Selva was Maurice Blackman, a South African Jew; he did valuable work later on, and is now professor at Imperial College, London, and a Fellow of the Royal Society. Soon another English pupil of mine, Thomson from Oxford, also arrived. I gave them little lectures on a bench in front of our house or in the woods of the narrow valley, Val Lunga. We were very proud of this little Selva University.

I never seriously considered going to Jerusalem, for the reasons mentioned in the letter, to which I should like to add a few words of explanation. My parents were both of Jewish extraction. My mother died while I was still a child. My father, who was Professor of Anatomy and Embryology at the University of Breslau, was a member of the Jewish community; he was a liberal of the previous century, for whom religious tolerance was natural. Though he suffered professionally more than once from anti-semitism, he refused to change his religion, for merely practical reasons. The atmosphere in his house was one of urbanity and tolerance. I grew up in this and have tried to preserve it in my own home. An involvement with Judaism can hardly be said to have existed. It was even less so in the case of my wife; although her father, the well-known lawyer Viktor Ehrenberg, was of Jewish descent, her mother was of Frisian stock, a daughter of the world-famous lawyer Rudolf von Ihering. My wife was in later years a Christian in more than name. In Edinburgh her conviction became even more strongly rooted when she joined the Religious Society of Friends (Quakers). Neither she nor our children had any ties with Judaism, other than love for Jewish relatives, and certainly none with Zionism or with Palestine.

We took the call to Yugoslavia seriously. I wrote to a colleague in Vienna whom I knew to be familiar with the Balkan countries. His reply was a humorous description of the situation in Belgrade: how everything depended on personal relations, and that it was far more important to entertain a Minister of State with a few amusing stories over a glass of wine than to do research, and so on. This deterred us.

Shortly afterwards came the invitation to England. The next letter, again from myself to Einstein, was written from Cambridge, where my wife had rented a small house.

68

Cambridge
8 March, 1934

Dear Einstein

I have had news of you from time to time through Weyl, just as you have probably heard in the same way about us from him. Today I am writing to you direct, because I would like to know if there is any prospect of assistance for exiled German scholars, and for physicists in particular, from America. You, with your warm heart, are no doubt following all these disastrous events in detail, but from a distance, after all. Here, where I am, it is all very real indeed. Almost every week some unfortunate wretch approaches me personally, and every day I receive letters from people left stranded. And I am completely helpless, as I am myself a guest of the English and my name is not widely known; I can do nothing except advise the Academic Assistance Council in London and the *Notgemeinschaft* [Emergency Aid Society] in Zurich. But neither of these institutions has any money. As a result of your address in the Albert Hall, Rutherford had hoped to get a movement under way which would produce greater amounts; but nothing much seems to have come of it. Most of the grants from the Academic Assistance Council come to an end in the autumn, and *cannot* be renewed. In the meantime many more have arrived in need of help, for whom nothing is available.

What I would like to know is this:

1. Is America still able to take people, and particularly younger people? In which professions? Could teachers of physics be placed? To whom would one have to apply? (Dugan Committee?)

2. Would it be possible for you to collect a really *large* sum by making use of your popularity, and to send it to Rutherford for the Academic Assistance Council? I would then devote my entire time and energy to make sure that it is used sensibly. (You would have to write to Rutherford and suggest that I should be asked to do this.) Frequently it is not the most capable but the most pushing who are given preference.

3. What other possibilities are there? Could one not start a publicity campaign in South America? What is the position in regard to Jerusalem?

The *Notgemeinschaft* in Zurich has, partly with my assistance, established connections with Russia and India, which offer good prospects.

I myself have been asked by Raman whether I would accept a professorship in Bangalore. But because of my predisposition to asthma, I would rather avoid any such abrupt change in climate as long as the Cambridge people want to keep me on.

I feel very much at home here, and can work better than in Göttingen. Hedi has not settled down as well; her health, particularly her nervous condition, is not at all satisfactory. My daughters are arriving in England in a fortnight's time and want to stay at home for the time being. Hedi will then enter a sanatorium.

The other day I sent you my paper which appeared in the *Proceedings of the Royal Society*. It is not yet satisfactory. I am very satisfied, however, with a second paper which is at present being printed; it contains a 'classical' treatment of my field theory, in which everything happens to fall into place most splendidly. You may not agree with it, as I have not dealt with gravitation at the same time. This is a matter of principle, in which I differ from the ideas expressed in your papers on the unified field theory. I hope soon to be able to develop my idea about gravitation. I have made some progress with the quantisation of my field equations, but I still face towering difficulties.

Are you going to come to Europe in the summer? I expect I will have to remain here for financial reasons. Hedi would very much like to know *Margot's address*. How is your wife? Please give my sincere regards to her and our colleagues at Princeton.

    Yours

      Max Born

While Einstein occupied a firm, highly paid academic teaching post at Princeton, my employment in Cambridge was only provisional. But I was soon given the 'degree' of Master of Arts (M.A.). and the title of 'Stokes lecturer'; I had a small room in the Cavendish Laboratory and did not have to give many lectures, which left me enough time for my own work. Our economic position was, however, very tight. I spent a great deal of my time in correspondence or discussions to try to accommodate exiled scholars.

Parting from Göttingen, and from all I had built up there, was bound to weigh heavily upon me. But I found some compensation in my scientific life, which flourished under Rutherford's leadership at the Cavendish Laboratory. I was also granted the hospitality (dinner rights) of two colleges, Gonville and Caius (of which I had been a member years ago as an 'advanced student'), and St. Johns (where Dirac was one of the Fellows). My wife had none of these things. She had been torn away from everything she knew and loved – landscape, language, friends, and the hometown where her parents and grandparents had lived. Cambridge offered her nothing but heavy domestic drudgery, and well-meaning invitations to afternoon tea. There is no letter from her to Einstein during this period.

As regards my research, the investigations mentioned in the letter concern an attempt, begun in Selva, to modify Maxwell's electrodynamics so that the self energy of the point charge is finite. In Cambridge I was fortunate in getting the Polish physicist Leopold Infeld as my colleague. The theory is usually referred to as the 'Born-Infeld theory' now. We gave it a generally relativistic look without pursuing this aspect of it any further. Einstein rejected the idea right from the beginning. We tried very hard to reconcile it with the principles of the quantum theory. But we did not succeed, and today, possibly with good reason, the whole thing has been forgotten. I then warmly recommended Infeld to Einstein, and he became his collaborator and assistant. They published a popular book, *The Evolution of Physics*,[23] which is brilliantly written and has helped to bring Einstein's ideas to a much wider public. The pinnacle of their scientific collaboration was the reduction of the laws governing the movements of celestial bodies to Einstein's field equations. These will be mentioned again.

69

Princeton, N.J.
22 March, 1934

Dear Born

It gives me great pleasure to see your handwriting again, even if the main cause of your letter is so regrettable. Unfortunately I can see no possibility of being able to contribute directly to the health of the English Assistance Fund, as I was able to do last year. I regret that, for a variety of reasons, it is impossible for me to hold travelling lectures in America.

It is particularly unfortunate that the satiated Jews of the countries which have hitherto been spared cling to the foolish hope that they can safeguard themselves by keeping quiet and making patriotic gestures, just as the German Jews used to do. For the same reason they sabotaged the granting of asylum to German Jews, just as the latter did to Jews from the East. This applies just as much in America as in France and England.

I am greatly interested in your attempt to attack the quantum problem of the field from a new angle, but I am not exactly convinced. I still believe that the probability interpretation does not represent a practicable possibility for the relativistic generalisation, in spite of its great success. Nor has the reasoning for the choice of a Hamiltonian function for the electromagnetic field, by analogy with the special theory of relativity, convinced me. I am afraid that none of us will live to see the solution of these difficult problems.

If at all possible, I am going to fritter away the summer somewhere in America. Why should an old fellow like me not enjoy relative peace and quiet for once? I hope that your position in England is now ensured for some time to come. Conditions are very difficult here, as the universities, which in the main have to live from hand to mouth on a combination of private contribution and diminishing capital, have to struggle for their existence, and for this reason many capable young local people are unemployed.

Kind regards
Yours
A. Einstein

Margot's address: 5 rue du Docteur Blanche, Paris 16me.

Einstein's objections to my ideas were twofold. The first was based on his rejection of the probability of quantum mechanics. This concerns a matter of principle. It did not really apply to the theory devised by Infeld and myself, because we ourselves did not in fact manage to make it fit in with quantum mechanics; he judged our efforts in this direction to be wrong in principle. Einstein's second objection concerned our original classical field theory, which was complete in itself and free from inconsistencies. It was based on the following analogy: in the special theory of relativity the kinetic energy of a particle, which in classical mechanics is proportional to the square of its velocity, is represented by a rather complicated expression; for velocities which are small compared with that of light it tends to the classical expression, but deviates from it when the velocity approaches that of light. In Maxwell's electrodynamics the energy density is a quadratic expression containing the field intensity. I replaced this with a general expression which approximates to the classical expression whenever the strength of the field is small compared with a certain field intensity, but diverges from it when this is not the case. From this it followed automatically that the total energy of the field of a point charge is finite, while it becomes infinite in the Maxwellian field. The absolute field has to be regarded as a new natural constant. Einstein did not find this analogical construction convincing. Infeld and I found it attractive for a long time. We abandoned the theory for completely different reasons, namely, because we did not succeed in reconciling it with the principles of the quantum field theory. In any case this constituted the first attempt to overcome the difficulties of microphysics by means of a non-linear theory. Heisenberg's theory of elementary particles, which is much talked about today, is also non-linear. But I am guessing.

70

'*Haus Simon*', *Neue Wiese*
Karlsbad
24 August, 1936

Dear Einstein

Please let me know as soon as possible how one should evaluate the work of Prof. Y. He has approached me and seems to be in great distress. I understand nothing of his work, but he seems to have had closer contact with you (and indeed has even written a book about you). My personal impression is that he is a poor wretch who rather overrates himself. But I may be wrong, and in any case I would like to help him. Please write to me completely objectively.

I am here to take the cure; my gall-bladder pains have already disappeared. I will be back in Cambridge in a fortnight's time (address: 246 Hills Road); please write to me there.

We are moving to Edinburgh shortly, where I have been appointed Darwin's successor.

During my holidays I spoke to many Americans (Franck, Ladenburg, Courant), who all talked to me about you. I am extremely sorry to hear that your wife is ill. My family are all well.

With kind regards
Max Born

My chief memory of my stay at this spa is my meeting with Chaim Weizmann, the Zionist leader. He accompanied me almost daily on the early morning constitutionals which were part of my cure, and I learned a great deal about the Zionist movement. The beneficial effect of the cure, however, lasted only a short time. A few years later I had to undergo a gall-bladder operation in Edinburgh.

My appointment to the University of Edinburgh is mentioned here for the first time. To us it meant the end of uncertainty, and the beginning of a new life in Scotland.

71

[undated]

Dear Born

Y. is a somewhat pathological case. He has an independent but unfortunately not very clear mind. His papers about surfaces contain much that is useful, even if it has unfortunately never been put in order or given clear form. He is a little difficult as a person. For example, he made use of our very casual personal acquaintance over many years to make money by writing a biographical book about me, though I had expressly forbidden him to do so. But he was having a very difficult time, and was constantly in some kind of distress; always, or almost always, without employment. At the same time his exaggerated opinion of himself makes it hard to help him, particularly as I am not sure whether he would do well in a subordinate position. But it is quite possible that his hard experiences have made him more amenable. Therefore, help him if you can, but be cautious with your recommendations to save yourself from possible reproach. He is able to do experimental and technical work, and seems at times to have supported himself by it in the past. Some time ago I tried to put a word in on his behalf with J. Franck. But he refused quite brusquely, on the grounds that one should make efforts to help more valuable people. But I believe that this attitude towards an older man, who is in great distress and who, after all, has certain merits, is far too harsh.

I am quite *extraordinarily* pleased that you have found a

permanent and highly respected chair in Edinburgh, and that you and your family are well. My wife is unfortunately very seriously ill. I personally feel very happy here, and find it indescribably enjoyable really to be able to lead a quiet life. It is, after all, no more than one deserves in one's last terms, though it is granted to very few.

Next term we are going to have your temporary collaborator Infeld here in Princeton, and I am looking forward to discussions with him. Together with a young collaborator, I arrived at the interesting result that gravitational waves do not exist, though they had been assumed a certainty to the first approximation. This shows that the non-linear general relativistic field equations can tell us more or, rather, limit us more than we have believed up to now. If only it were not so damnably difficult to find rigorous solutions. I still do not believe that the statistical method of the quantum theory is the last word, but for the time being I am alone in my opinion.

> With best wishes
> Yours
> *A. Einstein*

At the end of the letter, Einstein again rejects the statistical quantum theory, with the admission that he is alone in this. At the time I was quite certain that I was in the right on this question. All theoretical physicists were in fact working with the statistical concept by then; this was particularly true of Niels Bohr and his school, who also made a vital contribution to the clarification of the concept. However, I consider it unjustified that this is usually cited as having originated in Copenhagen.

72

84 Grange Loan
Edinburgh
24 January, 1937

Dear Einstein

Today I have to ask for your help in two different matters:
1. Prof. R. Samuel, a pupil of Franck's and mine from Göttingen; we did not regard him as outstanding in those days

(more than ten years ago), but he has developed well. He went to India, to the Muslim University of Aligarh, and created an up-to-date institute there under extraordinary difficulties (such as one could not imagine here). A new vice-chancellor (my wife calls him the most amiable rogue she has ever met) is getting rid of all non-Mohammedans; as a result, Samuel has to leave on April 1st. The beautiful institute, which we inspected last winter, is going to sink back once more into the lap of Allah. Samuel has been a convinced Zionist from his youth; his dearest wish is to live in Palestine. His wife, also a Zionist of long standing, and his son, are already there. Samuel is applying for a position as experimental physicist in Jerusalem (or elsewhere in the country).

As regards his suitability, it is like this: he is no genius, but intelligent and extremely energetic. The establishment of the institute in Aligarh is a considerable achievement. His papers are based on ideas of Franck's (the linking together of chemistry and spectroscopy). During the last few years he has tried hard to demonstrate experimentally that the original valency interpretation by Heitler and London is better than the so-called 'improvements' by Hund, Herzberg and Millikan.

At first I was very sceptical, but have become more and more convinced that Samuel's empirical material proves him right. London, who is very sceptical, shares my opinion. Be that as it may, the experimental material is valuable in itself because of the systematic selection of the materials and clean workmanship.

My motive for interceding so energetically on Samuel's behalf is as follows: a convinced Zionist of long standing, provided he is otherwise suitable, should be given precedence over people who want to go to Palestine for purely personal reasons. Moreover: a most unpleasant clique seems to be in control at the university in Jerusalem; people who lead rather lazy lives, and do not want to be disturbed. They object to Samuel as not being sufficiently distinguished; I believe the opposite to be true – he is too energetic for them. I think your word will still have influence there. I hope you did not take it amiss that I did not go there myself. I am just not a Zionist. I do not belong there; but Samuel wants to go there, and is entirely suitable. He wrote to me that, if all else failed, he would even settle there as a bricklayer or shoecleaner. I had a very detailed discussion with Weizmann this summer. He also takes Samuel's part; but this does not seem to be enough.

Please do something in this matter, if you think it right to do so.

2. Dr Hans Schwerdtfeger: young mathematician from Göttingen. Lone wolf, earned his university education by doing factory and similar work. Pure 'Aryan'. Was not popular with Weyl and Courant, as he used to go his own way. I believe him to be talented, but lacking in self-criticism; his enthusiasm has up to now been greater than his achievement. Herglotz had a good opinion of him; but he does nothing for his people. Schwerdtfeger is married to a young chemist of whom my wife is very fond, and they have a baby. Schwerdtfeger was a violent opponent of the Nazis right from the beginning, and has therefore no chance of a position in Germany in spite of his 'spotless' ancestry. It is people such as this whom we should help.

A friend of his, Cohn-Vossen, went to Russia and obtained a good post in Moscow in 1933. He tried to get Schwerdtfeger to follow him. Negotiations got under way; to facilitate them, S. went to Prague (one risks one's life in Germany if one has any contact with Russia). Hardly had he arrived there when he received the news that Cohn-Vossen had died. Thereupon the negotiations gradually came to an end. Schwerdtfeger and his wife and child were in considerable trouble. We helped a little, as did the *Notgemeinschaft* in London. Eventually, after a year, I succeeded in establishing a direct link with the Russians through my former pupil Weisskopf, who is now with Bohr and who went on a trip to Russia. He wrote of the great fear of German 'spies' which prevails there. But, in spite of this, the employment of S. might possibly be considered if someone like you or Langevin put in a word for him. I have written to Langevin, but have not received a reply. Therefore I address myself to you: could you write to Molotov, to Prof. Schmidt or to Garbunov, to the effect that S. has been highly recommended to you (you can use my name) as an absolutely honest, decent person, who has a burning desire to work in Russia; he as a mathematician, his wife as a chemist. Both would be satisfied with nominal positions. But if you do not want to do this, please say so openly; I can well understand that no one gladly gets involved in Russian affairs. The new trial against Radek and associates seems to me extremely disgusting.

My wife, who is beginning to get on to her feet again, sends her warmest regards. She would very much like to hear from Margot.

    With kind regards
     Yours *Max Born*

This letter is an example of the voluminous correspondence I carried on not only with Einstein, but with many people all over the world, on the subject of help for exiled scientists.

Samuel, as far as I know, did go to Palestine. After many vain attempts I eventually managed to place Schwerdtfeger in Australia, with the help of the great physicist Sir William Bragg, who came from there.

Weisskopf was one of my best pupils and one of the last of those who were working for their doctor's degree in Göttingen. He subsequently had a distinguished career, and was for many years head of the European Institute for Nuclear Research, CERN, in Geneva.

73

                  [undated]

Dear Born

First of all, I am extremely delighted that you have found such an excellent sphere of activity, and what's more in the most civilised country of the day. And more than just a refuge. It seems to me that you, with your well-adjusted personality and good family background, will feel quite happy there. I have settled down splendidly here: I hibernate like a bear in its cave, and really feel more at home than ever before in all my varied existence. This bearishness has been accentuated still further by the death of my mate who was more attached to human beings than I.

The tasks you gave me are no simple matter.

1. Palestine is unquestionably the right place for Samuel. But from the university's point of view, the first priority is to obtain a proficient theoretician, preferably London. I cannot appear on the scene with Samuel until this has been accomplished, because it would only add to the confusion. There is as yet no proper theoretician there, and while this is so it is going to remain a desolate place. But when the time comes, I am quite prepared to put in a word for Samuel, particularly as his organising ability could prove to be of great importance there.

It is really rather a comforting thought that in India, too, the all-too-human trait of knavery predominates. After all, it would be just too bad if this were to be the privilege of the proud white race. I believe that all creatures who can have young ones together are very much the same.

2. Schwerdtfeger. Nothing can be done for him here. This is because Weyl and Courant are up in arms at the suggestion. Besides, I have had a closer look at one of his papers, and have the impression of a lack of really profound questioning. Because of the widespread unemployment amongst local people, it is, in any case, very difficult to place anyone here, and if one does succeed, it usually means a lowering of status. But in this case I cannot even *attempt* it with a clear conscience.

Now Russia. After a certain amount of to-ing and fro-ing I was able to place one of my former assistants there satisfactorily, and am going to try and get in another very able and original man there, whose position here is threatened by the very considerable antisemitism in academic circles. But should I ever recommend a mediocrity to them, even just once, my credit there would be at an end, and I would never again be able to help. It is sad that one is forced to treat human beings like horses where it matters only that they can run and pull, without regard to their qualities as *human beings*. But what can I do? In the last resort it is precisely *humane* considerations which compel me to adopt this kind of attitude.

This would, however, not prevent me from giving a friendly account of Schwerdtfeger to Russia, if they could be induced to *ask me*. This is how it should be done. This is frequently more effective than if one takes the initiative oneself.

By the way, there are increasing signs that the Russian trials are not faked, but that there is a plot among those who look upon Stalin as a stupid reactionary who has betrayed the ideas of the revolution. Though we find it difficult to imagine this kind of internal thing, those who know Russia best are all more or less of the same opinion. I was firmly convinced to begin with that it was a case of a dictator's despotic acts, based on lies and deception, but this was a delusion.

Margot is spending the week in New York, and is hewing stone with unrivalled enthusiasm. She has really been saved by art, she could hardly have born her grievous human losses as well as her divorce without it. She often speaks of you with affection.

Kind regards to you and your family
Yours
A. Einstein

P.S. Infeld is a splendid chap. We have done a very fine thing together. Problem of astronomical movement with treatment of celestial bodies as singularities of the field. The institute has treated him badly. But I will soon help him through it.

The incidental way in which Einstein announces his wife's death, in the course of a brief description of his bear-like existence, seems rather strange. For all his kindness, sociability and love of humanity, he was nevertheless totally detached from his environment and the human beings included in it.

For me the most remarkable passage in the letter is the one about the all-too-human trait of knavery which ends with the confession: I believe that all creatures who can have young ones together are very much the same; a typical formulation of Einstein's rejection of racial discrimination and national pride.

It is typical of his kindness that he apparently suffered because he could only advance exceptionally able people by his recommendation as if they were horses. For my wife and myself it was brief remarks such as these which were, time and again, a source of renewed affection for Einstein the man.

The Russian trials were Stalin's purges, with which he attempted to consolidate his power. Like most people in the West, I believed these show trials to be the arbitrary acts of a cruel dictator. Einstein was apparently of a different opinion: he believed that when threatened by

Hitler the Russians had no choice but to destroy as many of their enemies within their own camp as possible. I find it hard to reconcile this point of view with Einstein's gentle, humanitarian disposition.

The 'good thing' which he and Infeld had done has been mentioned before. It concerns a fundamental simplification of the foundations of the general theory of relativity. Infeld described in a short autobiographical sketch of his[24] how the idea seemed so daring to him at first that he did not want to believe in it. At that time, the theory had two pillars. Firstly, the movement of mass points is determined by the geodetic lines of the space-time world; secondly, the metrics of this world satisfy Einstein's field equations. Now Einstein asserted that the first of these assumptions is redundant, because it follows from the field equations by going to the limit of infinitely thin, mass-covered world lines, on which the field becomes singular. The calculations were at first so extensive that only excerpts could be published, and the massive manuscript was deposited in the Institute for Advanced Study in Princeton. Shortly afterwards, and quite independently, the Russian physicist W. Fock (who had collaborated with me on several papers in Göttingen) and his students tackled the same problem in a somewhat different manner. This work was later incorporated in his well-known book on relativity. Einstein's theory, as elaborated by Infeld and Hoffman, was presented in an improved form after Einstein's death by Infeld and Plebanski in their brilliant book *Motion and Relativity*.[25] In his short autobiography, Infeld tells how Einstein had said to him more than once: 'here in Princeton I am considered an old fool'. He was regarded as an historical relic, and this at a time when he was engaged upon this great work.

74

84 Grange Loan
Edinburgh
11 April, 1938

Dear Einstein

Your paper with Infeld and Hofmann has impressed me enormously. I will not say that I understand it – that would need long and intensive study, for which I have not got time at present. But I believe I have understood the concept, the manner of approximation and the method of development, which treats the time and space components in different ways. In any case, the result is beautiful; it is the first really satisfactory deduction of the equations of motion from field equations. You know I have never concerned myself particularly with the theory; just enough to be able to lecture to average students.

Except for your fundamental work, it all seemed excessively formalistic to me, and, apart from a few papers by Weyl, not very profound. But this new work is both profound and beautiful. I shall keep studying it until I understand the details better. Infeld wrote to me the other day and said you were interested in my reciprocity speculations, and he would like material for a lecture. But I did not have anything decent available, and did not want to part with what I did have. This may not have been terribly nice. But this work is still in the early stages, quite unfinished, and over there you have, after all, so many terribly clever people who can do everything so much more quickly than my frayed old brain. On the other hand, I would have no hesitation about writing something on it for you personally, which you may also show to Infeld. It is like this:

The cosmic rays demonstrate the existence of a physical world in which the energy of the particles is many times that of their mass when at rest. The velocities are therefore almost c because

$$p = \frac{mv}{\sqrt{(1 - v^2/c^2)}}, \quad E = \frac{mc^2}{\sqrt{(1 - v^2/c^2)}} \quad .$$

This means that the v are not suitable physical parameters; so much can happen in a minute range of v, which contains an enormous range of p and E values. I interpret this in the sense that p and E cannot be reduced to, or measured by, v, but have an independent significance. There are other indications in support of this, but we cannot go into this here. [Nuclei with v of the order $c/5$ to $c/10$ (for protons or neutrons) are an intermediate stage.] The problem is to extend classical mechanics so as to include this hypothesis. I use the fact that the canonical transformations are symmetrical in x and p; e.g. if they are defined through the Poisson brackets:

$$(u, v) = \sum_k \left(\frac{\partial u}{\partial x_k} \frac{\partial v}{\partial p_k} - \frac{\partial u}{\partial p_k} \frac{\partial v}{\partial x_k} \right)$$

then the transformation $(x, p) \rightarrow (X, P)$ is canonical when

$$(X_k, X_l) = 0, \quad (P_k, P_l) = 0, \quad (X_k, P_l) = \delta_{kl} \quad .$$

If one now takes a line element $ds^2 = \sum_{kl} g_{kl}\, dx_k\, dx_l$

in x-space and carries out a canonical transformation, it becomes the eight-dimensional

$$ds^2 = \sum_{kl} (E_{kl}\, dx_k\, dx_l + F_{kl}\, dx_k\, dp_l + G_{kl}\, dp_k\, dx_l + H_{kl}\, dp_k\, dp_l)$$

where E_{kl} and H_{kl} are symmetrical and $F_{kl} = G_{lk}$. But this is, of course, not the most general case! There are four identities between the matrices E, F, G, H. They are best found as follows: first establish that canonically the following invariant *equations* exist between E, F, G, H; I am using matrix notation (matrices of matrices):

$$\begin{pmatrix} E & F \\ G & H \end{pmatrix} \cdot \begin{pmatrix} H & -G \\ -F & E \end{pmatrix} = \begin{pmatrix} \lambda & o \\ o & \lambda \end{pmatrix}$$

where λ is a 4 by 4 diagonal matrix. It is now very easy, viz. by $\lambda = o$, to characterise the case where ds^2 is reducible to the four-dimensional x-space. But if $\lambda \neq o$ one has a general case! This is precisely what I want. For, if λ is small (in c.g.s. units) it becomes conceivable that $\lambda \neq o$ applies to the 'real' mechanics, but that for less precise observations the limiting case $\lambda = o$ applies.

Fuchs and I are busy developing this new hyper-dynamics. We hope it will work. The characteristic feature is the appearance of a new natural constant for, since x and p are always treated as equivalent, a constant (H) of the dimension $[P]$ arises. Planck's constant (h) has the dimension $[x\,p]$. If we now equate

$$H = \frac{X_0}{P_0}, \quad h = X_0\, P_0,$$

then $X_0 = \sqrt{(H\,h)}$ and $P_0 = \sqrt{(h/H)}$ define an absolute length and an absolute momentum. A pure 'momentum mechanics' would be valid wherever $p \sim P_0$, i.e. $ds^2 = \sum_{kl} \gamma_{kl}\, dp_k\, dp_l$ (to a good approximation).

I have discussed this case in my papers (manuscript accepted for *Proc. R. Soc.*) and in the letter to *Nature*,[26] where I singled out rather arbitrarily a closed spherical p-space and discussed some of the conclusions. These are so reasonable that they have encouraged me in my delusions. In any case, I think it good fun to pursue them further; so please do not pour too much cold water on my head. When one lives in Europe – even here in far Caledonia – one has to have something which diverts one from political anxieties. How disgusting it all is. You are lucky to be over there.

Hedi is very well, having got over her eye operation. She is attending a Quaker meeting on the west coast with our son Gustav, and I am going to meet her there tomorrow for a few days' rest by the sea. Our elder daughter is happily married and living in the south of England; the second one is still studying in Vienna, and hopes to be able to hold out until her final exams in June. My brother was fortunately able to obtain a small post in St. Louis as Professor of Fine Arts. How is Margot? Kind regards to her, and to the Infelds, as well as to all our friends at the Institute, the Weyls, v. Neumanns, Veblens, Ladenburgs. Also please tell Robertson that I liked his papers very much. I wish he did not still bear me a grudge. I suppose he has reason, as I treated him badly when he was in Göttingen.

In old friendship
Yours
Max Born

My speculations about reciprocity, which I explain in this letter, have occupied me and a variety of collaborators for many years. The one mentioned here is the same Klaus Fuchs who later became notorious as an 'atom spy'. He spent many years at my Institute in Edinburgh, did excellent work and, if I remember rightly, obtained two doctorates, a Ph.D. and a D.Sc. (doctorate of philosophy and of science, of which the latter was more difficult to get and rated more highly). He was a quiet, friendly, likeable man. My wife and I are convinced that he acted from purely idealistic motives in the spy affair. He was a convinced Communist, and believed it to be his duty to prevent capitalist America from being able to dominate the whole world as the sole possessor of the atom bomb.

As regards my reciprocity theory, this is based on a demand for symmetry, requiring the fundamental laws of nature to remain unaltered when the four quantities – space coordinates and time – are interchanged with the four quantities – momentum components and energy.

All the efforts I made in Edinburgh at that time to deduce from this postulate concrete conclusions which could be proved experimentally were in vain. Later it was shown that this was due to the lack of suitable experimental material. Meanwhile great progress has been made in experimental research into elementary particles, and to my surprise and joy my old reciprocity principle now plays an important part in the interpretation of phenomena. Relations of that kind have been discovered quite independently in three different places, in the United States, Japan and Australia. Among the scientists involved is Yukawa, the great Japanese physicist and Nobel prizewinner, who predicted the existence of mesons. My former collaborator H. S. Green, Professor at the University of Adelaide, is working successfully in this direction and keeps me up to date. But I am unfortunately too old to be able to follow this line of research.

84 Grange Loan
Edinburgh
2 September, 1938

75

Dear Einstein

I would very much like to send you another peaceful letter about my physical and geometrical phantasies, but things political occupy my mind to such an extent that I feel compelled to write about them first of all. We hear such horrible things from Germany, and particularly from Vienna, where people are literally starving. Until recently I still had property and income in Germany, and we were able to use this to help not only a few of our relatives but others as well. Hedi, who has become a Quaker, has achieved a lot with the help of these good people. A short time ago, however, I learnt that my property in Germany had been confiscated by the secret police. Thus, even this chance of helping people has come to an end. This depresses me more than the general political situation and the threat of war. For you are probably right in your confidence in the deep-rooted stupidity of our one-time fellow-countrymen: they will once again succeed in having the whole world against them, and then attack – if not this year against the Czechs, then next year against the Poles or whoever it may be. And that will be the end of them. But what a horrible thought: all those hundreds of thousands of young men, who will perish as a result. I have two English sons-in-law, fine, peace-loving people (you know one of them, Maurice Pryce, who has become engaged to our Gritli). But one is unable to change the course of these events. They run their course like a thunderstorm.

I have in mind, however, another matter, where one might

perhaps be able to do something. Mussolini has passed a 'law', according to which all Jews who have settled in Italy since 1919 are required to leave the country within six months. It is not clear whether he did this in order to grovel before Hitler, or to do a favour to the Arabs in Palestine. I think this offers America a chance to take reciprocal action. Surely a certain amount of Italian emigration to America is still going on. Could one not get the American government to use this in order to apply some pressure on the Italians? And could you not address President Roosevelt? Simply to send back the same number of Italians as there are Jews forced to leave Italy would, I fear, hardly be possible. But it should be possible to construct some means of applying pressure. Of course, innocent people are bound to suffer again as a result, and I feel inwardly ashamed even to think of such a thing. But in the present situation there is really no other method but force against force. If the Western powers would only show by example that the methods of the dictators can also be used against them, they would probably have second thoughts.

Forgive me for disturbing the peace of your holiday by writing to you about these things. We are so close to these matters and events here that one cannot find peace. Hedi and I are alone at home at present, as the children are staying in different parts of Scotland. But we intend to go away for a short time in about a week to the west coast.

My idea of reciprocity pursues me constantly, although no-one else is taking it seriously. However, we did not succeed in giving it a useful form. One of Heisenberg's more recent papers in the *Zeitschrift für Physik* shows that he, too, has now realized that it is essential to limit the 'moment' p by an absolute constant. I was in Cambridge the other day at the meeting of the British Association, where I had a thorough discussion with Niels Bohr amongst others. The nuclear theory, which can be formulated in so beautifully unrealistic a way, gives him so much satisfaction that for the moment he is putting aside the question of the nature of the elementary particle, which I find so fascinating. Let us hear from you some time.

With kind regards, also to Margot, from Hedi and myself.

Yours

Max Born

A political letter. The prediction that the folly of the Germans would drive them into wild adventures and eventually to their ruin was confirmed by events.

My proposal to use the Italian immigrants to America as a means of applying pressure on Mussolini to mitigate the persecution of the Jews was somewhat naive. What I find of interest in this paragraph today is the shame I felt because it was not the real culprits who would be likely to be hit by such measures, but innocent people. It is precisely this which is so horrible about foreign politics, and what makes it so repulsive to any decent person.

The subject of the principle of reciprocity comes up again at the end, and in this connection a new paper of Heisenberg's is considered. Since those days he has switched from 'purely critical' observations to constructive ones. His non-linear spin theory of matter is a great gamble which has led to a number of successes. But time alone will show whether it is the real thing.

Department of Natural Philosophy
The University
Drummond Street
Edinburgh
31 May, 1939

76

Dear Einstein

I saw a report in the paper yesterday about a speech of yours on Palestine, and seize this opportunity to write to you once again. I quite agree with what you are supposed to have said, according to this report. Without wishing to defend the wavering and unreliable British policy, I am of the opinion that the Jews could do nothing more stupid than to assume an antagonistic attitude towards the English. The British Empire is still a place of refuge and protection for the persecuted, and particularly for Jews. I also completely subscribe to what you are reported to have said concerning the need for and the possibility of coming to an understanding with the Arabs. I am glad that you said what you did; your voice will be heard. I can only think my own thoughts in silence.

Hedi, at least, is doing something for the refugees. Her domestic servant office flourishes; she has already succeeded in saving many people from the Nazis, unfortunately virtually only women. My sister and other relatives have also escaped – except for a few unfortunate cousins. What can one do with a 55-year-old dentist? Unless he emigrates soon, the Gestapo will put him in a concentration camp. But his American registration number is 60,000!

My children are well provided for. I had an operation for removal of my gall bladder last April. The operation was a success, I have no more pain and am feeling fine, and I am able to work again. My Department is growing, I have a capable staff; next term there will be nine of them. We are working on a variety of things, nuclear structure, crystals, etc. I have written a paper about melting, which I have sent to Bridgman in America for publication, as I considered his high pressures in it. This is a new way of treating the thermodynamics of crystals (statistical mechanics), which is applicable up to very high temperatures and pressures. This work is being continued by some of my pupils. I hope also to be able to work on a new treatment of the solidity problem. I have not heard from Infeld for a long time; I do not even know his address. Franck wrote to me the other day quite contentedly from Chicago.

With kind regards, also from Hedi,
Yours
Max Born

There is little to say about this. P. W. Bridgman was Professor of Physics at Harvard University, the leading expert in the generation and handling of extremely high pressures, for which he received the Nobel Prize.

77

Department of Natural Philosophy
The University
Drummond Street
Edinburgh
10 April 1940

Dear Einstein

At the beginning of the war I wrote a letter to Niels Bohr in order to get news from Heisenberg. Today I have to write to you for news, if possible, about Niels himself. I am terribly worried. A year ago Niels was here – he received the Copley Medal of the Royal Society, our highest honour, and came to Edinburgh, where he stayed with us and gave us a lecture. He was quite excited and shocked by the indifference of most of the British people to the imminent danger of war, and he tried to convince all people he met (he met important people, of course) about the danger. He said to me confidentially that he believed his own little country to be in much greater danger than Great Britain, since it is so small and helpless, but that nobody would be spared to fight for its existence – though at that time many people here denied this and still believed in 'appeasement'. Well, he was right. You might be able to get news from him and his family. Let me know if you hear anything.

We are well so far. Hedi works very hard, as maternity nurse in a slum quarter in the morning, and in refugee and Quaker committees in the afternoon. At present she is in the country for a short holiday. We had both our daughters here for longer visits, one with her husband (M. Pryce, whom you know), the other with her fat and merry baby. My son is studying medicine here. I continue my work undisturbed; soon my department will be the only spot in Great Britain where theoretical work is still done.

My chief interest is concentrated on my 'reciprocity' idea; Fuchs and I have made nice progress, and Pauli, the super-critical man, wrote to me the other day: 'I think you are on the right track'. A series of papers will appear in June or July; but we have refrained from publishing short notes, as Landé does. He is working along the same lines (though with very primitive methods and rather unclear ideas). I am sure you will be interested in the thing because it is the proper way of unifying wave mechanics and relativity. There are many interesting mathematical features, but one of the main points is the discovery of representations of the Lorentz group by infinite (not finite) matrices which belong nevertheless to the Hilbert space (square integrable). I think that Wigner has some similar results in a very abstract way; but what we are trying to do is to show that these representations are connected with the 'structure' of the elementary particles. A letter is much too restricted a space for indicating these things even superficially.

In the summer term (starting next week) I am going to

lecture to my advanced students on general relativity, concentrating my attention on Fock's (the Russian) most interesting paper on the derivation of the equations of motion for finite bodies from the field equations. We have further quite interesting results on the thermodynamics of crystals, melting, etc. Fürth, from Prague, who is here as my guest, has found a most surprising connection between the tensile strength (breaking) of a solid and the heat of melting. The agreement of his formula with the empirical facts is perfect; the theoretical derivation is amusing, but will be criticised.

It is sometimes not easy to work under the strained conditions of war. But it is the best way to avoid worrying. We hear very little from American friends. Sometimes I think they consider us as lost outposts of civilisation. But I think that is quite wrong. This nation and France as well are tremendously strong and internally sound. But most of what we hear about American opinion seems to us strange. I am convinced that you look at the present struggle with the same attitude as I do.

Remember me to all friends in Princeton, Weyls, Veblens. Ladenburg, v. Neumann and the others.

Yours ever
Max Born

Pauli writes: 'I just got a letter from Guido Beck. He is in a camp (Camp de Chamberau, 27e Compagnie, Isère, France). He lost his post in Lyon (with Thiband) and needs money very urgently. Perhaps one could make a collection for him; it would facilitate his position very much. I shall try this here in Zürich.' I cannot do anything (export of money is not permitted, and we have innumerable liabilities).

Can you do it?
M. B.

This is the first letter in English. I was not more fluent in it than in German in those days, but after the outbreak of war it was more in accordance with my frame of mind.

My anxiety about Niels Bohr was well founded. After Hitler's army marched into Denmark, he was left in peace at first (as I found out later). When measures were taken in Denmark, as elsewhere, to exterminate the

Jews, he was warned in time (he was half Jewish) and escaped to Sweden. From there he went to America and, under a pseudonym, took part in the 'Manhattan Project', which led to the production of the first atomic bomb.

The work of the Quakers in saving Jews and other victims of persecution, in which my wife had a great interest, deserves the greatest praise.

The progress Fuchs and I made in the reciprocity investigations was probably, in spite of Pauli's approval, merely formal; as mentioned above, it has only quite recently (1965) really become physics.

Fock's paper on the deduction of the equations of motion in the general theory of relativity from the field equation was mentioned in connection with the paper by Einstein, Infeld and Hoffmann dealing with the same problem (commentary to letter No. 73).

Reinhold Fürth, Professor of Theoretical Physics in Prague, escaped to Great Britain with his wife after Hitler's invasion of Czechoslovakia, and was taken on by my institute, where he worked successfully and helped me with the teaching.

In my assessment of the strength of France and Great Britain, I was very much mistaken about France (which is understandable, as I did not know it well); but I was right where Great Britain was concerned.

Guido Beck was a gifted theoretical physicist. As far as I know, he was rescued when France was threatened, and found asylum in South America.

78

Department of Natural Philosophy
The University
Drummond Street
Edinburgh
10 May, 1943

Dear Einstein

A geographical colleague of mine, Dr Arthur Geddes, has asked me to write to you about the following matter: he has found a short essay of yours on the 'Meanders of Rivers in Alluvium, and the Earth's Rotation' (*Life as I see it*, Library Ed.). He is deeply interested in this problem and wishes to know whether you have published a full account of your considerations, or whether other people have followed your ideas. He could find no reference in the (rather scarce) literature in French, English, German which is available here. You would oblige me very much by letting me know what you are able to tell me. I take this opportunity to tell you about ourselves. Hedi had a serious operation last October and has recovered extremely slowly. But now she is almost well. Our son is now a doctor in a hospital and will join the forces in August. Our daughters both have two children each, and their husbands are in the Air Force and in the Admiralty. So we are four-fold grandparents. My department consists now only of Fürth and two half-time research students. But I have quite a lot of elementary teaching.

I have not done much research, but I watch what Schroedinger is doing with great interest. He writes to me regularly and I hope to visit him in Dublin during the summer. He has taken up an old paper of yours, from 1923, and filled it with new life, developing a unified field theory for gravitation, electrodynamics and mesons, which seems to me promising. But I suppose he has written to you about it.

I have just been informed that Joh. v. Neumann is in this country and will visit me next week, accompanying a man from the Admiralty for whom he will do some war research.

How is Margot? Give her our love.

Kind regards from both of us.

The war looks much better now, and I hope it will be over before Europe is completely destroyed. I had just a letter from Brillouin (Providence USA).

> Yours
>
> *Max Born*

I myself had once observed the meanderings of the great rivers, which is the subject I wrote to Einstein about at Dr Geddes' suggestion. It was during the Russian congress when we travelled down the length of the Volga.

I can no longer remember the towns, which now lie a few kilometres from the river, while it is quite obvious that they were originally built on its banks. The explanation of the phenomenon by means of the so-called 'Coriolis forces', which the rotation of the earth exerts upon bodies which have a component of motion in a south-north or north-south direction, is trivial and universally known. I cannot quite understand what induced Einstein to write anything on this subject, or why Dr Geddes should have been interested in it.

I can no longer remember anything about the contents of Schroedinger's unified field theory. My correspondence with him was sporadic and explosive. It would languish for a while; then there would be an out-break of letters from him, often one every day, so that I found it difficult to keep in step with my replies. I have a clear recollection of the series of letters about the general theory of relativity and its generalisation, but I cannot remember their contents. In the end, when I left Edinburgh (1954), I had a mountain of Schroedinger's letters and have destroyed most of them – because of lack of space in my tiny study in Bad Pyrmont. Today I realise how silly this was; for even if there was much chaff amongst the corn, there were also some precious grains, turns of phrase which were truly characteristic of Schroedinger.

John von Neumann was a Hungarian mathematician who spent some time in Göttingen soon after the discovery of quantum mechanics. He then published a book which today is regarded as a standard work on the sub-ject. It contains the rigorous proof of the mathematical concepts and methods used by Heisenberg, Jordan and myself. He represents the matrices I introduced as operators in an infinite dimensional space, the so-called 'Hilbert-space'. For this I used results of Hilbert's, although I was aware that the basic premises made in physics were less than those cus-tomary in the mathematics of this space up to that time. Von Neumann succeeded in the anything but easy task of finding rigorous proof amongst the further suppositions. His book contains other results of importance and useful creative concepts. During the Nazi period he emigrated to America, became professor at the Institute for Advanced Study at Princeton and worked there with Einstein and Weyl. He was considered to be the greatest mathematician in America, and possibly in the whole world. Unfortunately he contracted an incurable disease while still comparatively young, and died an agonising death.

79

2 June, 1943

Dear Born

My remark about the influence of the curvature of rivers and of the Coriolis force on the erosion of waterways was only a casual one. I have not published anything further on the subject, as I am convinced that the idea must have been known for a long time. I have, however, never searched the literature.

I was very interested in your news about yourself and your family. The multifariousness of our destinies is really remarkable.

Schroedinger was kind enough to write to me himself and tell me about his work. At one time I was rather enthusiastic about this trend of thought. Its weakness lies in its rather artificial and weak construction from the point of view of affinitive space. Moreover, the connection between the antisymmetrical curve and the electrical properties of space results in a linear relation between electric fields and charge densities. I have of course written to Schroedinger about it in detail.

I myself am engaged in a rather daring attempt to get to a unified physics, after trying vainly so many times before. Certainly, to make real progress will require a mighty leap forward in our thinking.

Kind regards to you and yours
Yours
A. Einstein

80

84 Grange Loan
Edinburgh
15 July, 1944

Dear Einstein

Our newspaper, *The Scotsman*, had a note about you: that you have called upon intellectual workers to unite and organise some protection against new wars of aggression and to secure their influence in the political field. I was very glad when I read that, for I feel that you are the only man who could do anything in this direction, as your name is known to everybody in the world. Of course, we are all getting old and have the desire to rest and to be left alone, and there are not many younger fellows.

Concerning myself, I had a kind of breakdown last winter from which I have not quite recovered. It was the result of many causes: a little overwork, the stress of the war in general and the extinction of the European Jews, the transfer of my son to the Far East (he is after many adventures quite safe on a pathological course in Poona, India), etc. But the most depressing idea was always the feeling that our science, which is such a beautiful thing in itself and could be such a benefactor for human society, has been degraded to nothing but a means of destruction and death. Most of the German scientists have collaborated with the Nazis, even Heisenberg has (I learned from reliable sources) worked full blast for these scoundrels – there are a few exceptions, e.g. v. Laue and Hahn. The British, American, Russian scientists are fully mobilised and rightly so. I do not blame anybody. For under the given circumstances nothing else can be done to save the rest of our civilisation. Yet I think that we must have an international organisation and, even more important, an international code of behaviour or ethics (like the very strict rules which the British physicians have inside their profession), by which our scientific community could act as a regulating and stabilising power in the world, not, as at present, being no more than tools of industries and governments. There is a definite ethical standard upon which all religions agree, Christian, Jewish, Moslem and Hindu. But some branches of biological science, logically backward and based on poor evidence, have been tools in the hand of criminal politicians for throwing us back in the state of the jungle. There must be a way of prohibiting a repetition of such things. We scientists should unite to assist the formation of a reasonable world order. If you have any definite plans please let me know. I am rather powerless, sitting at this pleasant but backward place. But I should try my best. Fowler, who would be the proper man to take the initiative in this country, is unfortunately very ill; he had a breakdown much worse than mine. I do not know where Niels Bohr is at present. I should like to get in touch with him. Here in Britain it is very difficult to keep up connections with people. Travelling is possible only in the most urgent cases, and meetings in the South are restricted by the flying bombs.

But the military situation is excellent and we hope the European part of the war will be over soon.

Hedi is quite well and sends her best wishes to you and Margot. My son is a medical officer in the army and has seen a lot of India. My daughters and their families are all right, though one of them is living in an area over which the flying bombs are passing and occasionally dropping.

I have tried, together with my Chinese pupil Peng, an excellent man, to improve the quantum theory of fields, and I think we are on the right track. Schroedinger on the other hand has improved your and other people's attempts to unite the different fields in a classical way. I think the next step should be a combination and merging of these two approaches. But I am too old and worn out to try it.

With kind regards and best wishes

Yours ever

Max Born

In writing about the responsibility of the scientist I have said more than once that the news of Hiroshima affected the issue decisively. This is true in so far as a new situation existed from that day on. It was no longer merely a question of ethics, whether political differences can ever justify technical mass murder, but of the continued existence of civilization itself, perhaps even of life on the earth. This letter shows that the ethical question, and the abhorrence of war waged with technical means, had been occupying me for a long time.

I would like to add a few more words on this subject here. It was during a meeting of the British Association that I first learnt of the possibility of developing a weapon of enormous effectiveness by splitting uranium nuclei with the help of a chain reaction, a technique which had just been discovered by Hahn and Strassmann. Before that, Leo Szilard, a Hungarian physicist who had worked with Einstein for some time, had appeared on the scene. He was completely obsessed with the idea of a nuclear explosion. As the discovery of the splitting of the atom had taken place in Germany, he was haunted by the fear that Hitler might be able to develop this horrible weapon, and he talked of nothing else. This was the first occasion I heard of fission, chain reactions, neutron exploitation, and so on. It alarmed me but, for all that, seemed a long way off.

Then the war really started. After Dunkirk, all Germans in Great Britain were interned, irrespective of whether they were Nazis or victims of Nazi persecution. I escaped this fate, as I had become a British subject a few weeks before the outbreak of the war. But my German collaborators, Klaus Fuchs among them, were interned, and had to spend the next few months in camps, first on the Isle of Man and later in Canada. There their political reliability was investigated, and those who passed the test were sent back to England.

Thus, Fuchs returned to my Institute after a few months and took up his work again. But a little later he received a letter from Peierls, a German physicist who had emigrated and had become a professor in Birmingham. He asked Fuchs whether he would like to collaborate on an important, top-secret war project. I knew at once that this could only mean one thing; nuclear fission. As the possible consequences of the development of such a means of destruction filled me with horror, I tried as hard as I could to dissuade Fuchs, but in vain. His hatred of the Nazis was boundless, and he was glad to be able to do something against them. So he went to Peierls in Birmingham, and later accompanied him to the United States; what followed is common knowledge.

I myself was never directly invited to take part in the fission project. I had never done any work in nuclear physics; but so many other branches of physics were tied up with it that I could certainly have collaborated if I had offered my services.

Thus I was spared any real temptation to participate; this is where my fate was different from Einstein's. At the time I wrote this letter to Einstein, about a year before Hiroshima, we still knew next to nothing about the Manhattan Project. It was not until much later that I found out that it was Einstein who, under pressure from Szilard and a number of other physicists, had written a letter to President Roosevelt which had set the whole thing in motion. I assume that Einstein, too, did not subsequently receive much further information about the progress of the project. Einstein, like Szilard, was motivated by the idea that Hitler must be prevented from being the first to use this weapon. That it should then be used against defenceless people was a horrible thought for him and one which cast a shadow over the evening of his life. Einstein's fate shows more clearly than almost any other in history that even the greatest intellectual powers and the purest of intentions are no protection against having to make a decision between two possible courses of action, both equally detestable.

Had all this been known to me, I would hardly have written the preceding letter. I had been under the impression that Einstein was an absolute pacifist, like the Quakers, with whom I came into frequent contact through my wife, who had become a member of the Society of Friends. But this he was not. He hated the use of force, particularly when it was directed against non-combatant, defenceless people. He considered no political or economic ideology, no state, no constitution to be worth the sacrifice of masses of human lives. But the events of our lifetime had taught him, and me, that the ultimate ethical values, on which all human existence is based, must, as a last resort, be defended even by force and with the sacrifice of human lives. We never again had an opportunity of exchanging our ideas on the subject. But I am convinced that we would have understood one another. The following letter, his answer to my suggestion, confirms this.

81

Dear Born

I was so pleased about your letter that to my surprise I feel compelled to write to you, although no one is wagging a finger at me to do so. But I cannot write in English, because of the treacherous spelling. When I am reading, I only hear it and am unable to remember what the written word looks like.

Do you still remember the occasion some twenty-five years ago when we went together by tram to the Reichstag building, convinced that we could effectively help to turn the people there into honest democrats? How naive we were, for all our forty years. I have to laugh when I think of it. We neither of us realised that the spinal cord plays a far more important role than the brain itself, and how much stronger its hold is.

I have to recall this now, to prevent me from repeating the tragic mistakes of those days. We really should not be surprised that scientists (the vast majority of them) are no exception to this rule, and *if* they are different it is not due to their reasoning powers but to their personal stature, as in the case of Laue. It was interesting to see the way in which he cut himself off, step by step, from the traditions of the herd, under the influence of a strong sense of justice. The medical men have achieved amazingly little with a code of ethics, and even less of an ethical influence is to be expected from pure scientists with their mechanised and specialised way of thinking. It is, of course, quite correct for you to allot the relevant priesthood to Niels Bohr. For there is some hope that he would dissociate his priestly side from physics, and use it in some other way. Apart from this, I do not, however, expect much from such an undertaking. The feeling for what ought and ought not to be grows and dies like a tree, and no fertilizer of any kind will do very much good. What the individual can do is to give a fine example, and to have the courage to uphold ethical convictions sternly in a society of cynics. I have for a long time tried to conduct myself in this way, with a varying degree of success.

Your 'I feel too old. . . .' I am not taking too seriously,

because I know this feeling myself. Sometimes (with increasing frequency) it surges upwards and then subsides again. We can after all quietly leave it to nature gradually to reduce us to dust if she does not prefer a more rapid method.

I have read your lecture against Hegelianism with great interest. It represents to us theoreticians the quixotic element, or should I say the seducer? Where this evil or, rather, vice is altogether missing, the inveterate philistine rules. I am therefore confident that 'Jewish Physics' is not to be killed. Moreover I have to confess that your deliberations remind me of the beautiful proverb: 'Junge Huren – alte Betschwestern' [Young whores – old bigots] particularly when I think of Max Born. But I cannot really believe that you have completely and honestly struggled your way through to the latter category.

We have become Antipodean in our scientific expectations. You believe in the God who plays dice, and I in complete law and order in a world which objectively exists, and which I, in a wildly speculative way, am trying to capture. I firmly *believe*, but I hope that someone will discover a more realistic way, or rather a more tangible basis than it has been my lot to find. Even the great initial success of the quantum theory does not make me believe in the fundamental dice-game, although I am well aware that our younger colleagues interpret this as a consequence of senility. No doubt the day will come when we will see whose instinctive attitude was the correct one.

With kind regards to you and your family (now freed from flying bombs)

Yours

A. Einstein

The incident of twenty-five years ago, which Einstein remembers here, was as follows: when the German Supreme Command suddenly capitulated towards the end of 1918 and the revolution broke out all over Germany, I was in bed with influenza and thus only witnessed the events in Berlin from a distance. Just after I had recovered, Einstein rang me up (the telephone functioned even during the wildest days) and reported that a student council had been formed at the university, modelled on the workers' and soldiers' councils (German soviets). One of its first actions had been to depose and lock up the Rector and some of the other dignitaries. Einstein, because of his left-wing political views, was believed to have some influence with the more radical of the students, and he was asked to negotiate with the 'council' in order to bring about the release of the prisoners and the restoration of reasonable order. Einstein had discovered that the student council met in the Reichstag building, and asked me whether I would accompany him. I accepted despite the weak state I was in after my bout of influenza.

First there was the long march from my house in the Grunewald to Einstein's in the Bavarian quarter, for there were no trams or buses running in our district; then three of us – Einstein had asked the psychologist Max Wertheimer to come too – went by tram to the Reichstag. I will not go into the difficulties we had in penetrating the dense crowds which surrounded the Reichstag building and the cordon of revolutionary soldiers, heavily armed and red-beribboned. Eventually someone recognised Einstein, and all doors were opened.

Once in the Reichstag building, we were escorted to a conference room where the student council was in session. The Chairman greeted us politely, and asked us to sit down and wait until an important point in the new statutes for the university had been dealt with. So we patiently waited and listened. Eventually the point at issue was settled and the Chairman said: 'Before we come to your request, Professor Einstein, may I be permitted to ask what you think of the new regulations for the students?' Einstein thought for several minutes, and then said something like this: 'I have always thought that the German universities' most valuable institution is academic freedom, whereby the lecturers are in no way told what to teach, and the students are able to choose which lectures to attend, without much supervision and control. Your new statutes seem to abolish all this and to replace it by precise regulations. I would be very sorry if the old freedom were to come to an end.' Whereupon the high-and-mighty young gentleman sat in perplexed silence. Then our business was discussed; but the student council decided that it had no authority in the matter, and referred us to the new Government in the Wilhelmstrasse, issuing us with a pass for this purpose.

Accordingly we walked on to the Reich Chancellor's palace. This was a hive of activity. The footmen of the Emperor's time still stood in corners of the passageways and stairs but, apart from them, the people running about the corridors were more or less shabbily dressed and carrying briefcases – socialist delegates and delegations from the workers' and soldiers' councils. The main hall was full of excited people talking in loud voices. But Einstein was recognised at once, and we had no difficulty in getting through to the newly appointed President Ebert, who received us in a small room and said that he would appreciate that he was unable to pay attention to minor matters that day, when the very existence of the Reich itself was in the balance. He wrote a few words on our behalf to the appropriate new minister, and in no time at all our business had been concluded.

We left the Chancellor's palace in high spirits, feeling that we had taken part in a historical event and hoping to have seen the last of Prussian arrogance, the Junkers, and the reign of the aristocracy, of cliques of civil servants and of the military, now that German democracy had won. Even the long journey back to the Grunewald, mostly on foot, could not dampen my elated mood.

In those days we believed in the triumph of reason, of the 'brain'. We had yet to learn that it is not the brain which controls human beings but the spinal cord – seat of the instincts and of blind passions. Even scientists are no exception to this.

Einstein had criticised Max Laue earlier on (Letter No. 3) but in this letter he gladly acknowledges his bravery towards the Nazis.

Einstein did not think much of an 'ethical code'. The words contained in this letter about Bohr, about 'the feeling for what ought to be, and what ought not to', and about the role of the individual in the society of cynics, are of profound wisdom.

Finally, Einstein concerns himself with my lecture 'Experiment and Theory in Physics'.[30,31] Scientifically, we had indeed drifted far apart. He concentrated on speculations about his unified field theory, while I tried to keep a tight reign on my inclination to speculate. My little book is a sharp attack against certain papers by the astronomers Eddington and Milne, who both, though in completely different ways, tried to solve the enigma of the world of atoms and of the cosmos by means of pure thought alone. I still, to this day, believe my arguments to be reasonable but, on the other hand, Einstein is quite right in that empiricism alone, without bold ideas, does not get one anywhere. He is a master who finds the right proportions.

The last paragraph deals again with the fundamental dice-game in quantum mechanics, and is probably the best and most lucid formulation of Einstein's point of view. I have discussed it thoroughly in my book *Natural Philosophy of Cause and Chance*[32] and there is no need to go into it again.

82

84 *Grange Loan*
Edinburgh
9 October, 1944

Dear friend Albert Einstein

It was wonderful to get a letter from you; that is, it was Max who got it. I have read it several times, and once again had that feeling of liberation which I used to get from our talks during the war. Somehow all the essentials are said in it, and I feel as if I were standing in crystal clear air on the top of Mount Everest. In the last few years, I have thought again and again about two things you once said to me. When I asked you whether you were at all afraid of death (when you were so serene during your serious illness), you said: 'I feel such a sense of solidarity with all living things that it does not matter to me where the individual begins and ends'. You also said: 'There is nothing in the world which I could not dispense with at a moment's notice'. For me these are very 'religious' remarks in the idiom of the twentieth century. I hope you do not mind my calling them that. It is a joyous consciouness of submission to a law allied with a stern sense of responsibility for ethical convictions. As to the latter: to *live* one's ethical convictions before one is reduced to dust again is something which you simply cannot renounce. I hope you will not regard this as a sermon – the Quakers (I've been one for the last six years) have no sermons. Nor have I become a *Betschwester* [bigot]. I am very bad at praying, as I think that we have no right to it. Once we have recognised how we *should* live, we can pray through the very quality of our life; and if the quality of our lives is not up to that level, in spite of our awareness, then we are even less entitled to pray with words. But usually there is this awareness of unity with God and with all living things. I, too, am unable to believe in a 'dice-playing' God, nor am I able to imagine that you believe – as Max has just told me when we were discussing it – that your 'complete rule of law' means that everything is predetermined, for example, whether I am going to have my child inoculated against diphtheria or not, etc. . . .

Things would then be as in Omar the tentmaker:

> 'That I would drink during my lifetime
> God has known for all eternity. . . .'

I have forgotten what follows, but it must have been: where then is ethics, the consciousness of striving?

You could probably explain this to me with just a few of those vigorous words of yours.

Just a fortnight ago I wrote two remaining sonnets to add to the three I wrote in India in 1935, where I try to express the thought that love alone binds and liberates one (from the ego) at one and the same time. They came into being from Indian 'non-attachment'. It seems to me that you have achieved such non-attachment – but how? You have landed yourself in a fine pickle with that letter of yours! I hope it has been pre-determined that you are going to answer me on this!

You are quite right in your attitude towards ageing – that we can simply leave it to nature to reduce us to dust again. What Max was trying to express must have been that feeling of being 'used up' which we are both constantly aware of now, and which is constantly being confirmed by certain facts: for example, by the fact that neither of us is any longer physically capable of coping with the constant calls for help from our daughters, who want us to put them up with their babies for weeks on end. I have just had one such visit, lasting four weeks, from Gritli and Sylvia (eighteen months old) which led to a mighty breakdown on my part. Gritli wanted to have a rest, just when I was entirely without help in the house; then too, Maurice came home on leave, and I had to do absolutely everything (and wanted to do it) – cooking, washing-up, shopping and queuing, looking after the baby, etc. etc. . . . Also, I can draw up quite a list of illnesses and operations since we came to Edinburgh – six months of pleurisy, an operation for detachment of the retina, and finally, less than two years ago, a major gynaecological operation for the removal of (your expression) my complete production centre with all accessories. You once said: 'where you females are concerned, your pro-duction centre is not situated in the brain' – you see how well all your shameful sayings are fixed in my memory! Yes, all these illnesses, together with the constant wear and tear caused by the vastly increased difficulties of everyday life, as well as three years of voluntary nursing service, have all contributed to the feeling of 'being used up'. This feeling of being old and tired is different from the 'normal' ageing process, which still seems to exist in America, far removed from the war. To recover from our kind of 'ageing', it would have to be *peace-time* again, with one's children and friends once more in peace-time occupations, when one would no longer have to be a constant witness of suffering.

Your letter – just as in the old days, during the last war, your cheerful objectivity – has done me a power of good. I wish I could hear you roar with laughter once again! How is my little Margot? Did she ever receive my letter with the Hiddensee photos? Wish I could see you all again sometime!

God bless!

Your old friend

Hedi

My wife's answer to Einstein's letter was written a few days before mine, but both were apparently sent off at the same time. She uses the familiar 'Du' to address Einstein here, which she had never done before. This familiarity may have been brought about by their feeling of mutual affinity. This letter, recollecting some of Einstein's remarks and contemplating on his philosophy of life, is indeed a testimony to our friendship and accord.

Although my wife had not been schooled in philosophy, her reservations about Einstein's attitude to nature hit the nail exactly on the head. Strict determinism seemed to us then, as it still does today, to be irreconcileable with a belief in responsibility and ethical freedom. I have never been able to understand Einstein in this matter. He was, after all, a highly ethical person, in spite of his theoretical conviction about predetermination. As far as I am concerned, the discrepancy between ethical freedom and strict natural laws – which even modern physics does not deny but merely conceives of in a different way – only became intelligible with the help of Niels Bohr's complementarity principle. How much longer will it be before the professional philosophers come to understand and adopt these ideas? I also mention the 'dice-playing God' in my letter. Today I still consider my objection, that Einstein's way of thinking in physics could not do without the 'dice-playing God', to be absolutely correct. For in classical physics the initial conditions are not determined by natural laws, and in every prediction one either has to assume that the initial conditions have been determined by measurement, or else one has to be content with a statement of probability. I basically believe that the first case is illusory; even the best of measurements offer only statistical evidence, which is more or less restricted by the scatter of the initial configuration. The letters which follow deal with this subject in greater detail.

83

10 October, 1944

Dear Einstein

Your letter gave both Hedi and myself great pleasure, and Hedi was so excited and stimulated by it that she replied straight away. In my case it takes a little longer.

I have not held any lectures for the last nine months, as I suffered a collapse in January from which I recovered very slowly, and today I lectured again for the first time after this long interval. I had to prepare myself for it, and eventually one single student turned up, whom I gave a private lesson. All the other fellows are somewhere in the army and navy or the R.A.F. Our expedition to the Reichstag building is still quite fresh in my memory. (Wertheimer was there, too, wasn't he?). In those days, I must admit, we completely misjudged the forces in German politics. But it was, after all, only by a hair's breadth that everything went as wrong as it did. Of course I agree with you completely that all human actions spring from the depths of an ethical feeling which is primary and almost completely independent of reason. But after agreeing with you on this point, I must now switch over to our disagreement in physics. For I am unable to separate the two and I cannot understand how you can combine an entirely mechanistic universe with the freedom of the ethical individual. Hedi, who knows nothing about physics, has all the same formulated it excellently in her enclosed letter to you. To me a deterministic world is quite abhorrent – this is a primary feeling. Maybe you are right, and it is as you say. But at the moment it does not really look like it in physics – and even less so in the rest of the world. I also find your expression, the 'dice-playing God', completely inadequate. You have to throw dice as well in your deterministic world; this is not the difference. You know what that difference really is, as well as I do, and if you are not in possession of all the arguments at the moment, give Pauli a cue, and he will trot them all out. I think first of all that you underestimate the empirical fundamentals of the quantum theory (I attach less importance to the mass of 'proof' than to single blatant instances, such as Gibb's paradox or the

Stern-Gerlach experiment); and secondly that your philosophy somehow manages to harmonise the automata of lifeless objects with the existence of responsibility and conscience, something which I am unable to achieve.

Now with regard to my anti-Eddington and Milne essay, it was written in accordance with the British style of courtesy. I myself would have summed it up as 'rubbish'. But something of that kind had to be written as Eddington is regarded as a kind of prophet in this country. I believe, though, that you have the right to speculate, but that other people do not, myself included. Did I sin so in days gone by (or rather, as you put it, whore)?

I have always appreciated your good Jewish physics, and have greatly enjoyed it; but I have done it myself on only one occasion, in the case of non-linear electrodynamics, and this was hardly a success. It is my honest opinion that when average people try to get hold of the laws of nature by thinking alone, the result is pure rubbish. Schroedinger may be able to do it. I would like to know what you think of his affine field theory. I find it all beautiful and ingenious, but is it true? He has now published his lectures about statistical thermodynamics (auto-graphed); I find them better and more substantial.

In spite of the war, I still have a small group of people doing scientific research here. Fürth too has done some experimenting; he has built a photoelectric microphotometer, as well as an harmonic analyser, which is also photoelectric. At the moment he is constructing a Fourier transformer which I have invented; this produces the Fourier coefficient curve for any given curve on the screen of an oscillograph. It would amuse you. We are also working on crystals and X-rays, but mainly on the improvement of the quantised field theory. You are, of course, absolutely right if you detest this in its present form. But I think that we (that is, my Chinese collaborator Peng and I) have already improved it considerably, and we are fairly certain that we will be able to discard everything unsatisfactory (diverging integrals, etc.). I believe it is going to be at least as beautiful as any respectable classical theory.

Unfortunately I am still unable to get much work done. My heart cannot stand the slightest exertion. For this reason I am not going to do anything further with regard to the matter which was the subject of my last letter to you and of your reply, particularly as your reply was not encouraging. Moreover, I do not know where Niels Bohr is, and therefore cannot appoint him referee in this business. You are probably right in saying that it is even more difficult for scientists than for ordinary people to develop a conscience and a sense of right and wrong. In regard to Laue, I have also heard that his conduct was decent and courageous. One can only hope that he will survive the last, and presumably the most gruesome, period of the war.

I hope that you will write again from time to time. A letter from you gives us the very greatest pleasure. It causes long discussions; for Hedi, as a Quaker, often interprets your remarks very differently from the way I do, old heathen that I am (I am not one really, in fact I am quite devout; it is only in comparison with Hedi). Give my regards to our friends in Princeton – Neumann, Ladenburg, Weyl and the caustic Pauli.

> In old friendship
> Yours
> *Max Born*

Fürth's experimental work contained only one idea of mine; this was the photoelectric Fourier transformer. Later on the Edinburgh branch of Ferranti developed this further, but it was not, however, introduced in practice.

84

3 March, 1947

Dear Born

If I were not a confirmed old rogue, with a fossilised bad conscience, I would not have been able to go for such a long time without writing to you. For firstly, your wife's poem about the Indian ideal of life made so deep an impression on me that I would not have been surprised if it had been written by old Goethe himself; secondly, I was very impressed with your contribution to that peculiar schoolmaster Schilpp's volume which is dedicated to me. It has so much warmth and proves so clearly that you consider my attitude towards statistical quantum mechanics to be strange and archaic. Finally, I particularly like your solicitude for your Chinese protégé's transportation; fortunately he has happily and silently slipped away from you without my intervention. I had consulted Weyl about him, and we both agreed that we would not have been able to solve the problem in the way you had suggested, and that I should approach the English ambassador, who would bring the matter honourably to a satisfactory conclusion. Fortunately I avoided making this step for several days, and then your letter arrived, releasing me.

I cannot make a case for my attitude in physics which you would consider at all reasonable. I admit, of course, that there is a considerable amount of validity in the statistical approach which you were the first to recognise clearly as necessary given the framework of the existing formalism. I cannot seriously believe in it because the theory cannot be reconciled with the idea that physics should represent a reality in time and space, free from spooky actions at a distance. I am, however, not yet firmly convinced that it can really be achieved with a continuous field theory, although I have discovered a possible way of doing this which so far seems quite reasonable. The calculation difficulties are so great that I will be biting the dust long before I myself can be fully convinced of it. But I am quite convinced that someone will eventually come up with a theory whose objects, connected by laws, are not probabilities but considered facts, as used to be taken for granted until quite recently. I cannot, however, base this conviction on logical reasons, but can only produce my little finger as witness, that is, I offer no authority which would be able to command any kind of respect outside of my own hand.

I am glad that your life and work are fruitful and satisfying. This helps one to bear the craziness of the people who determine the fate of *homo sapiens* (so-called) on the grand scale. Maybe it has never been any better, but one did not see it as clearly in all its wretchedness, nor were the consequences of the bungling quite as catastrophic as under present conditions.

Best wishes to you and your family

Yours

A. Einstein

My wife's 'Indian Sonnets' have been published in an anthology of her poems,[33] 'Stille Gange' [Silent Corridors]. 'Schoolmaster' Schilpp's volume is one of the series published in the United States called *The Library of Living Philosophers*, under this title: *Albert Einstein, Philosopher-Scientist*. Each volume of this collection begins with a short autobiography of the philosopher concerned; this is followed by critical reviews of his work by different authors, and ends with the subject's reply to his critics. I had undertaken to write about Einstein's statistical theories; this essay is also published in German in my book *Physik im Wandel Meiner Zeit*. Towards the end of the article I go into Einstein's attitude towards quantum mechanics, and contrast the empirical creed of his youth with his later inclination towards speculation. In an obituary that Einstein wrote for Ernst Mach,[34] he says: 'concepts which have proved useful for ordering things easily assume so great an authority over us, that we forget their terrestial origin and accept them as unalterable facts. They then become labelled as "conceptual necessities", "*a priori* situations", etc. The road of scientific progress is frequently blocked for long periods by such errors. It is therefore not just an idle game to exercise our ability to analyse familiar concepts, and to demonstrate the conditions on which their justification and usefulness depend, and the way in which these developed, little by little, from the data of experience. In this way they are deprived of their excessive authority. Concepts which cannot be shown to be valid are removed. Those which had not been coordinated with the accepted order of things with sufficient care are corrected, or they are replaced by new concepts when a new system is produced which, for some reason or other, seems preferable'. In my article in the Schilpp book I contrast this creed of his with his attitude towards quantum mechanics, by quoting from his earlier letters. The present letter can equally well serve as paradigm, particularly the paragraph which begins: 'I cannot make a case for my attitude which you would consider at all reasonable.' The decisive sentence is the one where he says: 'that physics should represent a reality in time and space, free from spooky actions at a distance'. I too had considered this postulate to be one which could claim absolute validity. But the realities of physical experience had taught me that this postulate is not an *a priori* principle but a time-dependent rule which must be, and can be, replaced by a more general one.

My article in the Schilpp book is not by any means the only one which deals with this subject. There is, for example, an article by Niels Bohr, in which he reports on some detailed discussions he had with Einstein. In the course of it he picks to pieces Einstein's ingenious thought-experiments, which were intended to refute quantum mechanics.

But even this difference of opinion in print did not interfere with our friendship in the slightest degree. Einstein expressly acknowledges the warm tone of my article.

I cannot now remember what was the point about the transportation of my Chinese protégé. I had a number of extremely gifted Chinese collaborators, who presumably wanted to return home because of the constantly increasing threat of war without having to pass through either Germany or Russia, but by way of America.

The last paragraph of the letter is a resigned complaint about the craziness and wretchedness of *homo sapiens*, which at that time (end of 1947) was becoming more and more obvious.

85   *Magdalen College, Oxford*
                                                      4 March, 1948

Dear Einstein

A few days ago I saw a film here about atomic energy, and there you were, as large as life, talking with that familiar and well-loved voice, and smiling your amiable, half-serious, half-cynical grin. I was quite moved – it will soon be twenty years since we last saw you. And when I wrote about this experience to Hedi in Edinburgh, she replied at once that she wanted to see the film as well. I am going to try and persuade the atomic physicists here to send the film there. It also contained some fine shots of J. J. Thomson and Rutherford but, though I have always greatly admired them, they are nowhere near as close to my heart as you are. As to the rest of the film, it is quite good, but it will not alter the course of world history very much. We've really put our foot in it this time, poor fools that we are, and I am truly sad for our beautiful physics! There we have been trying to puzzle things out, only to help the human race to expedite its departure from this beautiful earth! I no longer understand anything about politics: I understand neither the Americans, nor the Russians, nor any of the numerous little stinkers who are now, of all times, becoming nationalistic. Even our good Jews in Palestine have discredited their cause in this way. It is better to think about something else.

Today I gave the last of my Waynflete Lectures, in which *inter alia* I produced certain passages from your letter to me. I assumed that you would have no objection, as you did not return my manuscript in protest. My stay in a luxurious Oxford college was very pleasant. The (relatively) good food does not mean much to me; but the many conversations with a variety of intelligent people did, as well as the beautiful old town itself with its grey old buildings; visits to my daughter Gritli (her husband, Maurice Pryce, was unfortunately ill for almost the whole time) and playing with my grandchildren. Occasionally we played music on two pianos – all delightful things. I have prepared the lectures for printing in book form. Hedi stayed at home in order to re-arrange our house: moving the kitchen upstairs, to save us old people from having to climb so many stairs. She is happy because a religious (and very fine) article of hers has appeared in an Indian periodical. Could you not arrange to have her poems printed in a German periodical in America? They are very beautiful, aren't they, but here in England nobody understands German, and in Germany there are enough poets, more than the country can support. Much of Hedi's time is taken up with sending parcels to starving people in Germany. It is particularly the anti-Nazis who are suffering again at the moment. But then, we are rationed ourselves and so cannot do much to help.

What we are doing in physics will not interest you very much. We concluded our kinetic theory of liquids with a paper about the crazy helium II (which has not yet been published). One of my Chinese pupils is working on superconductivity, and I consider his theory (which is based on a few suggestions of mine) to be better than Heisenberg's. My collaborator Green is hard at work on elementary particles; he is a brilliant man, the best I have had since Pryce. All this keeps me reasonably young. I still have five more years in office, and then I have to retire on a pension, which is not enough to live on (it is a kind of insurance, and the amount depends on one's length of service), so I will probably have to go on working, right to my blissful end. Not a bad fate, really.

Although a letter from you gives me great pleasure, you need not reply unless you really feel like it. All the best, and kind regards to Margot.

Yours
Max Born

When I wrote 'we've really put our foot in it', I apparently still did not know that it was Einstein who, through his letter to President Roosevelt, had started it all off. Had I known, I would hardly have written this passage.

This letter comes from Oxford. The Vice-Chancellor of the old university, Sir Henry Tizard, known for his conflict with Lindemann-Cherwell over the technical conduct of the war, had personally invited me to hold the Waynflete Lectures while on a visit to Edinburgh. It was an honour I gladly accepted, although it meant a considerable amount of work for me. The lectures have been published under the title: *Natural Philosophy of Cause and Chance*.[32] They contain a report about the advance of the probability concepts into causal physics, which culminated in quantum mechanics. It also contains quotations from Einstein's letters which will be the subject of further comments.

The statistical mechanics of condensed systems, devised by Green and myself, which was intended to lead to a kinetic theory of liquids, has been summed up in a booklet called *A General Kinetic Theory of Liquids*,[35] and has made some contribution towards the development of this field. But the use of helium, which has a liquid phase that behaves curiously, was not as successful as we had hoped. The theory accepted today originated with the Russian Nobel prizewinner of 1962, L. D. Landau.

86

18 March, 1948

Dear Born

Today I was looking for something in my igloo, that is, on my desk in the Institute. I did not, however, find what I was looking for, but your letter instead, which I had taken to be printed matter (because of the large envelope), and had therefore left unopened together with many others. Now I have read it, of course, and moreover with such interest that I arrived home an hour late for lunch.

There are several misunderstandings in your quotations from my letters, presumably caused by my illegible handwriting, which distort the meaning as you will see from my marginal notes. But even if it has already been printed it is not a disaster because the 'patience of paper' will certainly be preserved in this case as well. I have got my own back by means of several caustic marginal comments, which will delight you; for I believe that you enjoy rough language, which after all goes with the Scottish climate.

It is really rather a pity that we cannot spend some time together at leisure. For I really understand very well why you consider me an impenitent old sinner. But I feel sure that you do not understand how I came by my lonely ways; it would certainly amuse you, even if there is not the slightest chance of your approving of my attitude. I would enjoy picking your positivistic philosophical attitude to pieces myself. But this is hardly likely to happen during our lifetime. I have greatly, although belatedly, enjoyed your and your wife's letters, and remain, with kind regards,

Yours
A. Einstein

I am only going to quote a few of the 'caustic comments' here. In the last chapter of my book ('Metaphysical Conclusions') I assembled some of the fundamental concepts of physics, which cannot be traced back to other more fundamental ones, but have to be accepted as an act of faith. I then continue: 'Causality is such a principle if it is defined as the belief in the existence of mutual physical dependence of observable situations. However, all specifications of this dependence in regard to space and time (contiguity, antecedence) and to the infinite sharpness of observation (determinism) seem to me not fundamental but consequences of the actual empirical laws'.

Einstein's marginal comment was: 'I am well aware that no causality exists in relation to the observable; I consider this realisation to be conclusive. But in my opinion one should not conclude from this that the *theory*, too, has to be based on fundamental laws of statistics. It is, after all, possible that the (molecular) structure of the means of observation involves the statistical character of the observable, but that it is expedient in the end to keep the basis of the theory free from statistical concepts.'

My text then continues: 'Another metaphysical principle is incorporated in the notion of probability. It is the belief that the predictions of statistical calculations are more than an exercise of the brain, that they can be trusted in the real world.'

Einstein comments briefly: 'I agree with this, of course.'

These comments are calm and matter-of-fact. But there are also some short, sharp remarks. My text deals with the question of whether the beauty and simplicity of a theory are of importance; it reads as follows: 'With regard to simplicity, opinions will differ in many cases. Is Einstein's law of gravitation simpler than Newton's? Trained mathematicians will answer yes, meaning the logical simplicity of the foundations, while others will say emphatically no, because of the horrible complications of the formalism.'

Einstein's comment on this is simply:

'The only thing which matters is the *logical* simplicity of the *foundations*'.

I agree with this, as a trained mathematician, but I am unable to condemn the other point of view entirely, After all, what really matters in the end is whose formulae do more justice to the observations, Newton's or Einstein's.

I then discuss what I call the 'principle of objectivity': 'It provides a criterion for distinguishing subjective impressions from objective facts, namely by substituting for given sense data others which can be checked by other individuals'. I have recently dealt in detail with this favourite idea of mine in an essay entitled: 'Symbol and Reality'.[36] Einstein's brief comment was simply: 'Blush, Born, Blush!'

Elsewhere I try to explain that the application of the objectivity principle can sometimes be out of place by using a work of art as an example (a Bach fugue), and he just comments: 'Ugh!'

At the end he adds a somewhat longer passage in his elegant handwriting, which I reproduce in its entirety: 'Remark: you should not interpret the omission of marginal comments in the latter part of your article as agreement. The whole thing is rather sloppily thought out, and for this I must respectfully clip your ear. I just want to explain what I mean when I say that we should try to hold on to physical reality. We all of us have some idea of what the basic axioms in physics will turn out to be. The quantum or the particle will surely not be amongst them; the field, in Faraday's and Maxwell's sense, could possibly be, but it is not certain. But whatever we regard as existing (real) should somehow be localised in time and space. That is, the real in part of space A should (in theory) somehow 'exist' independently of what is thought of as real in space B. When a system in physics extends over the parts of space A *and* B, then that which exists in B should somehow exist independently of that which exists in A. That which really exists in B should therefore not depend on what kind of measurement is carried out in part of space A; it should also be independent of whether or not any measurement at all is carried out in space A. If one adheres to this programme, one can hardly consider the quantum-theoretical description as a complete representation of the physically real. If one tries to do so in spite of this, one has to assume that the physically real in B suffers a sudden change as a result of a measurement in A. My instinct for physics bristles at this. However, if one abandons the assumption that what exists in different parts of space has its own, independent, real existence, then I simply cannot see what it is that physics is meant to describe. For what is thought to be a 'system' is, after all, just a convention, and I cannot see how one could divide the world objectively in such a way that one could make statements about parts of it.'

According to his letter, Einstein believes that I would disapprove of this attitude, even if we had the opportunity to discuss it personally. He calls my philosophical ideas 'positivistic', and would love to pull them to pieces. I myself certainly do not regard my philosophy as a variety of positivism if this implies that only sensory impressions have any claim to reality, and that everything else, not only scientific theories but also one's ideas about real things of daily life, is merely constructed, created for the purpose of establishing reasonable relationships between the various impressions of the senses. My reply to Einstein's comments is contained in a later letter.

87

84 Grange Loan
Edinburgh
31 March, 1948

Dear Einstein

Many thanks for the return of my manuscript with your marginal comments, and for your letter. It takes some time to get things printed here. Meanwhile the manuscript is nowhere near completion, and even if I should send it to the publishers in May it is unlikely to appear before January '49. This will enable me to make any corrections which seem necessary. I am very grateful to you for allowing me to reprint the two passages from your letters. I will make the corrections you suggest in their text, even though the wording of your original version was absolutely clear, while the second is entirely ambiguous. I have made a careful copy of your words; here is the result:

1. 'I firmly *believe*, but I hope that. . . .'
The words are curious, I admit. But the 'believe' has been underlined by you. I am leaving it out, and am going to replace it by: 'I hope. . . .'
2. Skin – as you are talking about the little finger, I took it to be 'hand'. But your reading is equally justified, particularly as it is in accordance with the writer's interpretation.

As to the rest, I will bear your earclipping and scolding with humility. There is nothing to be done. But in order fully to understand what you are criticising, one has to be familiar, of course, with the six preceding lectures as well. But I am quite sure that they would not have helped to convert you to my point of view either. I will make good use of your remarks and, if I can find the time, improve my wording. I am very sorry indeed that you do not like my 'observational invariants'. They are descendents of Wertheimer's *Gestalt*, in a new form. I think quite highly of it. But I am annoyed that you reproach me for my positivistic ideas; that really is the very last thing I am after. I really cannot stand those fellows. Again, my sincere thanks.

Hedi and I are travelling to France the day after tomorrow. First to Bordeaux, where a congress on light dispersion and the Raman effect is taking place. Raman and I are to receive honorary doctorates there. This is very funny, as for the last three years we have been engaged in a violent feud about crystal theory. That is, he has encouraged his pupils to attack me in *Nature*, and I have answered back rather energetically at times. Now we shall have to keep the peace and allow ourselves to be honoured. He is used to it, I am not. In the case of quantum mechanics, which you think so little of, the adulation has alighted entirely on Heisenberg and Schroedinger. And yet Heisenberg did not even know what a matrix was in those days (he was my assistant, that is how I know). By the way, he visited us last December, as pleasant and intelligent as ever, but noticeably 'Nazified'. I have recently talked to him again in Oxford. Once more we are on the same trail: superconductivity. He has published a theory which we consider absolute rubbish. We first of all carefully deduced the kinetic theory of dense matter (liquid and solid bodies), and then explained helium II very satisfactorily, and are at present engaged in producing a decent theory of superconductivity. It all seems to work out quite well. Do you really believe that the whole of quantum mechanics is just a phantom?

Do come over to Europe some time. In England and Scotland little has been destroyed, and even in France enough has been left intact. How beautiful are the ancient towns, churches and castles of pre-machine days! Hedi and I were in Switzerland last summer, and were completely intoxicated with the loveliness not only of the landscape but also of the small towns such as Berne, Lucerne, Thun, etc. Oxford, too, is not to be despised.

Or have you, with your leaning towards puritanism, lost the ability to enjoy such impressions?

With kind regards, also from Hedi

Yours

Max Born

When I used the expression 'observational invariants' in my book, I meant the following: when one sees a bird flying away, what one really perceives is usually a bird, recognisable as such, which then becomes smaller and smaller until one can no longer distinguish any details and finally sees only a small point. All the same, one is aware that one is looking at the same bird all the time. Thus there is something constant and invariable in totally different sensual perceptions, which one's brain deals with unconsciously. This is what I call the 'observational invariant'.

Wertheimer was the same man who accompanied Einstein and me to the Reichstag during the revolution, as described in the commentary to letter No. 81. He was one of the founders of the Gestalt theory, together with Köhler, Hornbostel and others, which teaches that perception consists, not of sense perceptions which coexist side by side, but of the recognition of complete and meaningful *Gestalten*.

The meeting with Sir C. V. Raman in Bordeaux was most dramatic. At his invitation we had spent the winter of 1935–36 at the Indian Institute of Science in Bangalore, where I gave some lectures. We had got on well together, apart from some minor differences of opinion, and had become friends, or so I thought. He even tried to obtain a permanent position for me there, but spoilt this plan by some rather clumsy manoeuvring. Although he had regularly attended almost all my lectures on the dynamics of crystal lattices, he developed a very primitive theory of his own about lattice vibration, and induced his pupils to attack me in *Nature*. In Bordeaux, after a friendly greeting, we clashed almost immediately; he was running down the theoreticians who want to make experiments, when I said: 'And what about experimentalists who try their hand at theory?' This made him see red; during the banquet, at which my wife sat next to him, he declared that I had insulted him to such an extent that he would have to leave, and she had great difficulty in dissuading him. The tension persisted for the whole of the congress. And even later, during a meeting of Nobel prizewinners in Lindau, he cut us as much as possible.

My opinion of Heisenberg was probably not justified. Later on he explained to me what his work had been during the Hitler period and how this had governed his relations with the regime. In the meantime (1969) objective evaluations of German work on the splitting of the atom during the war have appeared, in particular that by the English historian David Irving,* which confirms Heisenberg's statement and justifies his behaviour. As I have said before, nothing much came of our theory of the super-fluid phase of helium, and of the superconductivity of metals.

88

5 April, 1948

Dear Born

I am sending you a short essay which, at Pauli's suggestion, I have sent to Switzerland to be printed. I beg you please to overcome your aversion long enough in this instance to read this brief piece as if you had not yet formed any opinion of your own, but had only just arrived as a visitor from Mars. I am not asking you to do this because I imagine that I can influence your opinion, but because I think that it will help you to understand my principal motives far better than anything else of mine you know. However, it tends to express the negative aspect, rather than the confidence I have in the relativistic group as represent-ing a heuristic limiting principle. In any case, I will be extreme-ly interested to hear your counter-arguments, beyond the obvious fact, of course, that quantum mechanics alone has up to now been able to encompass the wave-particle character of light and matter.

With kindest regards
Yours
A. Einstein

Quantum Mechanics and Reality

In what follows I shall explain briefly and in an elementary way why I consider the methods of quantum mechanics fundamentally unsatisfactory. I want to say straight away,

---

* David Irving, *The Virus House*[37] (pseudonym of a German nuclear research laboratory in Berlin). Also the issue of *Bulletin of the Atomic Scientists*[38] devoted to the 'German atom bomb', which, in addition to a leading article by the editor, E. Rabinovich, contains contributions by Heisenberg himself and by Hans Suess (once a member of the German nuclear research team, now Professor of Chemistry in the University of California at San Diego).

however, that I will not deny that this theory represents an important, in a certain sense even final, advance in physical knowledge. I imagine that this theory may well become a part of a subsequent one, in the same way as geometrical optics is now incorporated in wave optics: the inter-relationships will remain, but the foundation will be deepened or replaced by a more comprehensive one.

I

I consider a free particle described at a certain time by a spatially restricted ψ-function (completely described – in the sense of quantum mechanics). According to this, the particle possesses neither a sharply defined momentum nor a sharply defined position. In which sense shall I imagine that this representation describes a real, individual state of affairs? Two possible points of view seem to me possible and obvious and we will weigh one against the other:

(a) The (free) particle really has a definite position and a definite momentum, even if they cannot both be ascertained by measurement in the same individual case. According to this point of view, the ψ-function represents an incomplete description of the real state of affairs.

This point of view is not the one physicists accept. Its acceptance would lead to an attempt to obtain a complete description of the real state of affairs as well as the incomplete one, and to discover physical laws for such a description. The theoretical framework of quantum mechanics would then be exploded.

(b) In reality the particle has neither a definite momentum nor a definite position; the description by ψ-function is in principle a complete description. The sharply-defined position of the particle, obtained by measuring the position, cannot be interpreted as the position of the particle prior to the measurement. The sharp localisation which appears as a result of the measurement is brought about only as a result of the unavoidable (but not unimportant) operation of measurement. The result of the measurement depends not only on the real particle situation but also on the nature of the measuring mechanism, which in principle is incompletely known. An analogous situation arises when the momentum or any other observable relating to the particle is being measured. This is presumably the interpretation preferred by physicists at present; and one has to admit that it alone does justice in a natural way to the empirical state of affairs expressed in Heisenberg's principle within the framework of quantum mechanics.

According to this point of view, two ψ-functions which differ in more than trivialities always describe two different real situations (for example, the particle with well-defined position and one with well-defined momentum).

The above is also valid, *mutatis mutandis*, to describe systems which consist of several particles. Here, too, we assume (in the sense of interpretation Ib) that the ψ-function completely describes a real state of affairs, and that two (essentially) different ψ-functions describe two different real states of affairs, even if they could lead to identical results when a complete measurement is made. If the results of the measurement tally, it is put down to the influence, partly unknown, of the measurement arrangements.

II

If one asks what, irrespective of quantum mechanics, is characteristic of the world of ideas of physics, one is first of all struck by the following: the concepts of physics relate to a real outside world, that is, ideas are established relating to things such as bodies, fields, etc., which claim a 'real existence' that is independent of the perceiving subject – ideas which, on the other hand, have been brought into as secure a relationship as possible with the sense-data. It is further characteristic of these physical objects that they are thought of as arranged in a space-time continuum. An essential aspect of this arrangement of things in physics is that they lay claim, at a certain time, to an existence independent of one another, provided these objects 'are situated in different parts of space'. Unless one makes this kind of assumption about the independence of the existence (the 'being-thus') of objects which are far apart from one another in space—which stems in the first place from everyday thinking – physical thinking in the familiar sense would not be possible. It is also hard to see any way of formulating and testing the laws of physics unless one makes a clear distinction of this kind. This principle has been carried to extremes in the field theory by localising the elementary objects on which it is based and which exist independently of each other, as well as the elementary laws which have been postulated for it, in the infinitely small (four-dimensional) elements of space.

The following idea characterises the relative independence of objects far apart in space (A and B): external influence on A has no direct influence on B; this is known as the 'principle of contiguity', which is used consistently only in the field theory. If this axiom were to be completely abolished, the idea of the existence of (quasi-)enclosed systems, and thereby the postulation of laws which can be checked empirically in the accepted sense, would become impossible.

III

I now make the assertion that the interpretation of quantum mechanics (according to Ib) is not consistent with principle II.

Let us consider a physical system S_{12}, which consists of two part-systems S_1 and S_2. These two part-systems may have been in a state of mutual physical interaction at an earlier time. We are, however, considering them at a time when this interaction is an at end. Let the entire system be completely described in the quantum mechanical sense by a ψ-function ψ_{12} of the coordinates $q_1, \ldots$ and $q_2, \ldots$ of the two part-systems (ψ_{12} cannot be represented as a product of the form $\psi_1 \psi_2$ but only as a sum of such products). At time t let the two part-systems be separated from each other in space, in such a way that ψ_{12} only differs from o when $q_1, \ldots$ belong to a limited part R_1 of space and $q_2, \ldots$ belong to a part R_2 separated from R_1.

The ψ-functions of the single part-systems S_1 and S_2 are then unknown to begin with, that is, they do not exist at all. The methods of quantum mechanics, however, allow us to determine ψ_2 of S_2 from ψ_{12}, if a complete measurement of the part-system S_1 in the sense of quantum mechanics is also available. Instead of the original ψ_{12} of S_{12}, one thus obtains the ψ-function ψ_2 of the part-system S_2.

But the kind of complete measurement, in the quantum theoretical sense, that is undertaken on the part system S_1, that is, which observable we are measuring, is crucial for this determination. For example, if S_1 consists of a single particle, then we have the choice of measuring either its position or its momentum components. The resulting ψ_2 depends on this choice, so that different kinds of (statistical) predictions regarding measurements to be carried out later on S_2 are obtained, according to the choice of measurement carried out on S_1. This means, from the point of view of the interpretations of Ib, that according to the choice of complete measurement of S_1 a different real situation is being created in regard to S_2, which can be described variously by $\psi_2, \underline{\psi_2}, \underline{\underline{\psi_2}}$, etc.

Seen from the point of view of quantum mechanics alone, this does not present any difficulty. For, according to the choice of measurement to be carried out on S_1, a different real situation is created, and the necessity of having to attach two or more different ψ-functions $\psi_2, \underline{\psi_2}, \ldots$ to one and the same system S_2 cannot arise.

It is a different matter, however, when one tries to adhere to the principles of quantum mechanics and to principle II, i.e. the independent existence of the real state of affairs existing in two separate parts of space R_1 and R_2. For in our example the complete measurement on S_1 represents a physical operation which only affects part R_1 of space. Such an operation, however, can have no direct influence on the physical reality in a remote part R_2 of space. It follows that every statement about S_2 which we arrive at as a result of a complete measurement of S_1 has to be valid for the system S_2, even if no measurement whatsoever is carried out on S_1. This would mean that all statements which can be deduced from the settlement of ψ_2 or $\underline{\psi_2}$ must simultaneously be valid for S_2. This is, of course, impossible, if $\psi_2, \underline{\psi_2}$, etc., should represent different real states of affairs for S_2, that is, one comes into conflict with the Ib interpretation of the ψ-function.

There seems to me no doubt that those physicists who regard the descriptive methods of quantum mechanics as definitive in principle would react to this line of thought in the following way: they would drop the requirement II for the independent existence of the physical reality present in different parts of space; they would be justified in pointing out that the quantum theory nowhere makes explicit use of this requirement.

I admit this, but would point out: when I consider the physical phenomena known to me, and especially those which are being so successfully encompassed by quantum mechanics, I still cannot find any fact anywhere which would make it appear likely that requirement II will have to be abandoned.

I am therefore inclined to believe that the description of quantum mechanics in the sense of I*a* has to be regarded as an incomplete and indirect description of reality, to be replaced at some later date by a more complete and direct one.

At all events, one should beware, in my opinion, of committing oneself too dogmatically to the present theory in searching for a unified basis for the whole of physics.

> *A. Einstein*

This short article[39] is so closely linked with the letter that I had to include it here. Also, my reply cannot be understood without it. The discussion is, of course, comprehensible only to those who have some knowledge of the development of modern physics and of its philosophical basis.

89

84 Grange Loan
Edinburgh
9 May, 1948

Dear Einstein

I am very sorry not to have replied at once to your letter of April 5th with the manuscript. I was in Oxford for two months, then at home for only a fortnight, and off again to France with Hedi to take part in two meetings, one in Bordeaux and one in Paris. After my return I had to look after my long neglected pupils, prepare my Oxford lectures for the printer, and write an official obituary on Planck for the Royal Society, a considerable task which has to be completed by the middle of June. This is why I am only just getting around to answering your letter. I am pleased that you seem to attach some importance to my opinion. I have the feeling that I hardly deserve it. But, if you like, you shall hear what came into my mind while reading your manuscript.

Let me begin with an example. A beam of light falls on to a plate of doubly refracting crystal, and is split into two beams. The direction of polarisation of one of the beams is determined by measurement: it is then possible to deduce that that of the second beam is perpendicular to the first. In this way one has been able to make a statement about a system in a certain part of space as a result of a measurement carried out on a system in another part of space. That this is possible depends on the knowledge that both beams have originated from one beam which has passed through a crystal; in the language of optics, that they are coherent. It seems to me that this case is closely related to your abstract example, which is apparently connected with collision theory. But it is simpler and shows that such things happen within the framework of ordinary optics. All quantum mechanics has done is to generalise it.

It seems to me that your axiom of the 'independence of spatially separated objects A and B', is not as convincing as you make out. It does not take into account the fact of coherence; objects far apart in space which have a common origin need not be independent. I believe that this cannot be denied and simply has to be accepted. Dirac has based his whole book on this. You say: The methods of quantum mechanics enable one to determine ψ_2 of S_2 from ψ_{12}, provided a complete measurement, in the quantum mechanical sense, of the spatial system S_1 exists as well. You evidently assume that ψ_{12} is already known. Therefore a measurement in S_1 does not really give any information about events occurring in far distant S_2, but only in association with the information about ψ_{12}, that is, with the help of additional earlier measurements. In the optical example, we have the information that both partial beams are produced from one single beam by one crystal.

Your example is too abstract for me and insufficiently precise to be useful as a beginning. 'Measurement' is often *loosely* defined in quantum mechanics. It means either the determination of the possible eigenvalues of a quantity, or the determination of the actual state corresponding to the particular eigenvalue of a system, or, more generally, the determination of the weight $|an|^2$ corresponding to the different eigenvalues $n = 1, 2, \ldots$ in the mixture $\psi(x) = \sum_n a_n \psi_n (x)$. It is not clear to me what you mean by 'measurement' in your example. I would find it more convenient to consider a real collision process, in which two originally independent particles collide and are deflected. The wave functions after the collision would then correspond to your ψ_1 and ψ_2. Moreover, it is relevant whether you mean a stationary current of falling particles or just two particles, one of each kind. In the latter case, nothing normally happens. But in addition to the direction of collision the times must be accurately known, and if they are so adjusted that deflection does occur, then it seems plausible to me that the particles are not independent after the collision. For in order for anything to happen at all, one must know and arrange so much before the collision. But if we are dealing with a stationary current of particles, with statistical arrival times at the place of collision, it is obvious that the statistics must have an effect on the distribution after the collision, i.e. the two partners are still not independent. I cannot really find any particular difficulty.

But I feel that I am not expressing my opinion as lucidly as I would like to do. Basically I am coming back again to the fact of coherence, which cannot be denied. But as the usefulness of mechanical analogues cannot be denied either, one must be content with a formalism which covers both. This does not go too much against the grain with me. I am therefore inclined to make use of the formalism, and even to 'believe' in it in a certain sense, until something decidedly 'better' turns up. I have expounded all this in some detail in my Oxford lectures, which you may have the chance to see one of these days. As for my expectation of 'something better' I am, of course, of a completely different opinion from you. For progress in physics has always moved from the intuitive towards the abstract. And this will probably remain so. Quantum mechanics and the quantum field theory both fail in important respects. But it seems to me that all the signs indicate that one has to be prepared for things which we older people will not like. I believe that even the days of the relativistic group, in the form you gave it, are numbered; the transportability of the line element is fine mathematically but, to my mind, physically unsatisfactory. Now, the divergencies in quantum mechanics seem to indicate that an absolute length does in fact exist in the world. I presume that this will have to be included in the general transformation group. We have gone to a great deal of trouble over this. My pupil Green, a highly gifted man (whom I am going to send to you in Princeton next year), may possibly make some progress with it; he has good ideas and great mathematical skill.

We are at present working on superconductivity, and I

think our theory is the right one. It is not so terribly complicated.

               With kind regards, also from Hedi.
                    Yours
                        Max Born

The root of the difference of opinion between Einstein and me was the axiom that events which happen in different places A and B are independent of one another, in the sense that an observation of the state of affairs at B cannot teach us anything about the state of affairs at A. My argument against this assumption is taken from optics, and is based on the concept of coherence. When a beam of light is split in two by reflection, double-refraction, etc., and these two beams take different paths, one can deduce the state of one of the beams at a remote point B from an observation at point A. It is curious that Einstein did not admit this objection to his axiom as valid, although he had been one of the first theoreticians to recognise the significance of de Broglie's work on wave mechanics and had drawn our attention to it. The axiom certainly does not apply to light; but if the movement of matter can be described as 'wave motion' – and it was Einstein himself, after all, who supplied some powerful arguments for this – then the concept of coherence can be applied to beams of matter: from this it follows that, as in the case of light, one can under certain circumstances draw conclusions about the state at B by determining the state at A. Einstein declared that any theory which could lead to such conclusions was incomplete. Therefore, in his eyes, the theory of light must be considered to be incomplete as well. He looked forward to the creation of a more profound theory which would do away with this state of imperfection. So far his hopes have not been realised, and physicists have good reasons for believing this to be impossible, based mainly on studies carried out by J. von Neumann (see commentary to letter No. 78).

Department of Mathematical Physics
The University
Drummond Street
Edinburgh 8
22 May, 1948

90

Dear Einstein

      Unlike my last letter, which I hope you received, this one has nothing to do with quantum theory, but with Palestine. You will say: 'Why does this concern you?' Indeed, when you wrote to me in 1933 suggesting that I should go to Palestine, I refused for the sake of my wife and children, who are entirely without any Jewish tradition. Also I had no clear picture of the situation in Europe. Later, I was in daily contact with Weizmann in Karlsbad for a number of weeks. I learned a great deal. However, I do believe that he could have saved many more Jews if he had accepted the offer of the English to give them a part of Kenya in East Africa. As things are now, Palestine is the only possible place of refuge. I was very sad when the Jews started to use terror themselves, and showed that they had learned a lesson from Hitler. Also I was so grateful towards my new 'fatherland', Britain, that I expected nothing evil from it. But it gradually dawned on me that our Mr Bevin is playing a wicked game: first the Arabs are supplied with arms and trained; then the British army pulls out and leaves the dirty business of liquidating the Jews to the Arabs. Of course, I have no proof that it is so. Moreover, I detest nationalism of every kind, including that of the Jews. Therefore I could not get very excited about it. But gradually it has become quite obvious to me that my worst suspicions were correct. A leading article in today's *Manchester Guardian* openly attacks Bevin for doing precisely what I had suspected. I am feeling very depressed, for I am completely powerless and without influence in this country. The main purpose of this letter is to tell you that you have my wholehearted support if you take any action to help. Could you not induce the American government to act before it is too late? The Russians would cooperate and this could perhaps help to reduce the tension between America and Russia. Let me know what people think of this business in your part of the world.

With kind regards, also from Hedi

Yours

Max Born

91

1 June, 1948

Dear Born

Your Palestine letter has moved me very deeply. Without any doubt, you have summed up Bevin's policy correctly. He seems to have become infected with the infamy germ by virtue of the post he occupies. You have, however, rather too optimistic an idea of the opportunities I have to influence the game in Washington. The latter can be summed up with the maxim: never let the right hand know what the left is doing. One thumps the table with the right hand, while with the left one helps England (by an embargo, for example) in its insidious attack.

Your letter about the interpretation of the quantum theory goes into quite a lot of detail but does not keep to my logical system, so that I am unable to reply without fatiguing you with tiresome repetitions. Perhaps one day we will have that personal discussion after all. I should just like to add that I am by no means mad about the so-called classical system, but I do consider it necessary to do justice to the principle of general relativity in some way or other, for its heuristic quality is indispensable to real progress.

Kind regards
Yours
A. Einstein

My Palestine letter and Einstein's reply hardly require comment. The assessment of Bevin's Palestine policy was quite correct. But he did not take into account the toughness and desperate determination of the Jews, who succeeded in getting the better of the Arabs.

As regards Einstein's remarks about physics at the conclusion of his letter, his reproach that I had not kept to his logical system seems to me quite unjustified. He was so thoroughly convinced that his ideas were right that he could not accept any different method, while he for his part reproached me for doing the same. We had come to different philosophical points of view between which there could be no bridge. But, even so, I believe that I followed the teaching of the young Einstein, as defined by him in his obituary for Ernst Mach, which I mentioned in the commentary to letter No. 84.

92

84 Grange Loan
Edinburgh
23 January, 1949

Dear Einstein

This communication is intended mainly in reply to Margot's letter to Hedi. Please pass my enclosed letter on to her – you can, of course, read it. We are very pleased to hear that you are feeling better. Look after yourself and take it easy.

By the way, what has happened to the Schilpp book? I sent off my contribution to it more than two years ago, and it has still not been published.

I worked very hard during the last term and, I think, with success. Green and I have developed a theory for elementary particles, and I am convinced that it is correct, though I express myself a little more cautiously in the literature. You will not believe in it, however, for we use the quantum-mechanical 'spook' which you so much dislike. There are going to be two short letters of ours in the next issue of *Nature*.

Our idea is as follows:

Previously one knocked together a Lagrange function for each kind of particle (photons, electrons, protons, mesons, etc.) as best one could, introducing the mass arbitrarily as a characteristic constant. We believe that a completely different approach should be made. For it is certain that the number of different mesons is very large, probably infinite. The huge unknown is the Lagrange function L itself, not the solution of the associated mechanical problem. We find it from a very general principle: the laws of nature are invariant with respect not only to the relativistic transformations but also to the substitutions $x^\alpha \to p_\alpha$, $p_\alpha \to -x^\alpha$ where x^α denotes space-time coordinates and p_α energy and momenta. Classically this is of course meaningless, but quantum-mechanically it makes sense because now $p_\alpha = -i\hbar \dfrac{\partial}{\partial x^\alpha}$.

It boils down to the fact that your fundamental invariant $x^\alpha x_\alpha = R$ is replaced by the symmetrical quantity $S = R + P$ where $P = p^\alpha p_\alpha$. S is an operator, the integral eigenvalues of which are the distances and the eigenfunctions of which are substantially the Lagrange functions L. (x_α and p_α must of course be measured in 'natural' units.) This indeed produces infinitely many Ls,

and the masses of the known mesons are calculated correctly.
No offence!

>Kindest regards
>Yours
>*Max Born*

Margot's letter contained the news of Einstein's serious illness.
The Schilpp book did eventually appear in the same year (1949).
The physical information which comprises the greater part of my letter
is based on the idea which I had already submitted to Einstein in an
earlier letter, and which we called the 'reciprocity principle'. But our
considerations went off in a new direction, and this, as previously stated,
has recently assumed renewed importance in connection with the theory
of elementary particles.

93

[*undated*]

Dear Born

Thank you very much for your friendly words. I am once again
crawling about quite cheerfully. But the machinery isn't much
good any longer. The Schilpp affair is temporarily buried because Schilpp is at present busying himself somewhere in Germany. When he returns, something will happen. I am truly sorry
to hear that your wife's nerves are in such a bad state. Her poem
about the Indian philosophy of life made such a deep impression
on me at the time. It shows a noble mind and a genuine poetic
talent. I am sorry to hear that you are worried about the mean
pension. However, this sort of thing is virtually an obligation in
Scotland, for the sake of all those jokes about the nation's
thrifty habits. Here, too, the pensions are none too generous
nowadays, as a result of inflation. I have more or less understood your theoretical hints. But our respective hobby-horses
have irretrievably run off in different directions – yours, however, enjoys far greater popularity as a result of its remarkable
practical successes, while mine, on the other hand, smacks of
quixotism, and even I myself cannot adhere to it with absolute
confidence. But at least mine does not represent a blind-man's

buff with the idea of reality. My whole instinct rebels against it irresistibly. My hope of talking it over with you once more before my departure is unlikely to be fulfilled. Perhaps I can still arrange for the institute to send you an invitation.

     Kind regards and wishes

        Yours

          A. E.

Einstein's handwriting in this letter clearly shows the effect of his illness, and is difficult to read in parts. But in spite of his premonition of death he lived for another six years.

His remark about retirement pay is funny, but unjustified. There is no pension to professors in the whole of Great Britain, except for a kind of compulsory insurance, to whose premiums the universities make quite considerable contributions. Anyone who serves for a long period of time thus receives a more or less adequate old age pension. As I became a professor at Edinburgh rather late in life, that is, at the end of my fiftieth year, I could only expect a small pension. The university was no doubt unable to make an exception by increasing the amount in my case, to avoid creating a precedent. As regards the parsimony of the Scots, we never encountered it anywhere. It only exists as a subject for jokes, and probably originated during the time when Scotland, in comparison with England, was relatively poor and forced to economise.

Einstein's hope that we would see one another once more before his 'departure' and discuss things was not to be fulfilled.

94

12 April, 1949

Dear Borns

    I was delighted with the wonderful photographs, the contributions on causality and probability, and the interesting article on how to overcome the moral decay of contemporary life. You, dear Born, have exposed to public view the frivolous remarks I made in my letter. The entire subject dealt with in your book has been very well integrated into the framework of development, and I understand your point of view very well. All the same, I am convinced that your principles, which are at present shared by almost everyone, will not stand the test of time. You did the right thing in your letter when you expressed the wish that you could be invited to the institute for a longish period. As a matter of fact, I did advocate this, but I lack influence, as I am generally regarded as a sort of petrified object, rendered blind and deaf by the years. I find this role not too distasteful, as it corresponds fairly well with my temperament.

Your thesis, Mrs Born, that liberation from the bondage of the self constitutes the only way towards a more satisfactory human society, I regard as absolutely right. But is it not also a fact that one cannot put everything down to the individual, as the social orientation of the individual is bound to wither in a society geared to ruthless competition? The effort to improve must therefore take both these sources of human behaviour into account.

Now you ask me what my attitude is towards the simple life. I simply enjoy giving more than receiving in every respect, do not take myself nor the doings of the masses seriously, am not ashamed of my weaknesses and vices, and naturally take things as they come with equanimity and humour. Many people are like this, and I really cannot understand why I have been made into a kind of idol. I suppose it is just as incomprehensible as why an avalanche should be triggered off by *one particular* particle of dust, and why it should take a certain course.

Kind regards and wishes
Yours
A. E.

Einstein explains the failure of his efforts to obtain an invitation to his institute for me, by claiming that he was regarded as a kind of petrified object. I am sure that I, too, was regarded as the fossilised relic of a bygone epoch. Two fossils at the same time were too much for the up-to-date gentlemen at the institute.

95

The Institute for Advanced Study
Princeton
New Jersey
8 January, 1950

Dear Born

The mischief in the press about my latest paper is very annoying. I have no copies of the manuscript, which is to be reprinted in the course of the next few weeks as an appendix to my booklet, *Meaning of Relativity*.[40] I will send you an offprint.

Meanwhile, my warmest greetings to you, as one of my favourite antipodes.

from Your
A. Einstein

At that time the American papers, and consequently many European ones as well, made much of a statement Einstein had made in one of his papers to the effect that the unified field theory expounded in it was, in his opinion, satisfying and probably conclusive.

I received a newspaper cutting on a postcard, dated 12th January 1950, which, together with some unintelligible 'elucidations' (in English), contains the four basic equations:

$$g_{ik} = 0; \quad \Gamma = 0; \quad R_{lk} = 0; \quad g^{is}_{,s} = 0$$

This is a typical example of the Einstein-idolatry, which he rejected at the conclusion of his previous letter with words little short of desperation.

96

Dpt. of Mathematical Physics
(Applied Mathematics)
The University
Drummond St.
Edinburgh 8
3 September, 1950

Dear Einstein

The periodical *Nature* has sent me your book *Out of my later years* to review. I was not going to write to you until I had finished reading it. But I would like to tell you straight away how much I enjoy reading those beautifully lucid and concise articles. Hedi was wondering whether they exist in a German edition; she thinks it most likely that you wrote them originally in German, and that no translation could possibly do justice to your characteristic style. I have just read the 'open letters' between you and four Russians. One wonders whether these four gentlemen are now beginning to see that you are right that international anarchy is bound to lead to a terrible catastrophe, beside which all conflicts about social and economic issues appear trivial by comparison. But most likely they are so entirely cut off from everything non-Russian that they can form no independent opinion. I am acquainted with the state of mind of committed Communists from examples in this country. A local doctor is one of them. He is a very good doctor, good-natured and willing to help, and would not hurt a fly; but he is apt to remark glibly that no sacrifice is too great in order to achieve the realisation of Marxist ideals, not even the destruction of millions of human lives. To him everything printed in our newspapers, including the *Manchester Guardian*, is American propaganda, while his Communist rag, the *Daily Worker*, proclaims absolute truth. It is useless to argue with such people. It is unfortunate, however, that they are right in so many things: for example, that America, with us in tow, always supports governments in Asia which are reactionary and corrupt, bombs civilian populations, and never does any of the things which the economically backward countries themselves need and desire. The world is enough to make one despair. But it is possible that we are experiencing the crisis of the illness, and that recovery will follow. Churchill said in one of his last cautionary speeches: 'It is a miracle that the enormous Red Army has not yet overrun the whole of Europe, in spite of the atom bomb'. I think that maybe it is not a 'miracle' at all. It looks to me as if the Russians really do not want a major war; their peace overtures are not pure humbug. I have the feeling that neither the Russians nor the Americans can go on ir-ritating each other much longer, without the Europeans getting tired of it and going their own way. No one here wants to fight for Chiang Kai-Shek. I would very much like to hear your comments on world events.

I have also read the articles on physics in your book and enjoyed them very much, apart from our well-known difference of opinion on the subject of quantum mechanics. I have defined my position in regard to the argument of 'the incomplete description' in an article which I am going to send to you. In it I have the audacity to refer to you by claiming that this incompleteness is sometimes necessary, as, for example in the case of the theory of relativity.

Hedi and I spent three weeks in England, first in a small town called Lewes from where we paid a visit to Glyndebourne, and were allowed to see a rehearsal of *Figaro*. Then we went to Guernsey, one of the Channel Islands, where the weather was warm and southerly. Now we are back in cold Scotland once more, but enjoy the warming Festival of Music and Drama. We saw here the finished performance of *Figaro* given by the Glyndebourne Opera, and various other things. Our son Gustav married, in July, a Catholic girl from the Highlands. Hedi, by her tact and intelligence, managed to iron out various difficulties with her strictly orthodox and snobbish parents. My son-in-law, Maurice Pryce, will arrive in Princeton in October with his entire family, except for one son, and I hope you will get to know him and my daughter Gritli.

I am at present working on the completion of a book I began a year ago on the quantum mechanics of crystal lattices, together with a Chinese collaborator. The subject matter is completely beyond me by now, and I am glad if I can understand any of what young Kun Huang writes in both our names. But most of the ideas in it date back to my younger years. I see from the newspapers that Blackett has once again announced the discovery of several new short-lived mesons to the British Association in Birmingham. There is a paper of mine in the issue of *Rev. of Modern Physics* dedicated to you, where I make the existence of masses of short-lived particles of this sort seem plausible. The details of these calculations are probably wrong but the principle seems to have proved itself.

Hedi sends her kindest regards to you and Margot. Once more, many thanks for the book.

Yours
Max Born

4 September, 1950

Before I send this letter off, I want to add two comments. One of them concerns a paragraph in your book, where you explain the responsibility of the whole German people for the monstrous crimes of the Nazis. I did share your opinion, but have now come to another conclusion. I think that in a higher sense responsibility *en masse* does not exist, but only that of individuals. I have met a sufficient number of decent Germans, only a few perhaps, but nevertheless genuinely decent. I assume that you, too, may have modified your wartime views to some extent.

The other remark concerns your interpretation of the ψ-function; it seems to me that it completely agrees with what I have been thinking all along, and what most reasonable physicists are thinking today. To say that ψ describes the 'state' of one single system is just a figure of speech, just as one might say in everyday life: 'My life expectation (at 67) is 4.3 years'. This, too, is a statement about one single system, but does not make sense empirically. For what is really meant is, of course, that you take all individuals of 67 and count the percentage of those who live for a certain length of time. This has always been my own concept of how to interpret $|\psi|^2$. Instead you propose a system of a large number of identical individuals – a statistical total. It seems to me that the difference is not essential, but merely a matter of language. Or have I misunderstood you, do you mean something much more fundamental? If we were able to reach agreement on this point, there would seem to me also some hope of our reaching agreement on the question of 'incompleteness' as well. But more of this later.

    M. B.

Since this was written, there have been so many crises that it is hardly likely that anyone will remember the one of 1950. The state of the world is still just as 'desperate'. Perhaps the difficulty in communicating with Communists has been somewhat reduced. I still believe now, as I did then, that the Russians do not intend to overrun Europe without extreme provocation.
I had begun the book on crystals at the outbreak of war, in order to build up the theory of crystal lattices systematically on a quantum-mechanical

basis. But the task proved beyond my strength; I had to put the manuscript aside. Later I gave it to one of my talented Chinese collaborators, Dr Kun Huang, to read, and he declared himself willing to help me with its completion. As it happened, it was he who bore the main burden of the work, as described in my letter. It was only in the final stages that this once more fell to my lot. He was an enthusiastic Communist and, when the news of Mao Tse-Tung's victory over Chiang Kai-Shek was received, he wanted to take part in whatever happened, and he returned to China with his (English) wife, taking the last, still unfinished chapters of the book with him. After many exhortations he eventually returned it to me. I then had to get the large manuscript ready, check all the calculations, and read the proofs, etc., all by myself, which was not easy for me at the age of 70. The book, *Dynamical Theory of Crystal Lattices*,[42] is widely known and is fulfilling its purpose.

The news of the existence of many short-lived particles pleased me, as our reciprocity theory had predicted something of this kind. Today this theory seems also to contribute to their classification and to an understanding of their properties.

The postscript contains first of all an observation about the reponsibility of the masses. Einstein's reply to this is in the next letter. Then follows an attempt to put an end to the difference of opinion between us about the interpretation of quantum mechanics, by saying that it was due to an inaccurate, abbreviated expression. But this observation misses Einstein's most essential point, as the following letter clearly shows.

97

15 September, 1950

Dear Born

I am sorry that you have been bothered with my series of articles. Nothing they contain can lay any claim to originality; they are only jottings which I wrote, not because I wanted to, but in answer to certain demands made on me.

People such as your Bolshevik doctor come by their fantastic attitude as a result of their objection to the harshness, injustice and absurdity of our own social order (escape from reality). If he happened to be living in Russia, no doubt he would be a rebel there as well, only in that case he would take care not to tell you about it. Nevertheless it seems to me that our own people here make an even worse job of their foreign policy than the Russians. And the idiotic public can be talked into any-thing. And they really are very shortsighted, for technological superiority is transitory, and if it comes to an all-out conflict, the decisive factor is sheer numerical superiority.

There is nothing analogous in relativity to what I call incompleteness of description in the quantum theory. Briefly it is because the ψ-function is incapable of describing certain qualities of an individual system, whose 'reality' we none of us doubt (such as a macroscopic parameter).

Take a (macroscopic) body which can rotate freely about an axis. Its state is fully determined by an angle. Let the initial conditions (angle and angular momentum) be defined as pre-cisely as the quantum theory allows. The Schroedinger equation then gives the ψ-function for any subsequent time interval. If this is sufficiently large, all angles become (in practice) equally probable. But if an observation is made (e.g. by flashing a torch), a definite angle is found (with sufficient accuracy). This does not prove that the angle had a definite value before it was observed – but we believe this to be the case, because we are committed to the requirements of reality on the macroscopic scale. Thus, the ψ-function does not express the real state of affairs perfectly in this case. This is what I call 'incomplete description'.

So far, you may not object. But you will probably take the position that a complete description would be useless because there is no mathematical relationship for such a case. I do not say that I am able to disprove this view. But my instinct tells me that a complete formulation of the relationships is tied up with complete description of its factual state. I am convinced of this although, up to now, *success* is against it. I also believe that the current formulation is true in the same sense as e.g. thermo-dynamics, i.e. as far as the concepts used are adequate. I do not expect to convince you, or anybody else – I just want you to understand the way I think.

I see from the last paragraph of your letter that you, too, take the quantum theoretical description as incomplete (referring to an ensemble). But you are after all convinced that no (complete) laws exist for a complete description, according to the posi-tivistic maxim *esse est percipi*. Well, this is a programmatic attitude, not knowledge. This is where our attitudes really differ. For the time being, I am alone in my views – as Leibniz was with respect to the absolute space of Newton's theory.

There now, I've paraded my old hobby-horse once again. But it is your own fault, because you provoked me. I am glad to hear that your children are going to visit our dovecote. I have not changed my attitude to the Germans, which, by the way, dates not just from the Nazi period. All human beings are more or less the same from birth. The Germans, however, have a far more dangerous tradition than any of the other so-called civilized nations. The present behaviour of these other nations towards the Germans merely proves to me how little human beings learn even from their most painful experiences.

Kind regards
Yours
A.E.

This is probably the clearest presentation of Einstein's philosophy of reality. The last but one paragraph is particularly revealing. He calls my way of describing the physical world 'incomplete'; in his eyes this is a flaw which he hopes to see removed, while I am prepared to put up with it. I have in fact always regarded it as a step forward, because an exact description of the state of a physical system presupposes that one can make statements of infinite precision about it, and this seems absurd to me. It seems to me that I have followed Einstein's own way of thinking in accordance with his theory of relativity, which recognises the impossibility of locating any point in time and space absolutely, and therefore concludes that the concept of absolute place and time determination does not make sense. This is at the base of the whole of his mighty edifice. But he did not want to acknowledge the analogy of the situation in the quantum theory.

98

4 May, 1952

Dear Einstein

As you can imagine, the death of Ladenburg grieves me very much. He was my oldest and, until fate cast us into different countries, my closest friend, with whom I have corresponded all the time. Since we came to Scotland I have only seen him once briefly in London. Else Ladenburg wrote that you had spoken very movingly at the cremation ceremony. It is very painful to me that I was unable to be present. I hope that Else is materially well provided for. Perhaps you could give me some information about this some time.

A few days ago more sad news reached me—of Kramer's passing. He had of course been ill for a long time, and was not as strong and robust a man as Ladenburg. With him, too, I was on terms of close, though not quite as intimate, friendship. The last time I saw him was three years ago during a congress in Florence, when he was not at all well, and spent most of his time in bed. I had hoped to meet him in June at a conference on thermodynamics. So we old fellows become more and more lonely, and I am writing to you in order to keep intact the few remaining links with our contemporaries which still exist. Hedi and I have come throught the winter rather well. It is already the second time that we have spent the Christmas holidays in the Bavarian Alps (Oberstdorf), and the sun, snow, good food and Bavarian beer have worked like a fountain of youth. We intend to return there again next summer. My pension in Germany has been restored to me (as Professor Emeritus), and so I can afford these holidays. While there, we live entirely for ourselves, and only see close friends and simple people, such as maids, waitresses, peasants, who, there as elsewhere, are still pleasant and unspoilt.

I am engaged in completing two books, one with my Chinese collaborator, Dr Huang Kun, on crystal theory, and one about optics with a Czech, Dr E. Wolf. The American 'Custodian of Alien Property', who appropriated my German book on optics without paying any compensation, has actually demanded that we should apply for a licence for the *new* book (which is going to be much larger and more up-to-date). But the British government has taken up my case, and my publisher, Dr Rosbaud, whom you may remember, now hopes to fight it out with their assistance.

Freundlich was here yesterday and gave us a very lucid lecture about the state of light-deflection by the sun. It really looks as if your formula is not quite correct. It looks even worse in the case of the red shift; this is much smaller than the theoretical values towards the centre of the sun's disk, and much larger at the edge. What could be the matter here? Could it be

a hint of non-linearity? (The scattering of light by light?)
Have you done anything about this problem? Schroedinger is
pursuing these ideas – I have given them up.

 Hedi sends her best wishes; also to Margot.

  In old friendship
   Yours
    Max Born

Since those days when I lamented the death of two dear friends, thirteen
more years have gone by. In the meantime many more have died, including Einstein himself. Working on this correspondence helps me to
combat increasing loneliness.

The new book on optics was written at the instigation of the principal
of the University of Edinburgh, Professor Edward Appleton, himself a
physicist who had made a great name for himself by investigating the
upper layers of the atmosphere with the help of radio beams. He received
the Nobel Prize for this work. He told me that my old optics book of 1933
was being reprinted photomechanically in the United States and had sold
widely during the war because it contained material important to the war
effort – the spreading of radar waves along the earth's surface, for example.
I was unable to accept his suggestion that I should have the book translated into English, because it seemed to me to be out of date. So I decided
to write a new book in English, based on the old one, and I succeeded
in finding an excellent collaborator in Dr E. Wolf, now (1965) Professor
in Rochester, N.Y., U.S.A. This book, *Principles of Optics*,[43] was very
successful; the first edition of 8000 copies was sold out within a year, and
the third is now in preparation. The negotiations with the Custodian
of Alien Property in Washington had to be continued for several more
years. I had, after all, become a British citizen at the beginning of the war,
and I alone owned the copyright. The confiscation of the book was therefore completely unjustified. But several more years went by before I
received justice and compensation.

The astronomer Freundlich tried right from the start to obtain proof of
Einstein's theory of gravitation with the help of astronomical observations;
he first worked at the Einstein Tower telescope in Potsdam, and later,
after his enforced emigration in 1933, at St Andrews, a small university
not far from Edinburgh. At that time (1952) it did not really seem that the
predictions of the theory about the bending of light by the sun, and about
the red shift of the spectral lines, were correct. More recent observations,
however, have eliminated these difficulties. But this is not the place to
enlarge on them. A brief report can be found in the latest edition of my
book *Die Relativitätstheorie Einsteins*.[10]

99

12 May, 1952

Dear Born

First of all I must express my admiration for your wife's poems. Most of them are among the most beautiful I have ever come across. My compliments! You are right. One feels as if one were an Ichthyosaurus, left behind by accident. Most of our dear friends, but thank God also some of the less dear, are already gone. Ladenburg was taken very suddenly – apparently by a virus infection of the internal organs. He was a good man who did not take things lightly. During the last few years he even avoided reading the newspapers because he could not bear all the hypocrisy and mendacity any longer. Over there with you things seem on the whole to be cleaner and less wild.

It really is sweet of the Germans to pay you a pension which you can convert on the spot into sausages and beer. The victory over the cunning publisher is also rather gratifying. The generalisation of gravitation is now, at last, completely convincing and unequivocal formally unless the good Lord has chosen a totally different way of which one can have no conception. The proof of the theory is unfortunately far too difficult for me. Man is, after all, only a poor wretch. Freundlich, however, does not move me in the slightest. Even if the deflection of light, the perihelial movement or line shift were unknown, the gravitation equations would still be convincing because they avoid the inertial system (the phantom which affects everything but is not itself affected). It is really rather strange that human beings are normally deaf to the strongest arguments while they are always inclined to overestimate measuring accuracies.

Have you noticed that Bohm believes (as de Broglie did, by the way, 25 years ago) that he is able to interpret the quantum theory in deterministic terms? That way seems too cheap to me. But you, of course, can judge this better than I.

Kindest regards to you both

Yours

A. Einstein

My report on Freundlich's doubts about the astronomical confirmation of the theory of relativity left Einstein quite cold. He considered the logical foundations of his theory of gravitation to be unshakeable. The latest observations have proved him right.

It is curious that he does not acknowledge the analogy with quantum mechanics. He condemns the term 'inertial system' as a 'phantom' which affects everything but is not affected by anything. This must surely mean: as a hypothesis, produced *ad hoc* and uncheckable. But he would not admit that processes in the atomic world can be described by means of things which can be fixed in time and space, which are sturdy and real according to the standards of the everyday world, and which obey deterministic laws. The remark he makes about David Bohm's theory is connected with this. Although this theory was quite in line with his own ideas, to interpret the quantum mechanical formulae in a simple, deterministic way seemed to him to be 'too cheap'. Today one hardly ever hears about this attempt of Bohm's, or similar ones by de Broglie.

100

29 May, 1952

Dear friend Albert Einstein

This is just a little thank-you for your dear, kind words about my poems; after all, their sole significance and purpose is to give a little pleasure to someone. How happy I would be if I could see you and Margot again; but I'm afraid that wish will never be fulfilled, for if we old folks travel it is either to visit children and eight grand-children or to the tranquillity of mountains, meadows and forests. In Germany we live mostly very much by ourselves, but have several times invited children and children-in-law. And I have formed many connections with German Quakers. I also have my brother and his family still living in Germany, as well as two old aunts almost ninety years old and many cousins of both sexes. There are now 500 German Quakers; last July I took part in their annual meeting held in Bad Pyrmont, a really beautiful experience. This year Max is coming with me, provided he gets 'permission', to attend some of the sessions, but apart from that will just be 'holiday-making'. The German Quakers still address each other with '*Du*' while the English and American ones have abandoned 'Thou'.

Germany is and will remain a cause for concern. I, at least, have not torn up my roots so completely that I no longer feel 'responsible'. In some ways, surely, everyone shares the responsibility for everything. There can be no true 'world-citizenship' until everybody becomes very much more aware of this. The German Quakers fully realise this. It is, of course, the most decent of the Germans who are most profoundly conscious of German guilt. And there are many circles and classes of people working for reconstruction from the inside. Seen from outside, it is always the loud-mouthed and brutal which attract attention. By sinking one's roots into new ground one has, of course, grown away from it all in many essential respects, but one feels all the more responsible. It is a pity that one is so old and has insufficient energy for anything but a very modest effort.

By the way, Max is reading aloud to me from a very delightful book just now: the biography of Adolf v. Harnack, written by his daughter Agnes Zahn-Harnack. Do you know it? Harnack was undoubtedly a fine, energetic and upright man.

I hope that you and Margot are in good health. Old age is not so bad really, provided one does not have too many twinges. What have you got against being an Ichthyosaurus? They were, after all, rather vigorous little beasts, probably able to look back on the experiences of a very long lifetime.

In any case, we two old ones will go on thinking of you and Margot with unchanging loyalty, even if we should never be able to meet again.

> With all my heart
> I remain
> Your old *Hedi*

101

28 October, 1952

Dear Einstein

A few days ago I received a book by Dr Carl Seelig about you and Switzerland. As I happened to be in bed with a cold, I had time to read it right through, and liked it very much. Dr Seelig had written to ask me for a contribution to the book, and when he had assured me that you had agreed I copied some characteristic sentences from your letter, which he has now printed. I do hope that it is really all right by you. I have written to him to draw his attention to several inaccuracies (for example, he credited me with honours I do not have, and calls Wertheimer Paul instead of Max, etc.). The book took me back to old times and rekindled the desire to see you again. I met Courant in Göttingen this summer; he would very much like to invite me to New York, but I am afraid that will not be possible – for as I was born in Breslau, on the far side of the Iron Curtain, I am excluded from the U.S.A. by your 'McCarthy Act'.

I would like to know what you think of contemporary politics, particularly American. Seen from here, it all seems horrible – British politics included (for example, the Mau Mau uprising in Kenya). And then on the other side, the trial of tried and trusted Communists in Prague, with its strong anti-semitic overtomes; I am being bombarded with propaganda from China, wildly anti-American. My sensible Chinese collaborators, dear, fine fellows that they are, seem from their letters to have gone crazy politically since they returned to China. What a lovely, promising world! As I have eight grand-children, it matters to me; it could be a matter of indifference to you, were it not for your kind heart.

Next week I am due to hold a series of lectures at the University of London. Schroedinger was supposed to come for a public discussion that week. He dislikes the statistical concept of quantum mechanics, just as you do, but believes that his waves constitute the final deterministic solution. It is not quite as simple as that, however, and I'm afraid I would have been very hard on him had this discussion taken place. But unfortunately he had to undergo a serious operation for a perforated appendix, was in great danger, and is not strong enough to travel to London. Instead, there is now going to be a discussion with several philosophers, which promises to be a somewhat wishy-washy adventure. Afterwards we are going to celebrate my 70th birthday in Cambridge with the children and grand-children.

Hedi and I are going to spend our holidays in Oberstdorf again. Life in Germany is very pleasant after the austerity in this country (for those who have some money – I receive my pension). Nice, fine, good people exist there, too; most of them have suffered terribly during the Hitler period. I will have to retire from my academic chair in another 9 months' time, and then we are going to live for six months in Germany and six months here, for financial reasons. I want to finish two books before then. One of them, about crystals (with my Chinese collaborator), has just gone off to the Oxford University Press. The other one, about optics, is going to be ready in a year's time. Maybe it is silly to put so much work into these things. But for the bigger problems I am too old and too stupid. By the way, it causes me some amusement that Heisenberg has taken up my old idea of non-linear electrodynamics, and has applied it, *mutatis mutandis*, to meson fields.

Let me know from time to time what you are doing and how you are.

With kindest regards, also from Hedi
Yours
Max Born

The discussion with philosophers in London did in fact take place, and in Schroedinger's absence turned out to be wishy-washy as I had predicted. The discussions have been published in E. Schroedinger's 'Are there Quantum Jumps?'[44] and my own 'The Interpretation of Quantum Mechanics'.[45]

Schroedinger was, to say the least, as stubborn as Einstein in his conservative attitude towards quantum mechanics; indeed, he not only rejected the statistical interpretation but insisted that his wave mechanics meant a return to a classical way of thinking. He would not accept any objection to it, not even the most weighty one, which is that a wave in $3n$-dimensional space, such as is needed to describe the n particles, is not a classical concept and cannot be visualised.

Heisenberg's non-linear theory was intended to serve not only for meson fields but for all elementary particles. Today it is the centre of a great deal of interest.

102

84 Grange Loan
Edinburgh
26 September, 1953

Dear Einstein
  Very often I feel the need to write to you, but I usually suppress
it to spare you the trouble of replying. Today, though, I have
a definite reason – that Whittaker, the old mathematician,
who lives here as Professor Emeritus and is a good friend of
mine, has written a new edition of his old book *History of the
Theory of the Ether*, of which the second volume has already
been published. Among other things it contains a history of
the theory of relativity which is peculiar in that Lorentz and
Poincaré are credited with its discovery while your papers
are treated as less important. Although the book originated in
Edinburgh, I am not really afraid you will think that I could
be behind it. As a matter of fact I have done everything I could
during the last three years to dissuade Whittaker from carrying
out his plan, which he had already cherished for a long time
and loved to talk about. I re-read the originals of some of the
old papers, particularly some rather off-beat ones by Poincaré,
and have given Whittaker translations of German papers (for
example, I translated many pages of Pauli's Encyclopaedia
article into English with the help of my lecturer, Dr Schlapp,
in order to make it easier for Whittaker to form an opinion).
But all in vain. He insisted that everything of importance had
already been said by Poincaré, and that Lorentz quite plainly
had the physical interpretation. As it happens, I know quite
well how sceptical Lorentz was and how long it took him to
become a relativist. I have told Whittaker all this, but without success. I am annoyed about this, for he is considered a
great authority in the English speaking countries and many
people are going to believe him. It is particularly unpleasant in
my opinion that he has woven all sorts of personal information
into his account of quantum mechanics and that my part in it is
extolled. Many people may now think (even if you do not)
that I played rather an ugly role in this business. After all,
it is common knowledge that you and I do not see eye to
eye over the question of determinism. What is more, I have
written a small article which is shortly to appear in which I

give a theoretical interpretation of an idea of Freundlich's about stellar red shift, which could, if correct, cause difficulties for the relativistic interpretation. Therefore my feeling towards you is that of a cheeky urchin who can get away with certain liberties without offending you, But it may well seem less harmless to other people. Well, I had to write this and get it off my chest.

Hedi and I have just returned from Germany. We have been in Göttingen, attending the town's thousandth anniversary, when Nohl, Franck, Courant and I were given the freedom of the city. It was a harmonious celebration. Franck and Courant will be able to tell you about it. Afterwards we went to Bad Pyrmont, where we are building a small house where we can settle down and spend our old age. I am about to retire from my academic post. Life in Germany is quite pleasant again; the people have been thoroughly shaken up and anyway there are many fine, good people. We have no choice, as I receive a pension in Germany but not here. Hedi sends kindest regards to you and Margot.

In old friendship
Max Born

Sir Edmund Whittaker's book is a brilliant and historic philosophical work which I found extremely useful in my early years. During my time in Edinburgh we had become very close friends. It grieved me all the more that he should dispute Einstein's merits in the special theory of relativity. As far as Lorentz is concerned my account is, if anything, too kind; he probably never became a relativist at all, and only paid lip service to Einstein at times in order to avoid argument.

The celebration in Göttingen caused us quite a headache to begin with. Franck at first did not want to accept the invitation under any circumstances. Courant and I were in two minds; when we eventually decided to go, plain curiosity played a certain part in our decision, and Franck eventually joined us. Our choice of Bad Pyrmont as the place where we would spend our old age was really due to sentimental memories. During our engagement my fiancée's parents in Leipzig had sent her, together with two of her girl friends, to Bad Pyrmont for the sake of her health. At that time it was known specifically as a spa for women, renowned for the treatment of anaemia and so on. I was then a private lecturer in Göttingen and travelled every weekend by train to Pyrmont. There we spent some delightful days together, which we liked to remember later on. When we decided to return to Germany in 1953 we looked around for a quiet and beautiful place in the Black Forest and elsewhere. Finally we remembered the period of our engagement that we spent in Bad Pyrmont. We stayed there for a few weeks of our summer holidays and, as we liked it, searched for and found a plot on which to build our small house.

103

12 October, 1953

Dear Born

Don't lose any sleep over your friend's book. Everybody does what he considers right or, in deterministic terms, what he has to do. If he manages to convince others, that is their own affair. I myself have certainly found satisfaction in my efforts, but I would not consider it sensible to defend the results of my work as being my own 'property', as some old miser might defend the few coppers he had laboriously scraped together. I do not hold anything against him, nor of course against you. After all, I do not need to read the thing.

If anyone can be held responsible for the fact that you are migrating back to the land of the mass-murderers of our kinsmen, it is certainly your adopted fatherland – universally notorious for its parsimony. But then we know only too well that the collective conscience is a miserable little plant which is always most likely to wither just when it is needed most.

For the presentation volume to be dedicated to you, I have written a little nursery song about physics, which has startled Bohm and de Broglie a little. It is meant to demonstrate the indispensability of your statistical interpretation of quantum mechanics, which Schroedinger, too, has recently tried to avoid. Perhaps it will give you some amusement. After all, it seems to be our lot to be answerable for the soap bubbles we blow. This may well have been so contrived by that same 'non-dice-playing God' who has caused so much bitter resentment against me, not only amongst the quantum theoreticians but also among the faithful of the Church of the Atheists.

Best regards, also to your wife
Yours
A. Einstein

Einstein's reaction to my complaint about Whittaker's account of the theory of relativity proves his utter indifference to fame and glory.

Then follows the harsh expression 'land of mass-murderers'. This was his opinion, and he never deviated from it. He was never able to understand why I returned to Germany, and never approved of it.

It may thus be appropriate to say something about it here. During the war and for some time afterwards, particularly when the atrocities of Auschwitz, Buchenwald and Belsen became known, we were of the same opinion. But when we began to re-establish connections with our relatives and friends in Germany the matter took on a different aspect. Many of them had undergone terrible experiences and sufferings. My wife tried to help as much as the scarcity in Great Britain permitted.

My post in Edinburgh came to an end in 1953. The fact that I could not look forward to an adequate provision in my old age was not, as Einstein thought, due to 'Scottish parsimony'; all over England, as well as Scotland, there are no pensions for professors. There are only contributory insurance schemes whose yield depends on the length of one's service, which in my case had been too short. My income would have been less than that of an unskilled labourer. Another factor which influenced us was the tough Scottish climate, which for anyone not brought up there is hard to bear.

During this time (1947) I was offered the directorship of the Dublin Institute of Advanced Studies as successor to Schroedinger, who had been recalled to Vienna, his native town. I declined after lengthy negotiations, because I did not feel confident that my strength was equal to taking on a new task; besides, after five years in office I would still have reached retirement age and would have faced the same problem once again. In the meantime I had been reinstated in Göttingen as Professor Emeritus on full salary. Quite some time went by before it was decided to allow this to be paid in foreign countries.

The first sortie into Germany was to be made by my wife. She had been invited to Göttingen by the philosopher Herman Nohl to give a talk there on British democracy as we had experienced it. But she was prevented from making the journey, which would have been subsidised by the Foreign Office in London, because on her arrival at King's Cross station in London all her luggage was stolen.

In 1948 I was awarded the Max Planck medal of the Deutsche Physikalische Gesellschaft (German Physical Society). This had been founded at Max von Laue's and my instigation a short time before we emigrated. The annual general meeting of the society was held in September 1948 in Clausthal-Zellerfeld. We took part and were given a friendly reception, but we were at that time still regarded as visitors from England, watched over and taken care of by the occupying power.

The impression made on us by the Harz mountains, and the small towns such as Goslar which had not been destroyed, was deep and moving. In the following few years we spent our summer holidays in Oberstdorf in the Allgäu.

In 1953 the town of Göttingen celebrated its thousandth anniversary. Franck, Courant and I were among those who were to be given the freedom of the city on this occasion. Franck wanted to turn it down at first, but after a lengthy correspondence we decided not to reject this gesture of reconciliation. The celebrations took place with due solemnity and friendliness, and even the sceptical Franck found no reason to complain. He paid frequent visits to Göttingen later on, and it was during one of these that he died (in 1964).

After these experiences we decided to settle down in Germany. In choosing Bad Pyrmont we took into account its beautiful situation surrounded by wooded hills, the fact that as a watering place it was quiet and well cared for, the close proximity of Göttingen and, most important of all, the Quaker house, the headquarters of the Religious Society of Friends in Germany. My wife had joined this society in Edinburgh, and she had my full sympathy in this respect. The Quakers' creed had been one of strictest pacifism for many centuries, and because of this they had suffered greatly under the Nazi régime. We were certain not to find any mass-murderers amongst them. We wanted to live the quiet life, indoors with books and music, out-of-doors in the garden, the Spa's park and in the forests. But it turned out rather differently, because in the year we moved to our new home (1954) I was awarded the Nobel Prize. In this way my name became known all over Germany, and my voice was listened to. This resulted in a new task for the rest of my life.

Many of my German colleagues shared my anxiety about the future of mankind, because of the atomic bomb. Foremost among these were Otto Hahn, the discoverer of atomic fission, Max von Laue, C. F. von Weizsäcker and Walter Gerlach. They succeeded in bringing about the well-known 'Declaration of the Eighteen from Göttingen', which was directed against the atomic re-armament of the Federal Republic. My name appears on the document, and I had some part in its accomplishment, if not in its formulation. I felt it to be my duty to continue the task of enlightenment about the dangers of nuclear war and other technical developments, and the fight against war and militarism. I tried to do this by means of lectures, radio talks, television discussions and books. There would not have been any point in doing this in England. The British people are politically mature, and need no advice from an immigrant. The Germans however, have destroyed their national tradition by two lost wars, and the misdeeds of a criminal government. Here there was the chance of making one's influence felt. I regarded this work as my duty, but it also gave me pleasure. But today (at the end of

1965) it seems more than doubtful to me whether it has had any success. The unteachable are in the ascendancy again.

The matter of the presentation volume was as follows. On my retirement from my chair in Edinburgh the university organised a small celebration, where a presentation volume was handed over to me: 'Scientific Papers, presented to Max Born on his retirement from the Tait Chair of Natural Philosophy in the University of Edinburgh'.[45] It contains papers by friends and former pupils of mine. Among these, however, were not only adherents of my statistical interpretation of quantum mechanics, but also four outspoken opponents. The first of these was Schroedinger, although he dealt with a different theme. Our differences had already been thrashed out in the papers from the *British Journal for the Philosophy of Science* that I mentioned in my commentary to letter 101. Contributions also came from de Broglie, David Bohm and Einstein, which dealt with the interpretation of quantum mechanics. As these questions play quite an important role in the correspondence with Einstein which follows, I should like to enlarge upon them here so that I can deal briefly with them thereafter.

Schroedinger's point of view is the simplest; he thought that by his development of de Broglie's wave mechanics the whole paradoxical problem of the quanta had been settled: there are no particles, no 'quantum jumps' – there are only waves with their well-known vibrations, characterised by integral numbers. The particles are narrow wave-packets. The objection to this is that one generally (i.e. for processes which are classically described with the help of several particles) needs waves in spaces of many dimensions, which are something entirely different from the waves of classical physics, and impossible to visualise; that wave packets representing solutions of the Schroedinger equations do not propagate without change of shape, but disperse; and other similar objections. Schroedinger's point of view has, I think, definitely been abandoned today.

De Broglie, the creator of wave mechanics, and Bohm accepted the results of quantum mechanics just as Schroedinger did, but not the statistical interpretation. They tried to develop ideas in which the deterministic character of the elementary processes were preserved, assuming that concealed mechanisms exist which were hidden by the waves, or suggesting that the formulae should be re-written so that they looked like deterministic mechanical laws. These attempts did not get far; it seems to me that today (1965) they have virtually disappeared. Even Einstein considered this point of view 'too cheap' (letter 99).

His ideas were more radical, but 'music of the future'. He saw in the quantum mechanics of today a useful intermediate stage between the traditional classical physics and a still completely unknown 'physics of the future' based on general relativity, in which – and this he regarded as indispensable for philosophical reasons – the traditional concepts of physical reality and determinism come into their own again. Thus he regarded statistical quantum mechanics to be not wrong but 'incomplete'. His reasons were essentially philosophical and therefore difficult to shake, least of all by purely physical arguments. Nevertheless I tried to answer him, and thus a sharp but always friendly dispute arose, which is expressed in the following letters.

At the end of his letter, Einstein talks about the effect of his phrase, the 'non-dice-playing God', and uses the expression so typical of him, 'Church of the Atheists'. He had no belief in the church, but did not think that religious faith was a sign of stupidity, nor unbelief a sign of intelligence; he knew, as did Socrates, that we know nothing. One should tell this to the Communists when they claim that he shared their beliefs.

104

Department of Mathematical Physics
(Applied Mathematics)
The University
Drummond Street
Edinburgh 8
8 November, 1953

Dear Einstein

Your kind letter of 12.10.53 has reassured me that old Whittaker's peculiar pranks do not trouble you particularly. You say that it is unreasonable to behave like some old miser in defence of his property, who tries to hold on to the few pence he has managed to scrape together. I agree with you wholeheartedly, and I too have tried to keep my mouth shut whenever my own few coppers have disappeared into other people's pockets. But I have sinned against this good doctrine a little lately. I am sending you several of my papers on general themes, including my Guthrie lecture (given to the Physical Society, London), in which I have explained my contribution to quantum mechanics with as much modesty as I was able to muster, not only with regard to the statistical interpretation but also to the theory itself. That Heisenberg's matrices bear his name is not altogether justified, as in those days he actually had no idea what a matrix was. It was he who reaped all the rewards of our work together, such as the Nobel Prize and that sort of thing. I do not begrudge it him in the least, but for the last twenty years I have not been able to rid myself of a certain sense of injustice. Purely practical matters are involved, such as the return to Germany, for example, which you clearly regard with a certain amount of suspicion. You are wrong in casting aspersions on my dear Scots; the inadequate provision for the old age of teachers and professors is quite general all over Britain, and is just as wretched in Oxford and Cambridge. If anyone is to blame it is the Swedes, who could quite well have found out about my contribution to quantum mechanics. But that happened in the year of Heil-Hitler, 1933. Now they have realised it, apparently, for six months ago they made me a member of their academy. Though this does not help me with my practical problems such as the choice of a place to live. But to be quite honest, I must admit that I would probably return to Germany even if I had the chance to remain here. Hedi is still homesick for the Weser mountains and I, too, love the beautiful countryside around Pyrmont, where we are building a small house (which will have central heating, of course, which does not exist here, because the Scots are such hardy fellows that they do not worry about chilblains and arthritis). As for the people, I only want to tell you that the German Quakers have their headquarters in Pyrmont. They are no 'mass-murderers', and many of our friends there suffered far worse things under the Nazis than you or I. One should be chary of applying epithets of this sort. The Americans have demonstrated in Dresden, Hiroshima and Nagasaki that in sheer speed of extermination they surpass even the Nazis.

I must wait a little longer for the presentation volume to which you have contributed. It is to be ceremoniously presented to me on November 24th. I am keenly looking forward to your treatment of the assertions by Schroedinger and Bohm. You will find my comments on them in a small package of papers which is on its way to you. After the confession of my weaknesses contained in this letter, there is no need to tell you how much pleasure I derive from being thus honoured by the most distinguished members of my profession.

Hedi is in a nursing home at the moment. She suffered a little breakdown, caused by all kinds of family worries and an excessive burden of domestic and social obligations. I am all alone in the house and am muddling through somehow. She is improving, and may well return home in a few day's time.

If she knew that I was writing to you she would want to add her kindest regards to you and Margot.

Yours

Max Born

I have nothing to add to this 'confession of my weaknesses', except to wish that its publication today, when I am almost 86 years old and have been decorated with various honours, will not be held too much against me.

I still fully subscribe today to my reply to Einstein's 'the land of mass-murderers.' One would have to have been brought up in the 'spirit of militarism' to understand the difference beiween Hiroshima and Nagasaki on the one hand, and Auschwitz and Belsen on the other. The usual reasoning is the following: the former case is one of warfare, the latter of cold-blooded slaughter. But the plain truth is that the people involved are in both instances non-participants, defenceless old people, women and children, whose annihilation is supposed to achieve some political or military objective. The first of the terrible attacks on Dresden was carried out by British bombers; the Americans came later. I mentioned the Americans in my letter as Einstein was living in America. I am certain that the human race is doomed, unless its instinctive detestation of atrocities gains the upper hand over the artificially constructed judgment of reason.

105

26 November, 1953

Dear Einstein

The presentation of the volume was made yesterday during a little celebration at the university. It gives me tremendous pleasure that so many of my old friends and colleagues have contributed to it. For the time being I have read only a few of the articles – yours was the first, of course, and you are also the first to receive my heartfelt thanks.

Your philosophical objection to the statistical interpretation of quantum mechanics is particularly cogently and clearly expressed. But even so I must take the liberty of asserting that your treatment of the example (that of a ball rebounding between two walls) does not prove what you say it does: namely, that in the limiting case of macroscopic dimensions, the wave-mechanical solution does not become the classical motion. This is due to the fact that – forgive my cheek – you have chosen an incorrect solution which is inappropriate to the problem. When it is done according to the rules, it results in a solution which, in the limiting case (mass→∞), becomes exactly the classical, deterministic motion; although it always, of course, produces statistical statements of enormous probability only for finite (large) values of the mass. If one wants to describe a sequence of events, one has to use the 'time-dependent' Schroedinger equation:

$$\frac{\hbar^2}{2m} \frac{\partial^2 \psi}{\partial x^2} - \hbar\, \mathrm{i}\, \frac{\partial \psi}{\partial t} = 0$$

where $\hbar = h/2\pi$ (Planck's constant), and $m =$ mass; and not, as you are doing, the special case, that ϕ is proportional to $\mathrm{e}^{\mathrm{i}\omega t}$ ($\hbar\omega = E$); for this is appropriate to sharply defined energy, hence an indeterminate position.

The right solution in the range $0 < x < l$ is:

$$\psi(x, t) = \sum_{n=1}^{\infty} A_n\, \mathrm{e}^{\mathrm{i}\omega_n t} \sin b_n x$$

$$\text{where } \omega_n = \frac{\hbar\, \pi^2}{2ml^2}\, n^2, \quad b_n = \frac{\pi n}{l}$$

$$\text{and } A_n = \frac{1}{l} \int_0^l \psi(x, 0) \sin \frac{\pi n}{l}\, x\, \mathrm{d}x.$$

$\psi(x, 0)$ is the arbitrary initial state. This has to be selected to express: at the time $t = 0$ the ball is close to point x_0, with the approximate velocity v. Therefore $\psi(x, 0)$ has to be zero everywhere except within the small range about point x_0, and it also has to be asymmetrical about x_0, so that the value to be

expected for the velocity $\quad\dfrac{\dfrac{h}{\mathrm{i}} \dfrac{1}{\mathrm{i}} \displaystyle\int_0^l \psi \dfrac{\partial \psi}{\partial x}\, \mathrm{d}x}{m \displaystyle\int_0^l \psi^2\, \mathrm{d}x}\quad$ has a predetermined

value. One can easily add these $\psi(x, 0)$; with three arbitrary constants, one for normalisation, one for v and one for imprecision of the range about x_0. For example:

$$\psi(x, 0) = x(l - x)(\alpha + \beta x)\, e^{-(x-x_0)^2/2a}$$

(I do not know whether this function is convenient for calculations). The result is certain to be (one can see it qualitatively without calculations) that the wave packet $\psi(x, t)$ bounces to and fro in exactly the same way as a particle, while it becomes a little more indeterminate in the process. But these imprecisions become infinitesimally small as $m \to \infty$.

I am convinced that in this sense quantum mechanics also represents the motion of macroscopic single systems according to deterministic laws. I am going to carry out a thorough calculation of it with my collaborator (which is not easy to do formally), and will send you the result. Ultimately you will certainly admit that I am right, and when that happens it will somehow have to be made known to the readers of the presentation volume.

I more or less agree with what you said about de Broglie, Bohm and Schroedinger. Incidentally, Pauli has come up with an idea (in the presentation volume for de Broglie's 50th birthday) which slays Bohm not only philosophically but physically as well.

Another letter of mine is on its way to you by ordinary mail. With sincerest thanks and kindest regards, also from Hedi,

Yours

Max Born

Every quantum theoretician would probably recognise that my objection to Einstein's example was correct. It formed the basis for my printed reply which was subsequently published, and which will be the subject of further discussion. But, as Einstein pointed out in his next letter, it misses the point of his basic philosophical thoughts.

106

Dear Born

Today I received (and read) your letter, as well as your printed material, which I intend to read thoroughly too. I was very pleased that you have taken my simple ideas seriously and did not dismiss them with a few superficial remarks like most people.

I must say first of all that your point of view surprised me. For I thought that an approximate agreement with classical mechanics was to be expected whenever the relevant de Broglie wavelengths are small in relation to the other relevant spatial measurements. I see, however, that you want to relate classical mechanics only to those ψ-functions which are narrow with respect to coordinates and momenta. But when one looks at it in this way, one could come to the conclusion that macro-mechanics cannot claim to describe, even approximately, most of the events in macro-systems that are conceivable on the quantum theory. For example, one would then be very surprised if a star, or a fly, seen for the first time, appeared even to be quasi-localised.

But should one now adopt your point of view in spite of this, one should at least demand that a system which is 'quasi-localised' at a certain time should *remain* so according to the Schroedinger equation. This is a purely mathematical problem, and you expect that the calculations would bear out this expectation. But this seems quite impossible to me. The easiest way to realise this is to consider the three-dimensional case (of a macro-body), which is represented by a 'narrow' Schroedinger-function in relation to position, velocity *and direction*. There it seems obvious, even without a mathematical 'microscope', that the position must become more and more diffuse in the course of time. The one-dimensional case is similar, as the group-velocity depends on the wavelength. I think it would be a pity to waste your assistant's time when the result can never be in doubt. But if you are not convinced, by all means have the calculations done. Oppenheimer has extricated himself by claiming that the time required by the process of getting more and more out of focus would be on a 'cosmic' scale, and that one could ignore it for that reason. But one could easily quote some quite pedestrian examples where the divergence time is not all that long. I consider it too cheap a way of calming down one's scientific conscience. All the same it is not difficult to regard the step into probabalistic quantum theory as final. One only has to assume that the ψ-function relates to an ensemble, and not to an individual case; then one can use my example to describe, with the expected approximation (statistically conclusive), what classical mechanics also describes. According to the interpretation which you support in your letter, one has to regard this circumstance as a kind of coincidence. The interpretation of the ψ-function as relating to an ensemble also eliminates the paradox that a measurement carried out in *one* part of space determines the *kind* of expectation for a measurement carried out later in *another* part of space (coupling of parts of systems far apart in space).

One can safely accept the fact that, according to this concept, the description of the single system is incomplete, if one assumes that there is no correspondingly complete law for the complete description of the single system which determines its development in time.

Then one need not become involved with Bohr's interpretation that there is no reality independent of the probable subject.

I do not believe, however, that this concept, though consistent in itself, is here to stay. But I maintain that it is the only one which does justice to the mechanism of the probabilistic quantum theory.

I am very much looking forward to reading the rest of your ideas on matters of principle. You call these thoughts 'philosophical', but unjustifiably so in my opinion. I am quite satisfied if one has the machinery for making predictions, even if we are unable to understand it clearly.

   Kindest regards
    Yours
     A. E.

This letter marks the beginning of the period of mutual misunderstanding. Even today it seems to me that Einstein's reflections resulted from his inadequate knowledge of quantum mechanics. His statement that 'approximate agreement with classical mechanics is to be expected whenever the relevant de Broglie wavelengths are small in relation to the other relevant spatial measurements' is, of course, correct. The example he used to point out the weaknesses in quantum mechanics was that of a particle which bounces to and fro between two parallel, elastic and reflecting walls. He regards the distance between the walls to be the only relevant length to be taken into account. But this is only the case when nothing else is known about the position of the particle. Einstein now wants to compare the quantum mechanical with the classical treatment of this situation, where in the latter case it is taken for granted that the initial condition is known. The situation is somewhat different in the case of the analogous quantum-mechanical treatment, because of Heisenberg's relation of indeterminacy; the point of origin and the initial velocity can only be prescribed to an accuracy which is limited by this relation. But this one can and must do if one wants to compare the quantum-mechanical with the classical treatment. It is therefore both necessary and possible to state the range within which the particle initially lies; and this constitutes a second 'relevant measurement'.

The next consideration, concerning the question of whether a particle which is 'quasi-localised' at a certain time must remain precisely localised according to the Schroedinger equation, is based on a simple misunderstanding. I never expected this to be so for a moment. The initial imprecision of the velocity brings about an imprecision which increases in the course of time. It was precisely this point which was of such importance to me from the beginning, for it is equally valid for classical mechanics, and shows that the usual assertion, that this is deterministic, only applies when one admits infinitely precise statements about the initial position and the initial velocity; and this seems to me metaphysical nonsense.

Einstein admits that one can regard the 'probabilistic' quantum theory as final if one assumes that the ψ-function relates to the ensemble and not to an individual case. This has always been my assumption as well, and I consider the frequent repetition of an experiment as the realisation of the ensemble. This coincides exactly with the actual procedure of the experimental physicists, who obtain their data in the atomic and sub-atomic area by accumulating data from similar measurements.

The last sentence of this letter is characteristic of Einstein in his old age. The 'it does not make sense' itself only makes sense when related to a definite philosophy. The same argument was used by the opponents of the young Einstein, who alleged that the consequences of the relativity theory did not make sense; as for instance that if one of two twins goes on a journey through space while the other remains at home, the first, on his return, is younger than the other.

107

Goldsborough Hotel
Hills Road
Cambridge
22 December, 1953

Dear Einstein

It was very nice of you to write to me again and to go into the details of my letter. As a matter of fact, I was very impressed by your article in my 'presentation volume', and could not rest until I had found a final answer to it. Your example needed to be calculated exactly from beginning to end at some time or other. The learned gentlemen at your institute and in other places do not concern themselves with such trivial problems But it is not at all easy, and I really had to rack my brain. Then too we started to move house at the same time, and encountered considerable difficulties with both the German and British financial authorities, and so on. In the end I finished the work here in Cambridge, in an ice-cold hotel (as they all are in this country), where one is roasted in front by the fire while one's back freezes. But even so I managed to finish it and, what is more, all by myself, without the help of an assistant. You see, I have taken your warning to heart, but not out of sympathy for the man (or to prevent him from working in vain) but because I had the ambition to accomplish it by myself. It all turned out exactly as I had thought, and as I indicated in my last letter. The result is completely rigorous and incontrovertible, and it overcomes your objections, which are due only to the fact that these simple problems have not been considered thoroughly in any of the literature. You cannot do anything about it. But I hope to be able to convince you at last that quantum mechanics is complete and as realistic as the facts permit.

I am going to have the paper typed, and will hand it over to the Royal Society. I will send you a copy on thin paper and I will ask the publications assistant to accept anything you want to insert. His address is: Dr D. C. Martin, Assistant Secretary, The Royal Society, Burlington House, Piccadilly, London W.1.

I would be very pleased if you would like to add a few lines or pages, if you agree, or have some new objections; the old ones have, I believe, finally been settled. For many years your critical dissociation from the general business of quantum mechanics has been quite unbearable to me. Much happens there which is contestable, particularly in Princeton; but the foundations laid down by Heisenberg and myself are quite in order, and there is no other way. Perhaps it is presumptuous of me to contradict you, as you did not concede anything to Niels Bohr. But Bohr's expressions are frequently nebulous and obscure. I am simpler and possibly clearer. Well, do not hold it against me.

Kind regards from Hedi, also to Margot, and good wishes for Christmas and the New Year.

> Your old
> *Max Born*

108

1 January, 1954

Dear Born

Your concept is completely untenable. To demand that the ψ-function of a macro-system should be 'narrow' in relation to the macro-coordinates and momenta is incompatible with the principles of quantum theory. A demand of this kind is irreconcilable with the superposition principle for ψ-functions.* As against this the following objection, which also applies in almost every case, is only of secondary importance: that the Schroedinger equation in time leads to a dispersion of the 'narrowness'.

You claim that the latter does not apply to the system I have been considering. But I am convinced that this result (not very important when seen from the point of view of the problem in general) is based on a mistaken conclusion. I do not want to take part in any further discussion, such as you seem to envisage. I content myself with having expressed my opinion clearly.

With best regards and wishes for 1954

> Yours
> *A. Einstein*

*Let ψ_1 and ψ_2 be two solutions of the same Schroedinger equations. Then $\psi = \psi_1 + \psi_2$ also represents a solution of the Schroedinger equation, with an equal claim to describing a possible real state.

When the system is a macro-system, and when ψ_1 and ψ_2 are 'narrow' in relation to the macro-coordinates, then in by far the greater number of cases this is no longer true for ψ.

Narrowness in regard to the macro-coordinates is a requirement which is not only *independent* of the principles of quantum mechanics but, moreover, *incompatible* with them.

109

1c Howitt Road
Belsize Park
London N.W.3
2 January, 1954

Dear Einstein

I enclose a short paper of mine, which links up with your contribution to the presentation volume. I am grateful to you for having forced me to think your simple example over thoroughly in my own way. That I have thereby arrived at a result which is different from yours, you will have to accept into the bargain. Presumably you will stick to your own way of thinking. I am going to hand over the papers to be published in the *Proceedings of the Royal Society* and will, as I mentioned, tell the Secretary, Dr Martin, that you might want to add a reply. I would be pleased if you did, even if you are going to contradict me.

These considerations have provided the impetus for me to make a new advance in the direction of the elementary particles, with the help of the reciprocity principle which I formulated years ago. Nothing has come of it up to now, but this time it seems to be working, thanks to the simple realisation which I have drawn from the inspiration you gave me.

I am in London visiting my nephew, but am shortly going to return to Edinburgh, where I still have quite a lot to do. I am going to live with our doctor. Hedi is in Germany and I am going to follow her in four weeks' time. Our household in Edinburgh has been disbanded.

With best wishes for a happy New Year, and kindest regards
Yours *Max Born*

110

12 January, 1954

Dear Born
Thank you for sending me your paper for the Royal Society, from which I see that you entirely missed the point which matters to me most of all. As I do not feel inclined to appear before the *circus publicum* in the role of fencing master, but as on the other hand I wanted to give you an answer, I herewith send you the kind of reply I could have made. In this way, too, there may be some hope of your thinking the matter over dispassionately, a hope which has already melted away considerably.

With best regards
Yours
A. Einstein

The above paper by M. Born merely shows me that my contribution to the presentation volume dedicated to him did not succeed in formulating the problems I posed with sufficient clarity. In particular, I did not intend to raise objections against the quantum theory, but to make a modest contribution to its physical interpretation.

In the quantum theory the state of a system is characterised by a ψ-function which, in its turn, represents a solution of the Schroedinger equation. Each of these solutions (ψ-functions) has to be regarded, within the sense of the theory, as a description of a physically possible state of the system. The question is: *in what sense* does the ψ-function describe the state of the system?

My assertion is this: the ψ-function cannot be regarded as a complete description of the system, only as an incomplete one. In other words: there are attributes of the individual system whose reality no-one doubts but which the description by means of the ψ-function does not include.

I have tried to demonstrate this with a system which contains one 'macro-coordinate' (coordinate of the centre of a sphere of 1 mm diameter). The ψ-function selected was that of fixed energy. This choice is permissible, because our question by its very nature must be answered so that the answer can claim validity for every ψ-function. From the consideration of this simple special case, it follows that – apart from the existing macro-structure according to the quantum theory – at any arbitrarily chosen time, the centre of the sphere is just as likely to be in one position (possible in accordance with the problem) as in any other. This means that the description by ψ-function does not contain anything which corresponds with a (quasi-) localisation of the sphere at a selected time. The same applies to all systems where macro-coordinates can be distinguished.

In order to be able to draw a conclusion from this as to the physical interpretation of the ψ-function, we can use a concept which can claim to be valid independently of the quantum theory and which is unlikely to be rejected by anyone: every system is at any time (quasi-) sharp in relation to its macro-coordinates. If this were not the case, an approximate description of the world in macro-coordinates would obviously be impossible ('localisation theorem'). I now make the following assertion: if the description by a ψ-function could be regarded as the complete description of the physical condition of an individual system, one should be able to deduce the 'localisation theorem' from the ψ-function, and indeed from any ψ-function belonging to a system which has macro-coordinates. It is obvious that this is not so for the specific example which has been under consideration.

Therefore the concept that the ψ-function *completely* describes the physical behaviour of the individual single system is untenable. But one can well make the following claim: if one regards the ψ-function as the description of an *ensemble*, it furnishes statements which – as far as we can judge – correspond satisfactorily to those of classical mechanics and, at the same time, account for the quantum structure of reality. In my opinion the 'localisation theorem' forces us to regard the ψ-function generally as the description of an 'ensemble', but not as the complete description of an individual single system. In this interpretation the paradox of the apparent coupling of spatially separated parts of systems also disappears. Furthermore, it has the advantage that the description thus interpreted is an *objective* description whose concepts clearly make sense independently of the observation and of the observer.

A. E.

III

Dear Einstein

Your letter of January 12th gave me pleasure and relieved me of the anxiety which your last letter had caused me. Its tone was irritable and angry, as if you had regarded the difference of opinion between us as a personal attack. I am glad that you have now given me an objective reply, even if I by no means agree with your opinion and, what's more, for reasons which are objective and completely 'dispassionate'. I have understood your ideas, but I am convinced that your starting point is an untenable one: the ψ-function, which you rely on, is inappropriate to the problem you intend to deal with. Although it represents a solution of the Schroedinger equation and fulfils the boundary conditions, it does *not* satisfy the initial conditions. Indeed, it lacks, in your own words, the properties required for the description of an individual system. But *other* solutions produced by superposition exist which satisfy the initial conditions required when one wants to follow an individual system. This can, of course, only be done approximately, but the greater the mass m, the more accurate it is. I have just calculated this limiting transition $m \to \infty$, by using your example, and have found that it leads exactly to the classical description. The calculation is free from difficulty, and has been confirmed not only by my collaborators, but also by my successor, Prof. Kemmer, and by the critical and sceptical Schroedinger. If you are in any doubt, ask Johann V. Neumann to read the manuscript, or Weyl, who is probably now in Princeton.

You were probably affronted because I used the opportunity to hit out at classical determinism. But I am convinced that even this will eventually seem plausible to you too, if you take plenty of time to read it, and discuss it with Weyl and Neumann. In any case, you must not be angry with me. My intentions are sincere and objective, and my respect for you is undiminished, even if I do not share your opinion. But you need not write to me any more if you consider me a hopeless case. Should that be so, write to Hedi, who is delighted with every line she receives from you. She suffers from constant noise in one ear, and cannot sleep for this reason; she is taking a cure in the Harz mountains, where I am also going shortly.

I am taking part in another piece of heresy in company with Erwin Freundlich. It has already been printed, and I am going to send you a copy. Incidentally, Freundlich has been seriously ill, arterial thrombosis of the heart.

Hoping that you are not angry with me, with sincere regards

Yours

Max Born

The preceding letters show how two intelligent people can misunderstand each other while discussing concrete problems. Each was convinced that he was right and the other wrong. This happened because each proceeded from a different point of view, which he regarded as incontestable, and was thereby prevented from accepting that of the other.

In this situation it was fortunate that a third person intervened and acted as intermediary: Wolfgang Pauli. I have included three of his letters to me below. He has already appeared in this correspondence as my assistant in Göttingen, the first of a series of outstanding young people. He had then, when barely twenty years old, already written a great work, the article about the theory of relativity in the Encyclopaedia, which was for a long time the best representation of the theory of relativity and is today still regarded as one of the authoritative sources. Pauli became a professor in Zürich. He went to America during the second world war, as he feared that Switzerland, like other small countries such as Belgium, Holland and Norway, would also be overrun by Hitler's armies. He became a close friend of Einstein's and regarded himself, probably with some justification, as the designated 'successor' in theoretical physics. With me, too, he remained in constant contact, although mainly by letter.

Princeton, N.J.
The Institute for Advanced Study
3 March, 1954

I 12

Dear Mr Born

I am here on a brief visit. I intend to be back in Zürich by the middle of April. In my spare time I have read many things, including the 'Scientific Papers' which were dedicated to you on the occasion of your retirement. They contain some interesting contributions, and I think the photograph of you is very good. Einstein's article arrested my attention, of course, particularly as I was able to talk it over with him in person, which is much easier than a discussion by letter. He also told me that there had been some correspondence with you on this subject. I believe I am fairly well able to understand what *he* means, as I know both Einstein and quantum mechanics, but what *your* point of view was I could not quite see from Einstein's remarks. As I am interested in this matter in general, and in the discussion between you and Einstein in particular, I would be grateful if you could write a brief summary for me of the point of view represented by you (details are not important to me). It is clear that quantum mechanics must, in principle, be able to claim validity for small *macroscopic* spheres; their finer structure (atomic constitution) clearly does not come into play.

Now from my conversations with Einstein I have seen that he takes exception to the assumption, essential to quantum mechanics, that the *state of a system is defined only by specification of an experimental arrangement.* [By the way, Einstein says instead of 'specification of the experimental arrangement': 'that the state of a system depends on the way one looks at it'. But it boils down to the same thing. M. Born.] *Einstein wants to know nothing of this.* If one were able to measure with sufficient accuracy, this would of course be as true for small macroscopic spheres as for electrons. It is, of course, demonstrable by specifying thought experiments, and I presume that you have mentioned and discussed some of these in your correspondence with Einstein. But Einstein has the philosophical prejudice that (for macroscopic bodies) a state (termed 'real') can be defined 'objectively' under *any* circumstances, that is, *without* specification of the experimental arrangement used to examine the system (of the macro-bodies), or to which the system is being 'subjected'. It seems to me that the discussion with Einstein can be reduced to this hypothesis of his, which I have called the idea (or the 'ideal') of the 'detached observer'. But to me and other representatives of quantum mechanics, it seems that there is sufficient experimental and theoretical evidence against the practicability of this ideal.

For the rest, however, I believe that it represents pure logic.
Now I would very much like to know what you think of it.
     Kind regards
     Yours
       W. Pauli

113
          Bismarckstrasse 9
          Bad Pyrmont, Germany
          17 March, 1954

Dear Einstein

A letter inviting me to contribute to a collection of congratulatory messages for your 75th birthday arrived here too late. Please overlook the fact that my congratulations are too late as well – I wish you health, cheerfulness and the strength to work. I would so much like to see you again some time! For there is no one in the world for whom I have more profound admiration, and to whom I am more indebted, than you. This is not at all affected by our temporary difference of opinion. I have had several invitations to come to America recently, one for example to give the Messenger Lectures at Cornell University. But I was unable to accept any of them. We are only just settling down here, and cannot leave again so soon. Moreover, I have two books in preparation: one about the theory of crystals is at the proof stage, and the manuscript of the other on optics is almost completed. I cannot take on any further obligations such as the invitation to Cornell would inevitably involve. In addition I was born on the other side of the Iron Curtain and am a member of the Russian Academy of Sciences. This would mean that one would be treated rather horribly at the consulates. My successor in Edinburgh, Kemmer, did not get a visa for a short visit to America because he was born in St Petersburg more than forty years ago. But it is still possible that Hedi and I may one day come to the United States and visit you.

Pauli has written to me to say that you have talked to him about our correspondence. But it was not clear to him what it is

I am asserting, and he asked for information. Could you perhaps give him my manuscript? That would save me a great deal of trouble.

With best wishes and kind regards,

Yours

Max Born

This letter came from Bad Pyrmont, where we had moved at the beginning of 1954.

Among the invitations to America was one from the University of California at Berkeley (perhaps it arrived after this letter had been sent off). This tempted me, as I had come to know and love this area during previous visits, with its blue skies, orchards, mighty mountain ranges, magnificent coastline and friendly people. One of the reasons why I refused this invitation was that Edward Teller lived there. He used to work with me in Göttingen, but had in the meantime risen to become 'father of the atom bomb'. I did not want to have anything to do with him.

114

17 March, 1954

Dear friend Albert Einstein

There can never be enough opportunities to wish other people well, especially when the other person has meant so much and been so helpful as you were to me during our years in Berlin. You may not even be aware of this yourself. But whenever the war really got me down and I came to see you, something of your Olympian outlook on life rubbed off on me and, happy once more, I went on my way. Now we are all of us approaching those years of which Henriette Feuerbach in her *Altersgedanken* [Thoughts of Old Age] wrote that 'the spirit floats above still waters'. I now wish you, in unchanging loyalty and friendship, many years of peaceful old age and the spirit to enjoy them. When Max reached seventy, I was reminded of a poem which our then eight-year-old Irene wrote for my father's seventieth birthday. It began like this:

'Merkwürdig ist's auf dieser Welt
Wie lang ein Menschenkind doch hält! . . .'

['It is a strange thing in this world of ours that a human being lasts for such a long time'!]
But when one gets old oneself, it does not seem such a long time at all; particularly when, unlike you, one cannot look back upon so long a chain of products of one's mind as you are able to do, as one has spent so much of one's time dreaming and vegetating as I have done.

Give a kiss to dear Margot on my behalf.

As always
old Hedi

115

Princeton, The Institute for
Advanced Study
31 March, 1954

Dear Born

Thanks for your letter. I am writing from here after all, for when I get back to Zürich on April 11th I will probably find work waiting for me and will have no time. Also, Einstein gave me your manuscript to read; he was *not at all* annoyed with you, but only said you were a person who will not listen. This agrees with the impression I have formed myself insofar as I was unable to recognise Einstein whenever you talked about him in either your letter or your manuscript. It seemed to me as if you had erected some dummy Einstein for yourself, which you then knocked down with great pomp. In particular, Einstein does not consider the concept of 'determinism' to be as fundamental as it is frequently held to be (as he told me emphatically many times), and he denied energetically that he had ever put up a postulate such as (your letter, para. 3): 'the sequence of such conditions must also be objective and real, that is, automatic, machine-like, deterministic'. In the same way, he *disputes* that he uses as criterion for the admissibility of a theory the question: 'Is it rigorously deterministic?'

Einstein's point of departure is 'realistic' rather than 'deterministic', which means that his philosophical prejudice is a different one. His train of thought can be reproduced briefly *thus*:

1. A preliminary question: Do all mathematically possible

solutions of the Schroedinger equation, even in the case of a macro-object, occur in nature under certain conditions (*in my opinion this question has to be answered in the affirmative whatever happens*) or only in those special cases where the position of the object is 'exactly', 'sharply' defined?

Comment: If the latter class of solutions (which we denote $(\Delta x)^2 < L_0^2$) is described by K^0, it has the following attributes:

i. When $\phi_1(x)$ and $\phi_2(x)$ also belong to K^0, but their mean positions

$$\bar{x}_1 = \frac{\int x_1 |\phi_1|^2 dx}{\int |\phi_1|^2 dx}, \qquad \bar{x}_2 = \frac{\int x_2| \phi_2|^2 dx}{\int |\phi_2|^2 dx},$$

are widely separated, that is to say $(\bar{x}_2 - \bar{x}_1)^2 \gg L_0^2$, then (A) $C_1\phi_1(x) + C_2\phi_2(x) = \phi(x)$ does *not* belong to K^0.

ii. If $\phi_1(x, t_0)$ belongs at a certain time t_0 to K^0, then $\phi_1(x, t)$ no longer belongs to K^0 when $|t - t_0|$ is sufficiently large.

It therefore seems impossible to me to confine oneself *in principle* to the solutions of the Schroedinger equation of the special class K^0, and this cannot in principle be different for a macro-body than, let us say, for an H atom or for a single electron. For if quantum mechanics is correct, then a macro-body has in principle to show diffraction (interference) phenomena, and the difficulties are only going to be *technical* because of the small size of the wavelength.

In that case, however, one *also* needs the superpositions of type (A) from solutions of class K^0 which do not themselves belong to K^0. This is, for example, the case with interference phenomena, when a particle passes through two (or more) openings (in this case it does not matter whether they are 'spheres which are visible under the microscope' or 'electrons').

Up to this point, it seems to me, there is agreement.

2. Now to Einstein's *essential question: How are those solutions of the Schroedinger equation which do not belong to class K^0 (for example, macro-objects) to be interpreted in physical terms?*

Here Einstein's reasoning is as follows:

A. When one 'looks at' a macro-body, it has a quasi-sharply-defined position, and it is not reasonable to invent a causal mechanism according to which the 'looking' fixes the position.

Comment: Instead of 'looking at', I would say 'illuminating with convergent light', and instead of the further 'looking', I would say 'a suitable experimental arrangement'. Apart from that I am still in agreement, because in this case I do not consider that the appearance of the *definite position* or, what amounts to the same thing, its appearance *as a result of the observation*, can be deduced by natural laws.

Einstein's reasoning continues:

B. Therefore a macro-body must *always* have a quasi-sharply-defined position in the 'objective description of reality'. As those ψ-functions which do *not* belong to class K^0 cannot in principle be 'thrown away', and must *also* be in accordance with nature, the *general* ψ-function can only be interpreted as an *ensemble* description. If one wants to assert that the description of a physical system by a ψ-function is *complete*, one has to rely on the fact that *in principle* the natural laws only refer to the ensemble-description, which Einstein does not believe (not only in those at present known to us).

What *I* do not agree with is Einstein's reasoning B (please note that the concept of 'determinism' does not occur in it at all!). I believe it to be *untrue* that a 'macro-body' always has a quasi-sharply-defined position, as I cannot see any fundamental difference between micro- and macro-bodies, and as one always has to assume a portion which is indeterminate to a considerable extent wherever the *wave-aspect* of the physical object concerned manifests itself. The appearance of a definite position x_0 during a subsequent observation (for example, 'illumination of the place with a shaded lantern') above the opening in the figure* on the previous page, and the statement 'the particle is there', is then regarded as being a 'creation' existing outside the laws of nature, even though it cannot be influenced by the observer. The natural laws only say something about the *statistics* of these acts of observation.

As O. Stern said recently, one should no more rack one's brain about the problem of whether something one cannot know anything about exists all the same, than about the ancient question of how many angels are able to sit on the point of a needle. But it seems to me that Einstein's questions are ultimately always of this kind.

* The figure was not with the letter.

Einstein would not agree with this, and he would demand that the 'complete real description of the system' even before the observation must already contain elements which would in some way have to correspond with the possible differences in the results of the observations obtained by 'illumination with a shaded lantern'. *I* think, on the other hand, that this postulate is inconsistent with the freedom of the experimenter to select mutually exclusive experimental arrangements (for instance, radiation with long *parallel* light wavelengths!).

To summarise I should like to say this: while I have no objection to the formal calculations your manuscript contains – which incidentally, were not unknown to me – it completely bypasses the problems which are of interest to Einstein. In particular it seems to me misleading to bring the concept of determinism into the dispute with Einstein.

A further remark here, independently of Einstein, to illustrate the difference between classical mechanics and quantum mechanics when 'measuring' a 'path'.

A. *Classical mechanics.* Let us consider, for example, the determination of the path of a planet. One should measure the position *repeatedly* (at different moments of time t_0, t_1, . . .) always with the same accuracy Δx_0. If one is in possession of the simple *laws* for the motion of the body (for example, Newton's law of gravitation), one is able to *calculate* the *path* (also position *and* velocity at any given time) of the body with *as high* an accuracy *as one likes* (and also to test the assumed law again at different times). Repeated measurements of the position with limited accuracy can therefore successfully replace *one* measurement of the position with high accuracy. The assumption of relatively simple laws of force like that of Newton (and not some irregular zig-zag motion or other on a small scale) then appears as an idealisation which is permissible in the sense of classical mechanics.

B. *Quantum mechanics.* The repetition of positional measurements in sequence with the same accuracy Δx_0 is of *no use at all* in predicting subsequent positional measurements. For every positional measurement to an accuracy Δx_0 at the time t_n implies the inaccuracy

$$\Delta x_{t_n} \sim \frac{h}{m \Delta x_0}(t_{n+1} - t_n)$$

at a later time, *and destroys the possibility of using all previous positional measurements within these limits of error!* (If I am not mistaken, Bohr discussed this example with me many years ago.)

The main difference between the theories A and B, which is that in B information obtained as a result of earlier measurements can be lost after *one* measurement, has not been expressed clearly enough in your manuscript.

With kind regards
I remain
Yours
W. Pauli

Pauli's discussion of the fundamental difference between classical and quantum mechanics is now probably the common property of all physicists. But his formulations are so simple and striking that they deserve to be preserved here.
His next, shorter letter comes from Zürich. It is even more technical than the last one, but deserves to be reproduced here for the same reasons.

Physikalisches Institut der Eidg.
Technischen Hochschule
Zürich
15 April, 1954

116

Dear Mr Born

Having returned home safely, I found your letter of April 10th. I doubt, however, whether there is much more to be said.

1. *Einstein.* I entirely agree with your opinion that Einstein has 'got stuck in his metaphysics'; though I would call his metaphysics 'realistic', *not* 'deterministic'. It is *always* those wave functions which do *not* belong to the special class K^0* from which he wants to make a rope to hang quantum mechanics by, claiming: those solutions which do not belong to K^0 (which

---

* An example: $\psi = Ae^{i\alpha t} \cos Cx$. 'Class K^0' is just my abbreviation.

are the case *in general*) are 'only' an 'incomplete' ensemble-description of 'reality' because, according to his metaphysics, the place of a macro-object must *always* be 'quasi-sharply-defined' in the objectively real state (in quantum mechanics, however, this is only the case for the special solutions of class K^0, and only for limited time intervals).

Thus I have already tried in my last letter to explain Einstein's point of view to you. It is *exactly the same* in Einstein's printed work and in what he said to me. What is more, on the occasion of my farewell visit to him he told me what we quantum mechanicists would have to say to make our logic unassailable (but which does *not* coincide with what he himself believes): 'Although the description of physical systems by quantum mechanics is incomplete, there would be no point in completing it, as the complete description would not agree with the laws of nature.' I am not, however, altogether satisfied with this formulation, as it seems to me to be one of those metaphysical formulations of the 'angels on the point of a needle' type (whether something exists which nobody can know anything about).

2. *Independent of Einstein*. The solutions $C_1\phi_1(x) + C_2\phi_2(x)$, where $\phi_1(x)$ and $\phi_2(x)$ do not coincide: $\int f(x)\,\phi_1(x)\,\phi_2(x)\,\mathrm{d}x \sim 0$ in the *x-space* results in nothing other than classical mechanical ensembles (which can be described by densities P), but does so (after Fourier decomposition) in *the p-space*, as long as the phase α in $C_2 = C_1 e^{i\alpha}$ is well defined. There is, of course, *no* difficulty in this; on the contrary, it is satisfactory. After averaging over α one obtains a *mixture* (which cannot be described by a single wave-function, but – as in wave mechanics – by a density matrix P, after v. Neumann), which is then quite indistinguishable from a mixture in classical mechanics.

Einstein has, of course, no objection to ensembles in classical mechanics, as these admittedly represent an incomplete description of the system in the sense of *classical* mechanics. He is only interested in his assertion that the characterisation of a state by a wave-function ('pure case' after v. Neumann) is also 'incomplete', as the 'true objective state of reality' always has a quasi-sharp location (even when the wave-function does not have it).

Sincerely
Yours *P.*

These letters of Pauli's clearly show that my draft for a reply to Einstein's paper in my presentation volume was completely inadequate. I had failed to understand what mattered to him. When now, twelve years later, I try to think how this was possible, I can find only one explanation: as an unconditional follower and apostle of the young Einstein, I swore by his teachings; I could not imagine that the old Einstein thought differently. He had based the theory of relativity on the principle that concepts which refer to things that cannot be observed have no place in physics: a fixed point in empty space is a concept of this kind, in the same way as the absolute simultaneity of two events happening in different parts of space. The quantum theory came into being when Heisenberg applied this principle to the electronic structure of atoms. This was a bold and fundamental step which made sense to me immediately and which caused me to concentrate all my efforts in the service of this idea. It was, then, clearly incomprehensible to me that Einstein should refuse to accept the validity of this principle, which he himself had used with the greatest success, for quantum mechanics, and that he insisted that the theory should supply information about questions of the type of 'how many angels can sit on the point of a needle'. For this is what Einstein's requirement, that a physical state must have an objective real existence even when it proves impossible to postulate a principle for it, amounts to, as Pauli clearly explains. And he claims, moreover, that any theory which offends against this is incomplete. In an earlier letter he expressed this by saying that he was opposed to the philosophy of *esse est percipi*.

Pauli's analysis of our fundamental difference of opinion was the correct answer to Einstein's paper; I had to leave it to him to publish a reply. As far as I know he has never done so.

My own manuscript seemed to me to contain certain thoughts which I had not yet come across elsewhere. I rewrote it completely, with only casual allusions to Einstein's article; I did this by proceeding from his example of the particle oscillating between two elastic reflecting walls, developing it further mathematically, and using it to explain my own philosophical ideas about relativity and determinism.

At this time I received an invitation from the Danish Academy to contribute to a volume of the Academy's reports, which was to be published on the occasion of Niels Bohr's seventieth birthday. I therefore sent my paper not to the Royal Society in London, as previously planned, but to the Danish Academy in Copenhagen. It was published there under the title 'Continuity, Determinism and Reality'. In a letter from Zürich of 11th December 1955, in which he first of all tells me about the sudden death of Hermann Weyl, Pauli then writes as follows: 'Your paper in the Danish presentation volume to Bohr makes very pleasant reading now; its epistomological content has now become very clear, and I agree with all of it. I had used the mathematics of the example of the mass point between two walls, and of the wave-packets which belong to it, in my lectures in such a way that the transformation formula of the theta-function comes into play. But that is a mere detail.' It is more than a detail. It shows that Pauli had long been familiar with all I had to say. But this did not embarrass me. For ever since the time he had been my assistant in Göttingen, I had been aware that he was a genius, comparable only with Einstein himself. Indeed, from the point of view of pure science he was possibly even greater than Einstein, even if as an entirely different type of person he never, in my opinion, attained Einstein's greatness.

His remark about the theta-function made me take up this example later when I had moved to Bad Pyrmont. In a paper that I wrote with W. Ludwig,[47] the movement of the oscillating particle was represented not only by the superposition of Schroedinger waves (wave representation) but also by a solution in the form of integrals, which could be regarded as superposition of Gaussian distributions of decreasing sharpness (particle representation). The first form corresponds to the quantum domain proper, the second to the almost classical domain. Each of them can be transformed into the other by means of the theta transformations mentioned by Pauli. Up to this point it was certainly familiar to Pauli. What we added to it was a method which could be used to transform these two separate descriptions into a single one, which can be used and is valid for all velocities and all masses. I was familiar with this method from the theory of crystals, where it had been used with great success by P. P. Ewald to calculate electrostatic and electromagnetic potentials.

Although this problem deals with a case which is physically trivial and unimportant in practice, it gives a clear insight into the connection between classical and quantum mechanics, and seems to me to be more useful than any philosophising about the question. It should be brought into, and discussed in, every elementary lecture about quantum mechanics.

In the letters which follow, the controversy which has been described here is merely hinted at. In spite of its occasional bitterness, it did not leave even the slightest stain on our relationship.

I I 7

112 Mercer Street
Princeton, New Jersey
U.S.A.

Dear Born

    I was very pleased to hear that you have been awarded the Nobel Prize, although strangely belatedly, for your fundamental contributions to the present quantum theory. In particular, of course, it was your subsequent statistical interpretation of the description which has decisively clarified our thinking. It seems to me that there is no doubt about this at all, in spite of our inconclusive correspondence on the subject.

And then the money in good currency is not to be despised either, when one has just retired. With sincerest regards to you and your wife.

Yours

A. Einstein

The fact that I did not receive the Nobel Prize in 1932 together with Heisenberg hurt me very much at the time, in spite of a kind letter from Heisenberg. I got over it, because I was conscious of Heisenberg's superiority. By the time we returned to Germany this wound had long healed. My surprise and joy were thus all the greater, especially as I was awarded the prize, not for the work done jointly with Heisenberg and Jordan, but for the statistical interpretation of Schroedinger's wave function, which I had thought of and substantiated entirely by myself. It is not surprising that this acknowledgement was delayed for twenty-eight years, for all the great names of the initial period of the quantum theory were opposed to the statistical interpretation: Planck, de Broglie, Schroedinger and, not least, Einstein himself. It cannot have been easy for the Swedish Academy to act in opposition to voices which carried as much weight as theirs; therefore I had to wait until my ideas had become the common property of all physicists. This was due in no small part to the cooperation of Niels Bohr and his Copenhagen school, which today lends its name almost everywhere to the line of thinking I originated.

118

Dr Barner's Sanatorium
Braunlage, Harz
28 November, 1954

Dear Einstein

I read in the paper recently that you are supposed to have said: 'If I were to be born a second time, I would become not a physicist, but an artisan'. These words were a great comfort to me, for similar thoughts are going around in my mind as well, in view of the evil which our once so beautiful science has brought upon the world. Now they have given me the Nobel Prize, essentially for the statistical interpretation of the ψ-function, work which dates back twenty-eight years. I can really only think of one explanation for this: the intention was to honour something which has no immediate practical application, something purely theoretical. Linus Pauling received the chemical prize at the same time, a man known for his upright political conduct and his rejection of the misuse of scientific discoveries. (It was even rumoured here that he had not received an exit permit from the United States, but this does not seem to be true.) This could be chance, but it does appear to have been done on purpose, and that would be gratifying. It is for this reason that I am glad to go to Stockholm, although neither Hedi nor I will feel any the better for it. For we both suffer from heart complaints, and are only free from pain when we live very quietly. Hedi is at present in a clinic in Göttingen, in order to be revitalized a little; I am up here in the Harz mountains for the same reason. It is unlikely that I will manage to do any more scientific work (except for my optics book, begun eight years ago), and I am thinking of using my present popularity in two countries (here I am the 'German', over there the 'British' physicist) to try and arouse the consciences of our colleagues over the production of ever more horrible bombs. Even before I knew anything about the Nobel Prize I had written an article in this vein for the *Physikalischen Blätter*, which is widely read here. I am reading a book at the moment with the nice title *Kapitza, the Atom Tsar*, which contains a dramatic description of the development of nuclear explosives in Russia. It makes one feel quite sick. Kapitza himself comes out of it quite well; in those days he tried everything he could to put the brakes on and to take delaying action, in much the same way as his opposite number R. O. [Robert Oppenheimer] did on your side (if my information is correct).

Someone wrote and told me that you were ill. Please accept my best wishes for a speedy recovery, and do not trouble to reply. We understand one another in personal matters. Our difference of opinion about the incompleteness of quantum mechanics is quite insignificant by comparison.

If Hedi were here, she would join me in sending you her sincere regards.

        In old friendship
          Yours
            Max Born

Even today I cannot say with any certainty whether I was right that the simultaneous award of the Nobel Prize to Linus Pauling and myself had anything to do with the fact that neither of us had had anything to do with the practical application or the misuse of science for political purposes. For, after all, other scientists besides ourselves were honoured with the prize at the same time. The physicist Walther Bothe was one, and my assumption hardly applies to him.

We found the Nobel celebrations in Stockholm tiring but extremely enjoyable, and sustained no injury to our health as a result. The Nobel Prize has helped me a great deal in public appeals for reason in the use of scientific discoveries.

The book *Kapitza, the Atom Tsar* apparently did not circulate widely in Germany, in spite of its fetching title. I have never met anyone who knew it, and did not see it reviewed in any paper or periodical. The greater part of it is probably pure invention, for those few features of Kapitza's life which we knew about in detail were either not mentioned at all or misrepresented.

The next letter, the last I had from Einstein, refers to the beginning of my previous one where I mention a newspaper report according to which Einstein said that if he were to be born a second time, he would become not a physicist, but an artisan. I thought at the time that he was referring to the atom bomb. Here is Einstein's brief reply (typewritten; apparently he was already seriously ill).

119

17 January, 1955

Dear Born

    I enclose the text of my letter to the *Reporter*, which you have asked for. Just one comment. The hired hacks of an accommodating press have tried to tone down the impact of this statement, either by making it appear as if I regretted having been engaged in scientific endeavour, or by trying to give the impression that I had attached little value to the practical occupations I mentioned.

What I wanted to say was just this: In the present circumstances, the only profession I would choose would be one where earning a living had nothing to do with the search for knowledge.

Kind regards from

Yours

A. E.

Unfortunately I no longer possess the letter to the *Reporter*. When I gave an account of Einstein's letters (my own letters to him were not at my disposal at that time) to the meeting of Nobel Laureates in Lindau this summer (1965), I still believed, as I have just mentioned, that Einstein's remarks referred to the atomic bomb. In the meantime I have heard from the executor of Einstein's estate, Dr Otto Nathan in New York, that this is not so. Einstein's statement referred to the crisis of civil rights, which had been brought about by the appearance of Senator McCarthy. Any teacher or scientist who dared to express his political opinion freely and openly risked being asked to appear before the Committee of the Senate presided over by Senator McCarthy, and the loss of his position, if not worse. Anyone interested in this can read about it in the notes by Otto Nathan in the book *Einstein on Peace*[29] (pages 613, 614), which also contains the letter to the *Reporter* with the sentence that has since become famous because of its incorrect interpretation: 'rather to become a plumber or a peddler than a physicist'.

Bad Pyrmont
Marcardstrasse 4
West Germany
29 January, 1955

120

Dear Einstein

Many thanks for sending me the text of your letter to the *Reporter* so promptly. I can well imagine that the press people have tried to tone down the impact of your words.

I myself am forced to say that your text is not free of ambiguity. I took it to mean something other than you explained, but even this explanation does not satisfy me. For even when one selects a method of making a living which is independent of the search for knowledge, one must then also decide to keep one's knowledge to oneself, or to interchange ideas only privately amongst friends, as was customary during the 17th and 18th centuries, for otherwise others are still going to misuse the results for evil purposes, and I feel that one would then never be free of responsibility.

I think a great deal about these things, and have got in touch with Bertrand Russell. He has made an effective statement over the British radio, which is printed in the *Listener* of December 30th. I will let you know whether this discussion leads to any conclusions, of either a personal or a more far-reaching nature. A Japanese periodical has asked me to agree to the publication of my correspondence with Yukawa about the atom bomb, etc., and sent me a letter by Y. This did in fact actually appear, together with my reply (I am unable to read it, as I do not know any Japanese). It will not have amused any Americans who read it. But this is only a miserable beginning.

With kindest regards, also from Hedi

Yours

Max Born

This letter contains my attitude towards the 'plumber and peddler' question. It goes beyond Einstein's; even if one does not earn one's living by science, but publishes the results of one's research, one cannot rid oneself of the responsibility for the use which is made of them. I have stuck to this point of view right up to the present.

Hideki Yukawa is a brilliant theoretical physicist, the only Japanese Nobel prizewinner. He received this in 1949 for his prediction of the existence of a new kind of particle, called a meson (with a mass which is between that of an electron and a proton). I correspond with him and see him from time to time, for example at the meeting this year of Nobel prizewinners in Lindau (1965). We are united not only by our ideas about physics – he recognised my reciprocity principle as the leading heuristic idea in the theory of elementary particles – but also by our attitude towards the misuse of scientific research results for the purposes of war and destruction.

Einstein died soon after this last exchange of letters between us (on the 18th of April, 1955). In a letter to my wife, his step-daughter Margot describes her last visit to his sickroom: 'Did you know that I was in the same hospital as Albert? I was allowed to see him twice more and talk to him for a few hours. I was taken to him in a wheel-chair. I did not recognise him at first – he was so changed by the pain and blood deficiency. But his personality was the same as ever. He was pleased that I was looking a little better, joked with me, and was completely in command of himself with regard to his condition; he spoke with a profound serenity – even with a touch of humour – about the doctors, and awaited his end as an imminent natural phenomenon. As fearless as he had been all his life, so he faced death humbly and quietly. He left this world without sentimentality or regrets.'

With his death, we, my wife and I, lost our dearest friend.

REFERENCES

1. Einstein, A., 'On the electrodynamics of moving bodies', in *Ann. Phys. Lpz.*, **17**, 891 (1905).
2. Einstein, A., 'On a heuristic viewpoint concerning the production and transformation of light', in *Ann. Phys. Lpz.*, **17**, 132 (1905).
3. Einstein, A., 'The presumed movement of suspended particles in static fluids', in *Ann. Phys. Lpz.*, **17**, 549 (1905).
4. Born, M., *Der Mathematische und Naturwissenschaftliche Unterricht*, **9**, 97 (1956).
5. Born, M., *Ausgewahlten Aghandlungen*, Göttingen Akademie.
6. Born, M., *Physik im Wandel meiner Zeit*, Braunscheweig, 1957, 1966.
6a. Born, M., *Physics in my Generation*, Longmans, 1970.
7. Born, M., *Von der Verantwortung des Naturwissenschaftlers* (The Scientist's Responsibility), Nymphenburger Verlagshandlung, Munich, 1965.
8. Born, M., and Born, H., *Der Luxus des Gewissens* (The Luxury of Conscience), Nymphenburger Verlagshandlung, Munich, 1969.
9. Born, M., *Physikalische Zeitschrift*, **17**, 51 (1916).
10. Born, M., *Die Relativitätstheorie Einsteins*, Springer, Berlin, 1920.
11. Born, M., *Einstein's Theory of Relativity*, Dover Publications, New York, 1962.
12. Born, M., *Enzyklopädie der Mathematik*, Teubuer, Leipzig, 1920.
13. Herneck, F., *Albert Einstein*, Bookpublishers der Morgen, Berlin, 1933.
14. Rabindranath Tagore, *The Home and the World*, Macmillan, 1919.
15. *A. Einstein, A. Sommerfeld Briefwechsel*, Schwaber, Basel, 1968.
16. Born, M., *Physikalische Zeitschrift*, **11**, 1234–1257 (1910).
17. Seelig, C., *Albert Einstein*, Europa Verlag, Zurich, 1960.
18. Haldane, R. B., *The Reign of Relativity*, John Murray, London, 1921.
19. Born, M., and Jordan, P., *Zeitschrift für Physik*, **33**, 32 (1925).
20. van der Waerden, B. L., *Sources of Quantum Mechanics*, North Holland, Amsterdam, 1967; see also Hund, F., *Geschichte der Quantentheorie*, Bibliographisch. Mannheim, 1967.
21. Heisenberg, W., *Zeitschrift für Physik*, **35**, 879 (1925).
22. Born, M., and Hund, F., *Vorlesungen über Atommechanik*, Springer, Berlin, 1925.
22a. Born, M., and Hund, F., *The Mechanics of the Atom*, tr. J. W. Fisher, G. Bell and Sons Ltd, London, 1927; Fredk. Ungor, New York, 1960.

23. Einstein, A., and Infeld, L., *The Evolution of Physics*, Simon and Schuster, New York, 1938.
24. Infeld, L., *Bulletin of the Atomic Scientists*, Feb. 1965.
25. Infeld, L., and Plebanski, *Motion and Relativity*, Pergamon Press, Oxford, 1960.
26. Born, M., *Nature*, **141**, 328 (1938).
27. Einstein, A., *Mein Weltbild*, Amsterdam, 1934.
28. von Neumann, J., *Mathematische Grundlagen der Quantenmechanik*, Springer, Berlin, 1932.
29. Nathan, O., and Norden, H., *Einstein on Peace*, Simon and Schuster, New York, 1960.
30. Born, M., *Experiment and Theory in Physics*, University Press, Cambridge, 1943; reprinted by Dover Publications, New York, 1956.
31. Born, M., *Experiment und Theorie in der Physik*, Mosbach, 1969.
32. Born, M., *Natural Philosophy of Cause and Chance*, Clarendon Press, Oxford, 1949.
33. Born, H., *Stille Gänge* (Silent Corridors), Leonard Friedrich, Bad Pyrmont.
34. Einstein, A., *Physikalische Zeitschrift*, **17**, 101 (1916).
35. Born, M., and Green, H. S., *A General Kinetic Theory of Liquids*, Cambridge University Press, 1949.
36. Born, M., *Physikalische Blätter*, **20**, 554 (1964); **21**, 53 (1965).
37. Irving, D., *The Virus House*, New York, 1968.
38. *Bulletin of the Atomic Scientists*, June 1968.
39. Einstein, A., 'Quantum Mechanics and Reality', in *Dialectica*, 320 (1948).
40. Einstein, A., *Meaning of Relativity*, 4 lectures translated by Edwin Plimpton Adams, Methuen & Co., London, 1922, 6th ed. 1956.
41. Einstein, A., *Out of my Later Years*, translated by Alan Harris, Watts & Co., London, 1940.
42. Born, M., and Huang, K., *Dynamical Theory of Crystal Lattices*, Clarendon Press, Oxford, 1954.
43. Born, M., and Wolf, E., *Principles of Optics*, Pergamon Press, Oxford, 1959.
44. Schroedinger, E., *The British Journal for the Philosophy of Science*, 109, Aug. 1952; 233, Nov. 1952; 95, Aug. 1953.
45. *Scientific Papers presented to Max Born on his retirement from the Tait Chair of Natural Philosophy in the University of Edinbrugh*, Oliver and Boyd, Edinburgh/London, 1953.
46. Born, M., *Kong. Dansk Videnskabernes Selskab, Matematiskfysiske Meddelelser*, **30**, 1 (1955).
47. Born, M., and Ludwig, W., *Zeitschrift für Physik*, **150**, 106 (1958).

Index